SAN MIGUEL DE ALLENDE
& GUANAJUATO

FIRST EDITION

San Miguel de Allende & Guanajuato

Great Destinations Mexico

Kevin
Delgado

The Countryman Press
Woodstock, Vermont

ISBN 978-1-58157-090-8

Cover photo © Place Photography
Interior photos by the author unless otherwise specified
Book design by Bodenweber Design
Page composition by Susan McClellan
Maps by Mapping Specialists Ltd., Madison, WI © The Countryman Press

Published by The Countryman Press, P.O. Box 748, Woodstock, Vermont 05091

Distributed by W. W. Norton & Company, Inc., 500 Fifth Avenue, New York, NY 10110

Manufactured in the United States of America

10 9 8 7 6 5 4 3 2 1

El Campanero Bridge

Contents

9

Acknowledgments

There is a black and white picture on my sister's living room wall of a dark mustachioed man in the round straw hat of a farmworker. He is not smiling, nor does he look as though he has much of a sense of humor. However, I cannot help but smile every time I look at the picture. He is my grandfather, and that picture is one of the very few of him that exist. He was a shoemaker from Guanajuato who, against all common sense, uprooted his family from the only land they ever knew and trudged them north in search of a better life. It was an arduous journey, and at times extremely tragic, but after many years he found a new home in a cinder block shack along a dirt road in southeastern Wyoming. My older brothers and sisters would tell stories about him in his latter years; how he would walk along that dirt road where, by that time, many of his children had also settled, and how his grandchildren would run out to meet him. He didn't speak much English and his grandkids didn't speak much Spanish, but they were always happy to see him and he always seemed to have chewing gum ready to hand out. Unfortunately, I never met my grandfather but I always felt a certain connection to that picture. Perhaps it is his strong resemblance with my father, or the stories told to me by my aunts. But when I was older I traveled to Guanajuato with a sense of anticipation and found I could not walk along its streets without thinking of my grandpa. I still walk along the streets looking for that stern face in the people I pass, and it makes me smile. This book is for my grandparents and their children, Aunt Lupe, Aunt Dolores, Uncle John, Aunt Sadie, Uncle Joe, Aunt Francis, Aunt Isabel, Aunt Rose, Uncle Tony, and, of course, my dad.

I am forever in the debt of the cast of characters whose stories and insights have contributed to this book. Thanks especially to Mike Brady for all the rides to and from the border and for all the travel and photography advice. Thanks to John Harten, Greg Zsulgit, and the other Yampounding Sherpas, for your wisdom and for dragging me along on all those adventures. I am thankful for the kindness, support, and assistance of the hoteliers, restaurant owners, tour operators, and others whom I visited during my research. Thank you to Betty, Monica, and Robert, as well as to Penny and Todd for keeping an eye on the kids, and to Daniel, Summer, Riley, and Isabel for your patience; to my parents, for always giving me a chance; to my brothers and sisters (Mickey, D. J., Lori, Barbie, Davie, Teddy, Brian, Penny, Darren, Ryan, and Sean), for making me who I am; to my old buddy, Brian Schwartzkopf; to Mona Klausing, just for being there; and, notably, thank you Simon Lozano and Craig Sodaro for teaching me to write. And, of course, thank you Mary, for all you do for me.

— KD

Many of Guanajuato's streets have changed little since colonial times.

Introduction

When most people think about a Mexican vacation, an image immediately comes to mind. You're sitting under an umbrella on a white sand beach and looking out over a crystal blue sea, while sipping on a margarita that was just served to you by the same guy that carried your luggage to your room yesterday and served you breakfast today. That Mexico exists many places along the Pacific Coast, the Yucatán Peninsula, and very near the spot where you may have taken this book off the shelf at your local bookstore. This book isn't about that Mexico. This is about the state of Guanajuato, which is completely landlocked by a bunch of other landlocked states (well, Michoacán isn't completely landlocked, but you get the point). Moreover, it is not a place where you will find very many brand name hotels, and there are none at the center of the action. You will also not find any all-inclusive resorts with 24-hour buffets, or familiar fast food restaurants. In short, this book is about a place that is likely outside your normal comfort zone. No need to fret, however. In San Miguel de Allende, Guanajuato, and Dolores Hidalgo, you will find towns that are extremely safe and full of people who will welcome you as their guest and proudly show you the wonders of their cities. And there are wonders.

Even if you live along the east coast of the United States or Canada, you probably see very few buildings that are more than a couple hundred years old, and those that are old are likely surrounded by structures that were put up much more recently. However, a walk along the cobblestone streets of these Central Mexican towns is a rare journey in North America, because you are surrounded by entire blocks that exist much as they did in the 17th and 18th centuries. And while the residents of these towns have done much over the last century to preserve their historic treasures, it was a tumultuous and complicated course of events that allowed the buildings to survive into the 21st century.

Early on in the history of Spanish colonization, San Miguel de Allende became a fashionable place to live for the wealthy families of Central Mexico. The investment that these families put into their town can be seen all over the central district of that city today. As for Guanajuato, the vast wealth from massive veins of silver discovered in the surrounding hills fueled the investment in infrastructure that made this city one of the jewels of colonial Mexico. However, the good times didn't last. Political instability, war, and economic hardship in effect froze these cities in time. For a while many of Guanajuato's great architectural works fell into disrepair, with one of

San Miguel de Allende is filled with beautiful courtyards.

Dolores Hidalgo is known as the cuna de la independencia, or the "cradle of the independence."

its churches sitting in rubble for decades, while San Miguel de Allende was all but abandoned. On the other hand, Dolores Hidalgo came to be known as *la cuna de la independencia*, or "the cradle of the independence," because it was here that the priest Miguel Hidalgo struck the first blow for independence from Spain, in 1810. An interest in this history, as well as better times, brought rejuvenation to the region. And the beauty of its towns has been widely recognized. The entire town of San Miguel de Allende is a national monument, and Guanajuato is recognized as a world heritage site.

However, Mexico is peppered with beautiful colonial cities, where you can blow in for a few hours and wander around admiring the architecture before hitching the next bus to the beach. These cities are much more than that. They are worth a visit, not because of the life that went on here hundreds of years ago, but rather because of the life that is happening in them today. San Miguel de Allende is today a Mecca for artists, musicians, chefs, and creative people from around the world. In fact, they don't just come here to visit, they come to settle down; it is home to upwards of five thousand American and Canadian expatriates who have come here to study art, start businesses, and retire. The town is an artist colony with galleries all over the central district. You will find live music just about any night of the week, and restaurants serving cuisine from all over the world. An hour and a half away in the town of Guanajuato, you will find a city that is equally as vibrant, with a little green heart that beats to the rhythm of mariachi and Spanish *estudiantina* music. This little green heart is known as the Jardín de la Unión, a wedge-shaped square lined with low Indian laurel trees and outdoor cafes. This square is the scene of constant activity and a mix of young university students, foreign travelers, and well-to-do locals. A walk in any direction will lead you to another café-lined plaza, and the fact that the town is built in a steep valley with traffic flowing through a series of narrow underground tunnels means that walking is just about the most efficient way to get around. A detour through any of the town's numerous alleys is almost certain to let out into a plaza, where you will find still more people sitting at outdoor cafés enjoying the beautiful Central Mexican weather.

To top it all off, these towns are also famous for their many annual festivals, which draw visitors from throughout Mexico and from around the world. This is particularly true during Holy Week, and in the fall when the streets around the historic centers become crowded with merrymakers and vendors of all types. Yes, a trip to San Miguel de Allende, Guanajuato, or Dolores Hidalgo may take you out of your comfort zone, but what you will find once you're there is a world filled with the cultural wonders—sights, sounds, and tastes—that only Mexico can provide.

Closeup of mural by José Chávez Morado, in the Alhóndiga Museum

1

History

Guanajuato is the center of Mexico both geographically and culturally. A landlocked state in the heart of the Mexican Republic, it shares borders with San Luis Potosí and Zacatecas on the north, Querétaro on the east, the state of México on the southeast, Jalisco on the west, and Michoacán on the south. It is a relatively small state in terms of territory. With just over 19,000 square miles, it ranks 22nd among Mexico's 31 states. However, its cultural and geographical importance is undeniable.

When Spanish conquistadores arrived in Mexico in the 16th century, this territory was a backwater populated by bands of hunter-gatherer tribes. However, it was relatively close to Tenóchtitlan, the capital of the Aztecs, the most powerful indigenous tribe on the continent. Had Europeans arrived at the height of the Toltec or Mayan empires, Mexican geography would likely look much different today. However, the Spanish made the former Aztec capital their base of operations in New Spain, from which to set about conquering the continent. Trade routes to the northern territories ran through Guanajuato, making the early settlement of San Miguel el Grande an important stopover. Furthermore, Spanish explorers quickly discovered rich veins of silver in the mountains surrounding the present-day city of Guanajuato.

The economic activities that sprung from these circumstances led to a particularly independent streak among the residents of San Miguel, Guanajuato, and other nearby settlements. This important factor led to a local movement that culminated in Mexico's independence from Spain in the early 19th century. This region has also been home to many of Mexico's most notable figures, including the artist Diego Rivera, singer José Alfredo Jiménez, and former president Vicente Fox.

Guanajuato is one of those places where the history is apparent wherever you look. From the beautiful colonial houses along San Miguel's avenues, to the mines of Guanajuato, to the statue of Hidalgo in the center of the town square in Dolores Hidalgo, this place values its history and is eager to help you experience it for yourself.

Natural History

San Miguel de Allende and the town of Guanajuato are located in the central plateau of Mexico in a geographical region known as El Bajío, or the lowlands, which includes the low mountains of Sierra de Guanajuato and the plains to the south. While this region is primarily known for its unquestionable historic significance, its many monuments, and its cultural festivals, it also has a wealth of natural beauty. This aspect of the region tends to be overshadowed by fiestas and architecture, but visitors wanting to get away from the bustle

Monument to Miguel Hidalgo

Overlooking Guanajuato

of the tourist centers can find serene moments in the undeveloped areas along rustic mountain paths, or along the many springs that lie just outside of San Miguel de Allende.

This area of El Bajío lies along a transitional geographic zone between the plains and the mountains, as well as between the fertile basin of the Lerma River and the deserts that open to the north. Because of this varied geography, this region possesses a variety of important natural resources that are both beautiful and vital to the Mexican economy.

The Laja River Basin

The Laja River, an important tributary of the Lerma River, lies to the west of the city of San Miguel de Allende. This tributary, fed by the waters of the mountain ranges north of Guanajuato state, flows from north to south into a reservoir bottled up by the Ignacio Allende Dam, an enormous hydraulic breakwater just to the southwest of San Miguel that was inaugurated in 1967. The banks of the Laja River were the principal site of pre-Hispanic settlements in the region. In the 16th century, Franciscan monks also used this river as a route from the south by which to penetrate into the lands of the Chichimecas. The first foundation of the town of San Miguel took place right on the banks of the Laja River as well, in an area with abundant springs. Today, several old chapels that were built by early converted indigenous people still survive along the Laja, as well as the ruins of one-time haciendas, and demolished bridges and aqueducts.

Some of these early buildings, as well as Chichimeca ruins, lie submerged beneath the

The Laja river basin is full of vegetation and mineral springs.

waters of the Ignacio Allende Dam. Despite the loss of heritage sites that this dam has caused, today it provides ample recreational space for San Miguel residents, ideal for sailing, fishing, and other water sports. At the same time, it has gradually been transformed into a refuge for a variety of aquatic birds, many of which are endangered, such as herons, ibis, pelicans, wild ducks, and other migratory birds.

Above the Laja River Basin, between the famous sanctuary of Atotonílco and the Ignacio Allende Dam, is a cluster of springs and wells that the area's rural communities have relied on for centuries. Additionally, these springs have given life to a wide diversity of wild flora and fauna. Dense stands of reeds border marshes and streams formed by the springs, together with thick gatherings of mesquite, called "the tree of life" by the Chichimecas, due to its great value as lumber, food, and medicine. This forested region is home to many populations of multicolored birds such as blue grosbeaks, vermilion flycatchers, and great kiskadees.

Los Picachos Mountain Range

In the town of San Miguel de Allende, these are the mountains clearly visible if one gazes off to the southeast. For hundreds of years they have provided an important source of water for the surrounding communities. The peaks and canyons of these mountains are covered with thick woods, predominantly comprised of oak. In fact, as many as seven varieties of oak create shelter for a diverse natural ecosystem here. It has managed to survive, thanks

The city of Guanajuato is located in the foothills of the Los Picachos Mountain Range.

in great part, to the region's relative isolation from the runaway urban development that has taken place in areas such as Mexico City and Guadalajara.

However, since the 16th century the forested surface of the region has been drastically reduced through overgrazing, fires, and indiscriminate deforestation for lumber and fire-wood. The gradual loss of this vegetative cover and the excessive drilling of wells, princi-pally for farming, have contributed to the desertification of the area. Overdrilling has also lowered the water table in general and specifically caused the disappearance of many of the springs that have been so important to the area.

Today the mountain range of Los Picachos is a protected area, along with other nearby woodlands and ravines, such as La Márgara to the east and La Cañada de la Virgen to the west. In 1989 a territorial reserve of more than 200 acres, La Cañada de los Pajaritos, was set aside for the preservation of woodlands. Its name comes from a species of large blue birds, which abound here in noisy flocks among the oak groves. Other species that can be found here include eagles, coyotes, red foxes, and white-tailed deer, which have managed to survive extermination despite the activities of the poachers that have unfortunately operated here since it became a reserve.

Travelers looking for some outdoor fun can climb to La Cañada de los Pajaritos and return to San Miguel in the same day with relative ease. If you are interested in overnight adventures you can camp in the reserve, which is equipped with several shelters. From the heights of Los Picachos you will find a magnificent panoramic view in all directions.

The Los Picachos Mountain Range

Guanajuato Semidesert

At the time of the conquest, the area that is now San Miguel de Allende and Guanajuato was likely covered with temperate woodlands. Soon after, however, the process of deforestation began to result in a wide-ranging ecological change to a semiarid environment that today characterizes the region.

Calcareous and sandy soils have sustained an astonishing variety of cacti, including spiny garambullo, agaves valued for making tequila, yuccas with sword-shaped leaves, and "spoon plants," as well as prickly pear nopales. The majority of these desert plants flower majestically during the spring, when regular rainfall results in a carpet of multicolored flowers. Other plant species that have managed to survive here include mesquite, acacia, and morning glory. This flora comes together to create the classic image of the rural countryside of the Mexican high plateau, with rolling hills covered in grasslands, sparse trees, and cactus.

The foothills around San Miguel are also scarred by numerous deep and craggy ravines that slash the hills, mesas, and semidesert prairies of the surrounding countryside. These ravines also shelter their own variety of flora and fauna. Even aquatic plants grow in small pools of water shaded by native trees such as mulberry, copal, and walnut. The ravines also provide an ecological niche for several types of native birds, foxes, badgers, and armadillos. Unfortunately, like much of the rest of the area's natural beauty, these microhabitats are threatened by overhunting, overgrazing, and deforestation. These ravines formed at the foot of the Los Picachos Mountain Range, particularly the area of La Cañada de la Virgen (the Glen of the Virgin), 30 miles southwest of San Miguel de Allende. This is also the location of a rare archaeological site. Closer to San Miguel, El Charco del Ingenio

The Guanajuato semidesert is an area of rolling hills covered in grasslands, sparse trees, and cactus.

Botanical Gardens presents another example of the natural beauty you will find here. This site contains 135 acres of ravines set aside for the preservation of the region's ecological treasures. It is run by a nongovernmental group dedicated to restoring microhabitats and promoting the conservation of Guanajuato's natural resources.

These natural resources are plentiful. Despite the fact that Guanajuato does not have the white sand beaches of Cancún and Cabo, it does have plenty of natural beauty. Moreover, it is a beauty you can enjoy in peace and contemplation, so you are well rested when you are ready to return to your world.

CULTURAL HISTORY

Guanajuato is undeniably one of the most culturally and historically important regions in Mexico. For a place with no significant indigenous ruins, that is really saying something. However, when you walk the streets of Guanajuato, you are walking in the footsteps of Diego Rivera. When you stand in the town square of Dolores Hidalgo, you can almost hear the voice of Hidalgo himself calling out *El Grito* for the first time. And when you stare up at the Parroquia in San Miguel de Allende, you see the radical vision of Zafrino Gutiérrez as he conceived of a majestic church by looking at a postcard. But more than these famous examples, Guanajuato represents the iconic image of the small Mexican village with towering churches, open squares, grizzled expatriates, and peasant farmers leading their burros through town. Incredibly, to this day you will still find all of this, wandering along the streets of Guanajuato's towns.

Place of Frogs

Before the arrival of the Spanish conquistadores in the 16th century, the region of Mexico where San Miguel de Allende and Guanajuato are located was populated by several small bands of indigenous people who lived a nomadic way of life. At that time, these groups depended on hunting and gathering for their survival. These indigenous tribes made note of the numerous frogs in the area and referred to it as *Quanax-juato*, meaning "Place of Frogs," the sound of which the Spanish would translate to "Guanajuato." Although all of these groups are today commonly referred to as Chichimecas, there were actually ethnically distinct groups with names such as Cazacanes, Guamares, Copuces, and Guachichiles. The ancient Aztecs were the first to refer to these groups as Chichimecas, a pejorative term that implied that they descended from dogs. The Spaniards would use the word as an umbrella term to describe most of the indigenous groups scattered through large parts of Guanajuato, Jalisco, Zacatecas, San Luis Potosí, Aguascalientes, and Durango.

However, the culture of this region had not always been limited to small groups of hunter-gatherers. Populations closely connected to the advanced Mesoamerican cultures to the south occupied Guanajuato many centuries earlier. These early populations were organized into small communities that settled along the banks of the Laja River between 950 A.D. and 1110 A.D. and spread out around most of what is today the state of Guanajuato. These societies were linked by trade to the ancient city of Tula, and the great metropolis of Teotihuacán, located just north of present day Mexico City (not to be confused with the Aztec capital of Tenochtitlán). Moreover, there is evidence to suggest that this region was actually the northwestern frontier of the Toltec empire. Around the year 1100 A.D., agricultural practices seem to have ceased almost completely in Guanajuato, and by 1200 A.D. the urban centers of the region had been abandoned. The desertion of the northern provinces of the Toltec empire was due to a political power struggle between the followers of the feathered serpent god Quetzalcóatl and the Tezcatipoca, who ruled in the Toltec capital of Tula. This political strife was compounded by an extended drought in

this region, which provoked a mass migration out of Guanajuato to the central high plateau in Michoacán. As the great Mesoamerican cultures shifted to the southwest, Guanajuato was inhabited by more primitive migratory groups. Over the next 300 years, little changed in the way these groups went about their lives.

Pre-Hispanic art on display at the Alhóndiga Museum in Guanajuato

The churches of San Miguel de Allende are among the oldest structures in the region.

Sowing the Seeds of San Miguel

In 1521, after a bloody struggle between the Aztecs and the Spaniards led by Hernán Cortés, the Aztec capital city of Tenochtitlán fell to the conquistadores, to become the capital of New Spain and a base from which the Spanish conquistadors could conquer the rest of Mexico and beyond. However, even after the subjugation of Mexico's indigenous peoples, the Spaniards had to struggle arduously against native traditions, particularly with regards to religious practices. The exploration and colonization of the state of Guanajuato was initiated from the region of Michoacán to the southwest.

The first settlement in Guanajuato was the monastery of San Francisco de Acámbaro, established near the Lerma River on September 19, 1526, by monks from the town of Urúapan, Michoacán. From this location, Spanish missionaries set out to explore the Chichimeca lands to the north. In 1542, the Franciscan Friar Juan de San Miguel, from the monastery of Acámbaro, set out to the north along the Grande River and its tributaries on an expedition that explored as far as the Laja River. He intended to find an appropriate location to establish a town in the region, to serve as a center of catechization of the local indigenous populations. This expedition led him to the upper basin of the Laja River, where he constructed a small church called the Chapel of San Miguel Viejo and a small settlement called San Miguel de los Chichimecas. He left this settlement in the hands of his associate, Friar Bernardo Cossin, who struggled for years to convert the Copuces, one of the most violent indigenous groups in the region. Catholicism proved a difficult sell to the Copuces and in 1551 they set fire to the settlement, forcing the friar to find a new location from which to preach. He chose a spot several kilometers away, situated just above a slope that provided for better defenses. This location also contained a spring that would provide fresh water for the new settlement, which he called San Miguel El Grande. Today, this location is occupied by San Miguel de Allende, and the spring continues to provide water to the city.

The first building that Friar Bernardo Cossin raised on his new site was the Chapel of La Santa Cruz, which was located near the spring. The town of San Miguel El Grande gradually grew around the chapel, populated by groups of indigenous people coming from around Central Mexico. Today, this old section of San Miguel, located on the southeast edge of town, is known as the Quarter of El Chorro.

Early Economic Development

Beginning around 1550, the sparse Chichimeca populations in the territory of Guanajuato began to be displaced by indigenous groups from other parts of Mexico, such as Tarascans from Michoacán, Otomies from Querétaro, and Mexicas from the Mexico City region. These immigrants came to work on the cattle ranches in the area. As a result of the influx of migratory populations, the town of San Miguel El Grande and the surrounding area experienced a diversification of its workforce. The population that settled in San Miguel El Grande possessed skills in working with textiles and metals.

In 1555, Viceroy Don Luis de Velasco decided to invest in the development of the town of San Miguel El Grande to defend access roads leading to Zacatecas and San Luis Potosí, where silver and gold were already being mined. On his urging, 50 Spanish families relocated to the area, constructing a new settlement just to the north of the Quarter of El Chorro. In 1564, the Chapel of San Rafael was established on this site by Don Vasco de Quiroga. Its main plaza was situated on the spot where Plaza Civica Ignacio Allende is today located.

Throughout the rest of the 16th century and into the 17th century, Spanish monks and ranchers continued to colonize the territory of Guanajuato. The lands north of San Miguel El Grande were ideal for raising cattle, and in 1573, Viceroy Luis de Velasco granted vast swaths of land in the region of Guanajuato to several Spaniards for the purpose of establishing ranches. These land grants proved to be great sources of wealth for the families that received them, as well as fundamental in the economic development of the fertile plateau of northern Mexico in the 18th century. They sowed the seeds for the large cattle raising trade that became a well-respected way of life and produced Mexico's famous *jinetes*, or horsemen.

In the 17th century, the discovery and development of the Real de Minas of Santa Fe in Guanajuato created a new source of wealth in the area. At the time, the Spanish crown was engaged in war with other European powers, which weakened its ability to maintain economic relationships with New Spain. As exchanges between New Spain and the mother country decreased, the region of Guanajuato went through an economic and social reorganization, making it more self-sufficient. During this time, the town of San Miguel El Grande enjoyed a long respite from its obligations to the crown, resulting in political and economic power shifting to wealthy local families. The town was located adjacent to the zone that the colonial administration had designated to support the Real de Minas of Santa Fe in Guanajuato. The mines in Guanajuato made local cattle ranchers even more powerful because, in addition to being a source of agriculture, their animals were needed to provide a source of labor in the silver mines. Both cattle ranching and mining reached their peak in Guanajuato in the 18th century.

That the land in the territory of Guanajuato was ideal for agriculture, as well as its being centrally located between Zacatecas, Durango, and Mexico City, made the region an important resource throughout the 17th century. Furthermore, this region quickly became one of the largest producers of wheat in New Spain, making it the breadbasket of Mexico. The fields of Acámbaro, Celaya, Salamanca, Silao, and León became the most cultivated in all of New Spain. Wheat farming and corn cultivation was so prosperous that Guanajuato was often referred to as the granary of New Spain.

However, in the latter half of the 18th century silver mining became Guanajuato's main source of economic activity. The deposits of silver discovered in Guanajuato gave rise to an

Descendants of the ancient Chichimeca Indians continue to populate the region today.

Lucrative silver mines led to massive investment in the infrastructure of the city of Guanajuato.

increase in commercial routes through the territory, north to Santa Fe and San Luis Potosí, and west to Guadalajara. San Miguel El Grande was located at the center of this activity and became the focal point where mining products, farming products, and manufactured products all passed through.

Glory Years

In the 17th and 18th centuries, San Miguel El Grande was the residence of choice for many large landholders of Central Mexico. These rich Spaniards and Creoles left their mark on San Miguel, distinguishing it from other towns throughout the region by investing in local architecture and works of art. By 1750, San Miguel El Grande was home to one of the most prosperous populations in all of New Spain. Its city planners were forward thinkers, laying the town out in a checkerboard configuration with ordered streets and blocks of regular shapes and size. The

Old mine cars are now used to beautify the city of Guanajuato.
Mary Delgado

more wealthy residents of San Miguel El Grande built baroque-style homes and churches at the city center around the main square—the Plaza Mayor. The outskirts of town would have been peppered with simple adobe huts that served as residences of the Indians and *mestizos* (mixed race individuals). In terms of local businesses, the town contained several grocery stores, bakeries, and granaries. Owners of these shops were generally wealthy Creoles of Spanish heritage, and some were tied to the commercial monopolies managed by powerful interests in Mexico City.

In 1741, Guanajuato was granted the title of City by King Philip V of Spain. In 1786, New Spain was divided into 12 *intendencias*, one of which was the Intendencia de Guanajuato, with an area about the size of the present-day state of Guanajuato. By this time Guanajuato had become known for a broad range of products, such as ironwork and woolen goods. The excellence of textiles from this region combined with efficient production techniques made Guanajuato one of the largest centers for the production of textile goods in New Spain. In particular, the town of San Miguel El Grande became known for its high-quality saddles. This success also meant that San Miguel was developing into an autonomous regional economic power far removed from political influences in Mexico City and the

Wealthy old families and silver barons lived in relative luxury during the colonial period.   Mary Delgado

Spanish crown. This would be a key factor in the development of Guanajuato as the focal point of the Mexican struggle for independence from Spain. For its part, Guanajuato was the most important silver-producing city in the world. The Valenciana silver mine, located just outside the city of Guanajuato, was one of the richest silver finds in history. In the 18th century, this mine alone accounted for 60 percent of the world's total silver production. For this reason, Guanajuato flourished as the silver mining capital of the world for three centuries, producing nearly a third of the world's silver during this time.

Birthplace of Independence

In the late 18th century, Spain had once again turned its attention to its territories across the Atlantic and was attempting to regain control of the American colonies by enacting more stringent administrative rules, and by pressing for a higher percentage of economic resources. King Carlos III enacted what became known as the Bourbon Reforms, which were a series of measures designed to restrain the autonomy and power of local authorities and interests in New Spain.

In 1762, tensions with the English caused Spain to reorganize the military in its American territories. To guarantee loyalty, the crown initially sent continental forces to serve in New Spain. However, maintaining what were essentially foreign forces in its American territories put further strains on the already stretched Spanish treasury. Therefore, Spain was eventually forced to pare down the number of Spanish troops in New Spain and to use them instead to train forces made up of Creoles. In San Miguel El Grande, financial contributions for military training by the local populace were so great that the

Dolores Hidalgo is where the movement for independence began.

Schoolchildren gather for a tour of Miguel Hidalgo's house.

town was granted its own provincial regiment, known as the Dragoons of the Queen.

In September 1810, tension between the Spanish crown and the colonial establishment had brought Mexico to the cusp of a revolution. Spanish forces in the city of Querétaro learned of a conspiracy for independence in the town of Dolores, 25 miles north of San Miguel. As they prepared to take action, the wife of Querétaro's mayor sent word to the insurgents that danger was on its way. The messenger was a member of the Dragoons of the Queen named Ignacio Allende. A native son of San Miguel, he had become sympathetic with the Mexican independence movement and had attended secret meetings in Querétaro. He had secretly agreed to be a leader of the independence, should insurgency ever come to fruition. At midnight on September 16, Miguel Hidalgo, the parish priest in Dolores, rang the church bell and called for followers to take up arms and go with him to San Miguel. Soon a group of around seven hundred farmers, miners, and peasants left Dolores armed only with pickaxes and machetes. They stopped in the village of Atotonilco to gather more followers and a cloth with the picture of the Virgin of Guadalupe, the patron saint of Mexico. Afterward, Hidalgo marched through the streets of San Miguel carrying the standard of Guadelupe and leading an army of five thousand. Seeing the insurgents, the mayor of San Miguel immediately turned over the city to Father Hidalgo. This priest had envisioned a bloodless revolution in which the will of the people would overwhelm the powers-that-be throughout Mexico, just the way they had in San Miguel. Instead, he would lose his life within months. As for Allende, he quickly became one of the leaders of the rebellion, before being captured and executed in the city of Chihuahua. The severed heads

The Jardín Principal is the heart of San Miguel de Allende.

of Hidalgo and Allende, along with two other insurgents (Aldama and Jiménez), were brought back to the town of Guanajuato and hung in cages on the Alhóndiga building for the duration of the war. Quickly, Mexico's war for independence became a bloody class struggle, with the wealthy pitted against the poor, that dragged on for the next 11 years.

Years of Turbulence

Of course, the cause of Allende and Hidalgo did culminate in Mexico's independence from Spain. In 1824, the first Mexican constitution created the sovereign state of Guanajuato with the town of Guanajuato as its capital. The first governor, Carlos Montes de Oca, was a dedicated supporter of education in the state. He was the force behind the reopening of the original College of the Most Holy Trinity, founded by the Jesuits, and the old College of the Immaculate Conception, run by Oratorian priests. The latter was to become the State

Ignacio de Allende—Hero of the Independence

José Ignacio María de Allende y Unzaga was born in San Miguel El Grande on January 21, 1769. The son of a wealthy, landed Spanish father (Domingo Narciso de Allende) and a Creole mother (María Ana de Unzaga), Allende attended the prestigious school of San Francisco de Sales with Juan José Martínez de los Reyes, also known by the nickname of *El Pípila*. After graduation in 1795, Allende joined the Dragoons of the Queen as a lieutenant. The military exercises of the Dragoons were limited to drills and guard duty. However, in 1804, tensions between Spain and England began to rise and colonial troops were put on a heightened state of alert to protect against a possible English attack. This situation caused Allende's company to be transferred first to Mexico City and then to Veracruz. Along the way, Allende had a political awakening in which he became convinced it was time for Mexico to vie for independence from Spain. He returned to San Miguel at the end of 1808 and began attending secret insurgent meetings at various locations around the state of Guanajuato. In fact, Allende himself presided over several such meetings that were disguised as mere social gatherings, to hide their intentions from local authorities.

In September 1810, Spanish authorities in Querétaro learned of a burgeoning independence movement in the small town of Dolores, near San Miguel El Grande, and resolved to crush it. What these authorities did not know was that Allende had already agreed to lead the independence movement.

Ignacio de Allende is a deeply important figure in Mexican history.

The Pípila statue that towers over Guanajuato is a constant reminder of the Battle of the Alhóndiga.

As the authorities prepared to move on the conspirators, Allende rushed to Dolores, where the parish priest Miguel Hidalgo had been organizing a small independence movement. After several hours of heated debate, Hidalgo, Allende, and their associates decided it was time to take up arms against the Spanish.

In the early morning hours of September 16, 1810, the insurgents set out from the parish church in Dolores and headed toward San Miguel. Instead of offering resistance, the majority of residents of San Miguel joined the insurgency. Allende was able to convince his fellow soldiers in the regiment of the Dragoons to join the cause, and his influence helped convince San Miguel's populace to back the insurgency. The insurgents locked up the Spanish authorities in the school of San Francisco de Sales and quickly named new town authorities. Then, in the morning of September 19, they set out to expand their movement.

After the capture of the Alhóndiga de Granaditas in Guanajuato—the battle that made El Pípila famous—Allende decided to march on Mexico City. The insurgents were decimated at the Battle of the Bridge of Calderón and Allende reversed course, marching north, where he was captured in an ambush. He was taken to the city of Chihuahua where he was tried for insubordination and executed by firing squad on June 26, 1811. His corpse was decapitated and his head was taken back to Guanajuato where it was put on display at the Alhóndiga de Granaditas. In 1824, his remains were buried in the cathedral in Mexico City with honors reserved for viceroys and presidents. Two years later, the name of his hometown was renamed in his honor, from San Miguel El Grande to San Miguel de Allende. In 1925, his remains were moved once again to the Independence column in Mexico City.

The Parroquia de San Miguel is the archetypal symbol of San Miguel de Allende.

College of Guanajuato. Despite the fact that the 19th century was a politically unstable period in Mexico, the citizens of Guanajuato managed several important developments in the region. Dams and aqueducts were constructed to serve San Miguel and other towns, and an abundant amount of spring water allowed the urban zone to flourish. Local craft traditions continued to develop and a few industries, such as textiles and masonry, infused some life into local economies. On January 17, 1858, President Benito Juárez temporarily established the capital of the Mexican Republic in the city of Guanajuato, due to the constant persecution leveled against him by conservative factions. Later, during the period of the French Intervention, a garrison of French troops occupied the city of Guanajuato and the newly installed Emperor Maximilian of Hapsburg visited the city in September 1864. It was he who ordered the conversion of the Alhondiga de Granaditas into a prison.

The final decades of the 19th century were a time of increased development for the region. Foreign investors arrived and pumped money into mines, railways, tramways, telephones, electricity, public lighting, and public spaces such as the La Paz square and statue, Juarez Theatre, and the Hidalgo Market. In San Miguel, this developing prosperity manifested itself in public and private works that modernized and beautified the city, though in many cases it was at the expense of destroying 18th-century baroque buildings. It was in these years that the indigenous architect Zafrino Gutiérrez embarked on a radical modification of the baroque facades of the Parroquia and the adjacent church called La Santa Escuela, as well as the clock tower in the heart of the city and Las Monjas dome of the Iglesia de la Concepción (Church of the Conception). Basing these works on Gothic models, it is said that he was inspired by the images of European churches that adorned the postage stamps and postcards that were arriving in Mexico from Spain at that time. Additionally, other public spaces were modified in those years. The traditional open and paved Hispanic Plaza de Armas was converted to the Jardín Principal with its manicured trees and walkways, as it exists today.

This new age of prosperity in Guanajuato was short-lived and left in its wake a further centralization of political power in the landed elite as well as increased authoritarianism and decreased social equality. Civil war broke out throughout Mexico in 1910 with the Mexican Revolution. Political instability and uncertainty ended Guanajuato's mining boom, and San Miguel's prosperity once again went into a state of decline. Though these two towns kept themselves at the edge of the revolutionary conflict, they did not escape the constant incursions by military troops traveling to and from such revolutionary hotspots as León, just a few miles away. Many of San Miguel's wealthier families withdrew to safer cities while the working class drifted away, faced with hardship from the decline of the haciendas and of commerce, joining the ranks of armed bands or making their way toward the safety of the United States. Guanajuato lost more than 20 percent of its population, and in San Miguel, a remote location and dwindling resources had resulted in a town on the verge of abandonment. Other nearby towns such as Mineral de la Luz did indeed become ghost towns.

This time, though, the decline and depopulation was more gradual than it had been 100 years before. However, Guanajuato's stability took another hit in 1926 when stringent anti-cleric laws were put into place by President Plutarco Elías Calles (founder of the PRI political party). These laws resulted in the violent guerilla conflict known as the Cristero War. Being the staunchly Catholic region that it is, Guanajuato was one of the areas that most strongly opposed the new laws, and many battles were fought here.

There is a legend that says that the visitor who drinks from the springs of El Chorro is destined to return someday. This legend is used to explain how San Miguel has continued to bounce back from decline and stagnation time after time. By the late 1920s, the region began the long process of recuperation after many years of civil strife and political instability. Once again, visitors began to take notice of the beautiful surroundings and temperate climate that San Miguel had to offer. The town's population began to grow once again with the arrival of Spanish immigrants who began buying up land. However, unlike Zafrino Gutiérrez, their impact on the town's appearance would be limited. In 1926, the Mexican government declared the entire town of San Miguel de Allende to be a national historic monument, to preserve the town's colonial character.

Birth of an Artist Colony

The modern, sophisticated city of San Miguel began to take root on a rainy day in 1937 when Felipe Cossío del Pomar—an exiled Peruvian painter and art critic—stepped off the train that had just pulled into town. He was a friend of such notable artists as Diego Rivera and Alfonso Reyes and had once before been to San Miguel. His ambition was to create a Latin American art school rooted in popular culture and open to all trends of contemporary art. He came to San Miguel to take advantage of the city's reputation as a hospitable place—a place steeped in history that exemplified its colonial past—and one that was isolated from large urban centers as well as the surrounding countryside. He was so committed to seeing his vision to fruition that he was able to garner financial support for his school from Mexico's President, Lázaro Cárdenas. He chose a historic but oddly sacred site as the location of his school: The Convento de Concepción nunnery, located one block from the Jardín Principal, what is today the site of the city's Bellas Artes, or fine arts center. At the time, the building was partially demolished and occupied by a cavalry regiment of the Mexican army. Cossío offered the position of Art Director to an American artist and writer named Stirling Dickinson, who had also only recently arrived in San Miguel. Dickinson helped with advertising and promotion as well. He made several trips to various cities in the United States, where he distributed more than ten thousand fliers to universities and cultural centers. The School of Fine Arts of San Miguel de Allende was designed principally to cater to foreign students and wealthy students from Mexico's interior. However, the school also offered popular arts and crafts workshops for local residents of limited means. These workshops focused on preserving various ancestral crafts such as handmade textiles and ceramics that might have otherwise been lost. Thanks to Cossío's full Rolodex, the school hosted many distinguished speakers during its early years, such as Pablo Neruda, Jesús Silva Hérzog, and Diego Rivera. As the school expanded, Cossío acquired an old ranch from a famous bullfighter and turned it into residences for students, professors, and visitors alike. He adapted a huge water tank on the property into an Olympic size pool, complete with showers and dressing rooms, and remodeled the rooms around the center patio into eight apartments, modeling them on his Paris studio. He also commissioned a great arch to be built at the lower entrance to the school, atop of Calle Santo Domingo. The arch is a perfect replica of a 17th-century baroque arch in Cusco, Peru. However, in 1945 the Peruvian government announced that exiles could return home, prompting Cossío to return to his homeland.

Before he left, Cossío sold his school to a pair of Italian brothers, who promptly made an agreement with the U.S. government to offer special rates to recently returned soldiers who were interested in studying art. Unfortunately, these brothers embezzled the G.I. Bill money and drove the school into ruin. Nevertheless, San Miguel's days as a haven for expa-

American and Canadian expatriates have long been a part of San Miguel de Allende.

triate veterans were just beginning. In 1948, *Life* magazine published a story about veterans studying art in San Miguel, calling the city a G.I. paradise. The story told of apartments that rented for $10 a month, tended by servants, as well as 65-cent rum and 10-cent packs of cigarettes. Soon, over six thousand American veterans had applied to study art in San Miguel, more than half the number of the city's total population. By this time, the residents of San Miguel had begun to restore the city's colonial architecture and develop other tourist attractions, such as the nearby thermal springs. Some veterans brought their families while others married into local, well-established families. This trend would continue with the later arrival of retirees from north of the border, and names like Brooks, Dickinson, and Hawkins became engrained into the cultural history of San Miguel.

Felipe Cossío was once again sent into exile, in 1948. He returned to San Miguel and began a new art school located at the old residences of the de la Canal family, known simply as the Instituto Allende. Again, with the help of Stirling Dickinson as well as that of the retired governor of Guanajuato, Enrique Fernández Martínez, Cossío converted the old de la Canal mansion into an appropriate venue for an art school. In 1951, classes began at the Instituto Allende. Nearly all of the students were from the United States. Today, San Miguel de Allende has a thriving art culture that stands as a testament to the hard work of Cossío and his associates.

In the ensuing years, waves of students arrived annually from north of the border for accredited summer courses and, along the way, many decided to stay. Enterprising locals soon saw the need to teach the newly arrived foreigners the local language, and San

A handicraft shop in San Miguel de Allende

Miguel's language schools began to pop up. The Hispano-American Acadamy began by organizing classes in Latin American culture as well as symphonic concerts and chamber music. These events were used to restore the Angela Peralta Theatre, which was being used as a movie theatre at the time. In 1960, after more than 10 years of neglect, the School of Bellas Artes that was begun by Felipe Cossío was restored with a government grant, to coincide with the celebration of 150 years of Mexican independence. Little by little, and with very few resources, the school grew to include instruction in areas such as music, as well. As the city's expatriate movement continued in the counterculture years of the 1960s, it became a popular destination of beat writer Neal Cassady, as well as Ken Kesey, author of *One Flew Over the Cuckoo's Nest*.

Today the atmosphere and ambiance of San Miguel, inarguably favorable for creativity, attracts painters, writers, and musicians from around Mexico and around the world. Moreover, it has all the modern services any urban dweller has come to expect, but with the feel of a small town. Despite an expanding populace and the influx of commercial and tourist development, San Miguel continues to be an artist colony and a favored destination for expatriates. The artistic and cultural environment that has prospered in San Miguel for nearly 75 years has created a unique society very different from any other in Central Mexico. In fact, what most makes the city unique is the interplay between the traditional Mexican culture, which the city has built upon over the years, and the culture from north of the border, which has been brought here by expatriates from the United States and Canada. In fact, it has become a common saying among American retirees here that one goes to Florida to die and one goes to San Miguel to live.

The streets of San Miguel de Allende were not built for auto traffic.

2

TRANSPORTATION

San Miguel de Allende and Guanajuato are towns that can be appreciated only and truly on foot. It is only by walking that you experience the ambiance created by the colorful houses with carved arched doors, along with the open plazas of these towns. Fortunately, they are both towns that are compact, with hotels, bars, restaurants, and general points of interest situated around a central area, making them ideal for walking. Having stated that, there are also monuments, villages, and other interesting locations that are not within walking distance. You will not have any trouble finding public transportation to take you to these places, though many people like to have the convenience of having their own transportation at hand. Certainly, if you are coming from the southern border region of the United States, the state of Guanajuato is well within driving distance. In fact, this region has become a somewhat popular destination for RV enthusiasts, though I can't imagine trying to navigate an RV through the narrow streets of San Miguel, which were not even constructed with a four-door sedan in mind. However you choose to get here, you are sure to find that your best hours will be spent on your feet rather than behind the wheel.

GETTING TO THE AREA

By Air
The biggest challenge of a trip to San Miguel de Allende is probably just getting there. San Miguel de Allende is served by two international airports, though neither one is a convenient choice for anyone accustomed to the convenience of a big city airport nearby. On the bright side, your afternoon coffee in the Jardín Principal will never be disturbed by a jet streaming overhead. The first is Aeropuerto del Bajio (airport code BJX), about halfway between the town of Guanajuato and the city of Leon, the largest city in the state of Guanajuato. Therefore, if the town of Guanajuato is your primary destination, you will only have a 20-minute cab ride from the airport to your hotel in downtown Guanajuato. However, this airport is about 100 miles away from San Miguel, making it difficult to catch an early morning flight out of town. The airlines operating out of BJX include Continental Airlines, American Airlines, Aeromexico, and Delta Airlines. If you do happen to have an early morning flight out of BJX, it might be worth your while to plan on spending the night in the town of Guanajuato. Another option is the recently opened Aeropuerto Internacional de Querétaro (airport code QRO), which lies only 40 miles away outside of the beautiful colonial city of Querétaro. The choice of airlines serving this airport is not as extensive as at BJX, though it is served by Continental Airlines and Aeromexico, with daily

Though small, nearby airports are served by several Mexican and American airlines.   Mary Delgado

nonstop flights from Los Angeles and Houston.

You can arrange to be picked up from the airport through several of the local tour companies. The drivers are bilingual and will take you directly to the doorstep of your hotel, and will pick you up as far away as the Mexico City airport, for as little as 50 dollars per person. This option has the added benefit of providing you with a knowledgeable local tour guide with which to discuss the ins and outs of this beautiful place, just as your visit begins.

Customs and Immigration

Technically speaking, customs and immigration can be a real pain. You can mitigate some of this inconvenience by either driving in, or crossing the border and flying out of Ciudad Juárez, Tijuana, or some other Mexican airport. Crossing the U.S.-Mexico border on foot or by car is much less of a hassle than making your way through airport security these days. Furthermore, while a passport is required to fly into the United States from Mexico, citizens of the United States and Canada ages 19 or older need only a government-issued photo ID (such as a driver's license) along with proof of citizenship (such as a birth certificate or naturalization certificate) to enter or depart the United States by land or sea. Children ages 18 and younger need proof of citizenship, such as a birth certificate. Eventually, passports will be required for even that as early as 2009, though the deadline may be put back. For specific details of current passport rules, check out the Department of Homeland Security Web site (http://www.dhs.gov/xtrvlsec/crossingborders/whtibasics.shtm). The bottom line is that it is best to get a passport before you need it. Getting one via a rush application can be expensive.

Do not delay getting your passport. Recently passed laws have increased the wait time to months.

A tourist card is an official Mexican document declaring that you have stated that the purpose of your visit to Mexico is tourism and that your visit will last no more than 180 days. This document costs $20 and anyone staying in Mexico for more than 72 hours and traveling beyond the border zone (about 70 miles south) needs to have a tourist card. If you are driving into Mexico, you can get this document at the immigration station just across the border. If you are flying out of a Mexican airport, such as Ciudad Juárez, you will get this document as you pass into the boarding area of the airport. And if you are flying into Mexico from another country (such as Canada or the United States), the cost of this document is included in the price of your airfare and you will receive it, along with instructions on filling it out, while on the plane. Once you arrive, customs and immigration will stamp it, indicating that you are in the country legally.

Traveling with Kids

These historic towns in Central Mexico can be great places to take a break from your day-to-day responsibilities. On the other hand, you will probably find yourself constantly thinking it would have been great to bring the kids. If you do decide to take the kids along, there are extra hoops you will have to jump through. First, new passport requirements for U.S. citizens returning from abroad also apply to children. Getting a passport for a child under the age of 14 requires filling out additional documents as well as having both parents' consent

Children playing in an empty fountain, Plaza Reforma.

to their child being taken out of the country. That said, it is no longer necessary for single parents or unaccompanied minors traveling in Mexico to have notarized documentation authorizing travel as long as each child has a valid passport and tourist card.

Traveling with Pets

Bringing pets to Mexico is a common practice for those driving across the border. If you are flying in, airlines have their own rules about this, so you should check ahead. Mexico allows dogs and cats into the country as long as the owner has a notarized letter from a veterinarian stating that the animal is in good health and has the proper vaccinations. However, if you're driving, it's unlikely that this will be an issue.

Keep in mind that certain risks are to be considered before bringing an animal down to Mexico. Very few hotels allow pets, and those that do generally charge extra. (Be sure to check ahead when making reservations.) Hot weather can also become an issue with some animals. However, the biggest danger with regard to pets is that Mexican towns—from giant Mexico City to tiny towns—have a problem with stray animals. There is always an outside chance that your animal could contract a disease from one of these animals or that some mishap may occur. Unless you are prepared to constantly look after your pets, it might be a better idea just to leave them at home.

San Miguel de Allende has plenty of options for inexpensive public transportation.

By Bus

If flying is not the way you like to get around, traveling by bus can be a nice way to tour Mexico and see the countryside in the process. Although Hollywood movies have created an image of Mexican bus travel as that of riding in cramped quarters with several goats and a rooster, many Mexican bus companies provide a more comfortable experience than you'll find in the United States, at extremely reasonable rates. Luxury or first-class buses are modern, with comfortable reclining seats, and are extremely clean. They usually will play an American film, which will more than likely be dubbed in Spanish. Second-class buses are also very clean but usually lack a bathroom and video monitors. Plus, some second-class buses are notorious for being long rides, because they often stop and pick up passengers anywhere in the countryside.

Both Guanajuato and San Miguel de Allende have modern bus stations fairly close to where you want to be. In San Miguel, it is located on Calle Canal, about a half mile from the center of town. Any local bus marked "Central" heading west on Canal will make a stop at the bus station. Taxis from the bus station to the center of San Miguel are a bargain at 20 pesos during the day and usually 25 pesos at night. In Guanajuato, the bus station is located outside of the city core but a taxi into town will only cost you a few bucks, or you can take the city bus for about a quarter. When in the bus station, always be alert and attentive to your luggage and never leave it unattended. Buses for San Miguel leave from Querétaro about every 20 minutes during the day, and every hour or two in the evening. The trip takes about an hour. Flecha Amarilla has nine buses a day with service between San Miguel de Allende and Guanajuato.

If you are crossing the border in Texas, Transportes del Norte offers first-class bus service to and from Laredo, Texas. If you plan to travel by bus to or from Pacific beach towns such as Acapulco or Zihuatanejo, your best bet is to go through Morelia, Michoacán. You could also connect through Mexico City. However, the logistics of getting in and out of Mexico City will add several hours to your trip.

The first-class bus ride to San Miguel or Guanajuato from Mexico City takes between four and five hours from the city's Terminal Norte. Companies offering this service include Primera Plus, ETN, Satelite, and Omnibus de Mexico. These companies offer six daily first-class trips. Herradura de Plata offers buses that leave for San Miguel around every half hour. Be sure that you are buying a first-class ticket that is "directo." Nondirect trips can have several annoying layovers and bus stations are rarely interesting places to spend time. And a long ride on anything less than first-class can quickly turn into a nightmare.

By Car

You can get to San Miguel de Allende by driving south on Highway 51, which comes from the west through Dolores Hidalgo. However, if you're coming south from Texas, take Highway 85 past Monterrey to the Saltillo Bypass. Here, hop on Highway 57 and continue through Central Mexico into the state of Guanajuato. To get to Guanajuato, pick up Highway 110 out of Dolores Hidalgo or Highway 45 out of León. To get to Guanajuato from Mexico City, there are two routes. The first is to take Highway 57 north past Querétaro to Dolores Hidalgo, then take Highway 110

Bus Companies

ETN (ENLACES TERRESTRES NACIONALES)
(From U.S.: 011 52) 473-733-1579
www.etn.com.mx
This line offers luxury service to destinations including Mexico City, Monterrey, Morélia, Querétaro, and Zacatecas.

FLECHA AMARILLA
(From U.S.: 011 52) 473-733-1332
www.flecha-amarilla.com.mx
This line offers second-class service to Mexico City, Querétaro, Dolores Hidalgo, Celaya, and San Luis Potosí.

OMNIBUS DE MEXICO
(From U.S.: 011 52) 473-733-2607
www.odm.com.mx
This line offers first-class service throughout Mexico, including Ciudad Juárez, Guadalajara, Mexico City, and Zacatecas.

PRIMERA PLUS
(From U.S.: 011 52) 473-733-1332
www.primeraplus.com.mx
This line offers first-class service to many locations including Guadalajara, León, Morélia, and Querétaro. Primera Plus also offers second-class service to Guadalajara, Guanajuato, and León. Second-class buses do not have a bathroom, so plan ahead.

TRANSPORTES DEL NORTE
(From U.S.: 011 52) 473-733-1344
This line offers first-class service to destinations in the northern border region of Mexico including Monterrey and Laredo, Texas.

---

west to Guanajuato. The faster route, however, is to take Highway 57 north to Querétaro where you pick up Highway 45D west to Salamanca, where you follow Highway 45 north to Silao, and then take Highway 110 east. To get to San Miguel de Allende from Mexico City, take Highway 57 through Querétaro and continue north for about 25 miles. A sign points left to San Miguel de Allende. Exit and continue on that two-lane road for about 20 miles. When you get to San Miguel de Allende, take Salida a Querétaro to the center of town. The

Driving in Mexico may take some getting used to, so take your time.

quickest way between Guanajuato and San Miguel de Allende is Highway 110 south from Guanajuato. The more scenic route is Highway 110 north out of Guanajuato through Dolores Hidalgo.

Long distance driving in Mexico is a challenging experience, even for drivers who have plenty of experience driving long distances north of the border. Even the most modern Mexican highways are not engineered with the same eye toward safety that you find in the United States. Driving in larger Mexican cities can be an intimidating undertaking, with other drivers prying their way into the smallest opening in traffic and putting the onus on you to avoid a collision—as well as treating stop signs and traffic lights as mere suggestions instead of requirements. With regard to Mexico's open roads, these circumstances cease and the greatest danger is quite the opposite of intimidating traffic; here the biggest danger is complacency. One of the most common dangers is the livestock that commonly wander onto the road. This is generally not a problem if you are minding your speed. However, you do *not* want to come careening through a mountain pass to find a herd of cattle sitting on the road ahead of you. Another slightly related problem is the lack of guardrails that exist on the road, even where it winds along steep cliffs. Getting to Guanajuato by car from the U.S. border requires driving highways that weave through the mountains of Northern and Central Mexico. As you drive through areas such as these, it will become abundantly clear that the road was not engineered with the kind of safety standards that are common north of the border. Add to this the frequent potholes and the steep or nonexistent shoulder.

If I still haven't talked you out of it, taking Mexican toll roads from Nuevo Laredo to Guanajuato or San Miguel de Allende can add up to around $70 in toll fees. These roads are marked as *cuota* on road signs and maps. There are free highways that will take you to the area (marked as *libre*), but these roads are generally two-lane highways and not well maintained. This means stretches that are even more treacherous than normal, and you are guaranteed to encounter slow-moving trucks that will crawl along for miles before pulling to the shoulder or giving you the opportunity to pass safely.

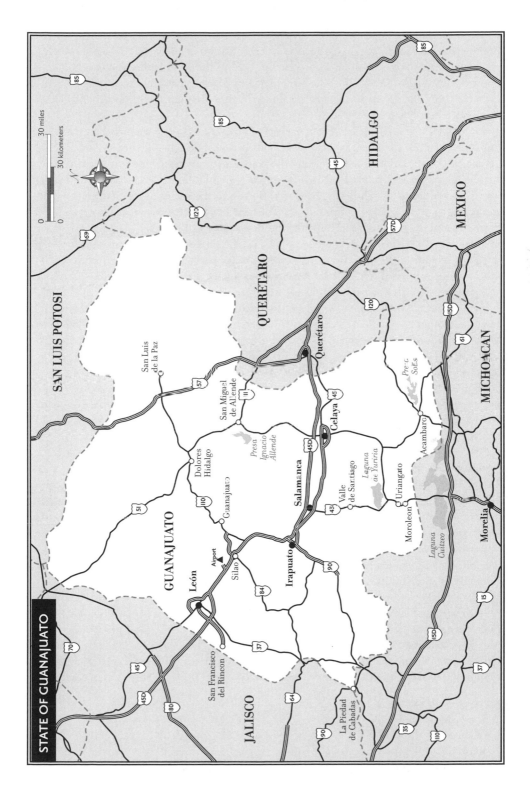

STATE OF GUANAJUATO

However, here is some advice that by now should be self-evident: Drive slowly. There may be times when you will have the urge to throw this bit of advice out the window—say, you have found yourself trailing a slow-moving vehicle for miles before you have the opportunity to pass, and you feel the need to make up some lost time. Resist this temptation. Getting in an accident will slow you down much more than driving safely and is liable to cost you more than time.

Do not drive at night. The dangers presented by narrow roads, wandering animals, and unprotected cliffs are exacerbated at night. This is especially true of animals, which congregate at the edge of the roadway where the grass grows greenest. One traveler told me that he has successfully navigated Mexican roads at night by sidling up behind trucks as a way of protection against loitering livestock. However, that seems like a lot of trust to put in the hands of the trucker in front of you. The best advice is to find a place to get some rest, and get going again in the morning when it's safe.

Speed limits are posted in kilometers. This can be a bit confusing if your speedometer does not include kilometers. However, since 60 miles per hour is roughly equal to 100 kilometers per hour, if you multiply the posted speed limit by 6 and drop the last zero it will give you a rough estimation of the allowed speed in miles per hour.

Keep in mind that while it can be a convenience to have your own car to travel between towns and other destinations, a car can easily turn into a hindrance here as well. Both San Miguel de Allende and (especially) Guanajuato are notoriously difficult places to find parking. Unless your hotel has private parking, you could have a tough time finding a place to leave your car. Remember that both Guanajuato and San Miguel are places where you can get from place to place just fine on foot. When driving, be sure to purchase Mexican insurance before crossing over into Mexico, since most U.S. auto insurance does not cover driving in Mexico. Mexican drivers tend to be aggressive, not to mention the fact that stop signs and traffic lights tend to be treated as mere suggestions rather than hard and fast rules.

Insurance

Under Mexican law, in the event of an accident motorists are required to have sufficient currency to cover damages, or insurance from a Mexican company. Non-Mexican insurance does not fulfill this responsibility. If you are involved in an automobile accident, you are basically considered guilty until proven innocent. You will be detained until the local authorities determine who is at fault. If this happens, it is a good idea to contact your nearest consulate immediately. You will be required to demonstrate financial responsibility. Financial responsibility is defined as being in possession of an inexpensive Mexican insurance policy or $5,000 to $10,000 in cash. Therefore, it is not a good idea to drive in Mexico without Mexican liability insurance. If you are renting a car, you will pay for this insurance through the rental company. However, if you are driving your own vehicle into Mexico, you'll need to purchase insurance on your own. This insurance is relatively inexpensive, and it comes with peace of mind. Plenty of companies offer this insurance at all major U.S.–Mexico border crossings and on the Internet. Here are a few just in case:

ADVENTURE MEXICAN INSURANCE
1-800-485-4075 (U.S.)
www.mexadventure.com
E-mail: info@mexadventure.com
P.O. Box 1469, Soquel, CA 95073

INSTANT MEXICO AUTO INSURANCE
1-800-345-4701; fax 610-690-6533
www.instant-mex-auto-insur.com
223 Via de San Ysidro, San Ysidro, CA 92173

MEXPRO MEXICAN AUTO INSURANCE
1-888-467-4639; fax 928-213-8476
www.mexpro.com
1300 South Milton Road, Flagstaff, AZ 86001

Military Stops

If you travel by road in Mexico, you will soon encounter being stopped at a military checkpoint. For the average American who is not used to such things, this can be a jarring experience. After all, you just came down here to have a good time, right? Just keep in mind that everybody goes through this, and it isn't really a big deal. Despite what you may have heard about corrupt cops demanding payola, Mexico's economy depends on the influx of tourist dollars. It would not be in their interest to have the authorities shaking down every tourist who comes along. As long as you've done nothing wrong, you have nothing to worry about.

These stops are actually largely the result of Mexico attempting to satisfy their allies from north of the border that they are doing everything in their power to stop the flow of drugs northward. Keep in mind that these young soldiers are just doing their job. Many of them come from the poorer parts of Mexico, and they are occasionally even illiterate—meaning that your political opinions about unwarranted searches could hardly have less significance to them. Therefore, it is best just to cooperate so you can be on your way.

Generally, you will be stopped for only a few minutes. The soldiers will likely ask to see your identification and to look in your trunk. It is always a nice gesture to offer them a cold soda on a hot day. Assuming that you are not carrying any drugs, guns, or other illegal paraphernalia, you will soon be on your way.

CAUTION: Do not forget that guns are illegal in Mexico. There have been cases of Americans unwittingly crossing the border into Mexico while in possession of firearms that are perfectly legal in the United States only to find themselves locked up for months and even years in a Mexican prison. *Do not take firearms into Mexico with you.*

Stopping for Gas

Petroleos Mexicanos—or PEMEX—is Mexico's state-owned nationalized petroleum company. Its midgrade gasoline, Magna Sin, is rated at 87 octane and should be fine for cars that run on unleaded regular in the United States. Mexican Premium is rated at 92 octane.

Though PEMEX stations are not as abundant as gas stations north of the border, you will find them in all major stops on your itinerary. They are generally open 24 hours a day, and they do not take credit cards; pesos or dollars only here. The upside to this is that PEMEX stations make a great place to break large bills since the attendants carry a lot of cash. Speaking of the attendants, they will pump your gas and clean your windshield if you need it. It is customary to tip them about 10 pesos, or $1USD.

Car Rental

Though it is quite likely that you will discover that a car is unnecessary and even inconvenient in San Miguel de Allende and Guanajuato, there is always the chance that you will be in a situation where you need one. In Guanajuato, the León airport is generally the best place to rent a car. Because San Miguel de Allende has no airport, none of the big companies that you are familiar with operate here. There are, however, a couple of smaller outfits that rent cars as well as ATVs and motorcycles. Of course, you could always rent your car at either the León or Querétaro airports, as well.

GUANAJUATO

ALAMO CAR RENTAL
472-748-2069
www.alamo.com
Carretera Silao-León Km 5.5
León International Airport
Open daily from 6 AM to midnight

AVIS RENT A CAR
472-748-2054
www.avis.com.mx
Carretera Silao-León Km 6.5
León International Airport
Open daily from 6 AM to 11:30 PM

HERTZ CAR RENTAL
472-748-2015
www.hertz.com.mx

Carretera Silao-León Km 5.5
León International Airport
Open daily 24 hours

SAN MIGUEL DE ALLENDE

HOLA RENT A CAR
415-152-0198
Plaza Principal #2
E-mail them at holarentacar@prodigy.net.mx
Open Monday through Saturday 9 AM to 2:30 PM and Sunday 4:30 PM to 7 PM

MOTO RENT
415-152-0023
Salida a Celaya, km 1 #97
Open daily 9 AM to 8 PM

GETTING AROUND GUANAJUATO

When packing for your trip to Guanajuato, a comfortable pair of walking shoes should be the first thing you stuff into your suitcase or backpack or attaché or whatever your bag of choice. When you are here, you will be doing a lot of walking. The Guanajuato that you have come to see is a compact old city located in a bowl-shaped valley, perhaps a mile across and a few miles long. Within this small area are a myriad of beautiful buildings, gorgeous vistas, and café-lined plazas. In the very heart of it—from east of Jardín de la Unión west to the tip of Plaza de La Paz, and a city block on each side—there are no streets open to traffic. Spanning out from there, there are only narrow one-way cobblestone streets where driving is at a snail's pace even when there is no traffic.

The town is actually served by an intricate series of underground roads that were originally constructed as a flood prevention system. Before they were built, the town would occasionally suffer terrible floods when rainwater would pour into the narrow valley where the city is located. In 1883, the construction on the first tunnel got off to a fitful start. However, after a major flood in 1905, city elders decided to commit themselves to the tunnel and to open other routes as well, drawing upon the city's mining resources to complete the job. In 1908, the Túnel de la Cuajín was completed with great fanfare. However, as the

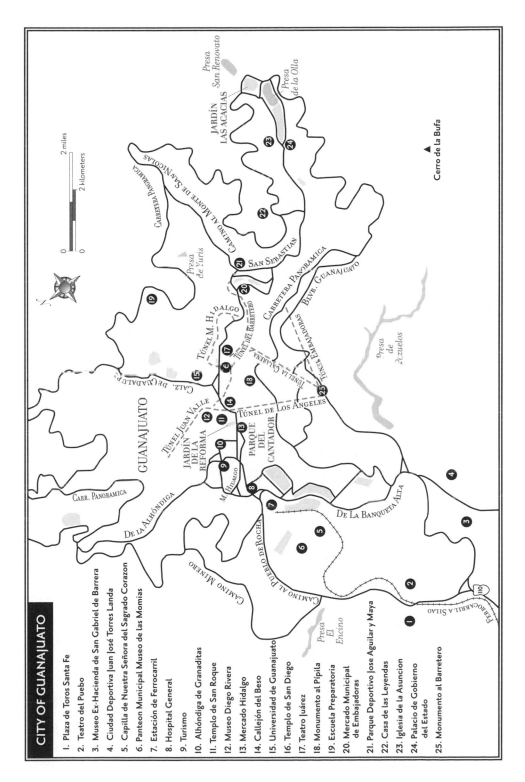

CITY OF GUANAJUATO

1. Plaza de Toros Santa Fe
2. Teatro del Puebo
3. Museo Ex-Hacienda de San Gabriel de Barrera
4. Ciudad Deportiva Juan José Torres Landa
5. Capilla de Nuestra Señora del Sagrado Corazon
6. Panteon Municipal Museo de las Momias
7. Estación de Ferrocarril
8. Hospital General
9. Turismo
10. Alhóndiga de Granaditas
11. Templo de San Roque
12. Museo Diego Rivera
13. Mercado Hidalgo
14. Callejón del Beso
15. Universidad de Guanajuato
16. Templo de San Diego
17. Teatro Juárez
18. Monumento al Pípila
19. Escuela Preparatoria
20. Mercado Municipal de Embajadoras
21. Parque Deportivo Jose Aguilar y Maya
22. Casa de las Leyendas
23. Iglesia de la Asuncion
24. Palacio de Gobierno del Estado
25. Monumento al Barretero

The sidewalks of Guanajuato can be narrow, steep, and elevated.

20th century progressed, it became increasingly clear that the town's streets, designed for horse and carriage, would not suffice with modern modes of transportation. Unwilling to tear up their historic city to build wider roads, Guanajuato's residents decided to modify the underground flood tunnels to accommodate traffic. By this time, the town's engineers had built a series of dams surrounding the city that redirected flood-prone rivers into underground caverns. The tunnels were then lit and paved with cobblestones and widened just enough for automobile traffic. Today, there are about 5 miles of underground roads that carry the majority of cars driving through the town center. These tunnels have also allowed the city to expand outside of the small valley, though there is little of interest outside of this compact center.

If you are driving, be sure to study road maps of the city and figure out exactly how to get where you're going before you set out for the first time. The tunnels are completely confusing if you're not familiar with them and, since they are all one-way, you could end up on a long and frustrating drive if you take the wrong tunnel.

In the center of town, it is perfectly safe to walk inside these tunnels. There is a pedestrian entrance on the west side of Jardín de la Unión next to the Templo de San Diego, several along Calle Alonzo, and one on Calle Positos near the Mesón del los Poetas hotel. Aside from the tunnels, the streets and alleyways of Guanajuato can seem like a convoluted maze. As such, you may want to take an afternoon to get lost in these streets just to see where they take you. Duck into one of the steep alleys—that can be as narrow as a few feet—

Guanajuato's historic downtown is served by a series of narrow one-way tunnels.

Guanajuato's tunnels were once used for flood prevention.

and you will invariably come out the other side to discover a beautiful plaza or an interesting street lined with shops and museums. To be sure, walks around Guanajuato range from the brisk to the strenuous. While the majority of the town's sites are within easy walking distance, there are a few that are further off, including El Pípila monument and Museo de las Momias. For these, you may consider taking the city bus or even springing for a taxi, which are plentiful here.

GETTING AROUND SAN MIGUEL DE ALLENDE

The vast majority of San Miguel's attractions are within walking distance of the center of town. That said, you will also find that it is common to get around town on ATVs as well, which might be a good option for anyone disinclined to walking. Although San Miguel's topography is nowhere near as hilly as the town of Guanajuato, it is situated on a mountainside. The streets are flatter on the north side of the city, making for relatively easy

A quiet early afternoon in San Miguel de Allende; note the cobblestones and elevated curb.

walking. On the south side, where wealthy neighborhoods are built around Parque Juárez, the streets are much steeper. Some of its streets here can have inclines as much as 20 degrees. Getting around can be a workout. Just keep in mind that it's good for you. Also, in addition to being beautiful, cobblestone streets are hard on the feet. Make sure you have a good pair of comfortable shoes. Luckily, if you forget them, this region is known for its shoes and buying a pair won't be a problem. And make sure to pay attention to where you are walking at all times. Many of the sidewalks are very old and not in the best shape. Curbs are not made to the same specifications in Mexico and can be several feet above the street in places. If you trip on an upturned pavestone in just the right spot, your vacation can take a bad turn very quickly.

If you have your own car, you might consider leaving it in a parking lot on the outskirts of the city. It's entirely unnecessary for getting around town and road conditions can be murder on your suspension. Keep in mind that driving in San Miguel can be a frustrating experience. The influx of well-to-do foreigners has also meant an influx of American

automobiles on roads that were never meant to support them. Even some two-way streets are far too narrow to realistically allow such traffic flows. In fact, in some parts of the city, burros are still used to deliver goods because they can do it much more efficiently than any truck. Parking is also famously scarce. A good alternative to driving your own car is to take one of the city's taxis, which are extremely inexpensive and reliable. Additionally, San Miguel has its own pleasant and reliable bus system that serves the entire town, including out-of-the-way areas like the Gigante supermarket or the bus depot.

Taxis

Taxis are a fairly inexpensive option for getting around. As with most taxi places in Mexico, taxis here generally charge a flat rate for transportation within certain zones. If you are unsure what the rate should be, be sure to ask the front desk clerk at your hotel. In general, however, the daytime fare within town is a little bit more than a dollar, and after 9 PM, the cost goes up to around 2 dollars. Keep in mind that taxi drivers will charge you double this price if you call them to pick you up. This covers the trip to come and get you as well as the trip to drop you off at your destination.

Taxis are generally plentiful in San Miguel and Guanajuato and you usually won't have any trouble finding one to wave down. Remember to always ask the price of the ride before getting in the car—or better yet, know the going rate and state that price to the driver in the form of a question. Even the most experienced travelers have been hit by the "gringo tax" every now and then. If the driver quotes you a price that seems too high, don't be afraid to say, "No gracias," and find another taxi.

GUANAJUATO

Central de Radio	473-732-9394
Radio Taxi Group	473-732-6649
Linea Dorado	473-734-1026

SAN MIGUEL DE ALLENDE

Radio Taxi	415-152-4501
Sitio Allende	415-152-0192
Taxi Express	415-152-4475
Tel-Taxi	415-152-3134

Be sure to settle on a price before taking a taxi ride.

The Casa Rosada lobby Courtesy of Casa Rosada

3

LODGING

In the 16th century, San Miguel de Allende was little more than a secluded stopover for weary travelers making their way along the Antiguo Camino Real silver route, between Zacatecas and Mexico City. There wasn't much here to offer, but what there was probably seemed like a great comfort to road weary travelers more than 250 miles from civilization. By the 18th century, San Miguel was infused with an air of sophistication; it likely seemed an impossible oasis, particularly after several days of travel by horse and wagon, along rocky roads through windswept badlands. By that time, several hotels had been established in San Miguel offering visitors comfortable accommodations that were not available anywhere else for hundreds of miles.

Even today, with the nearest international airport around 40 miles away, San Miguel de Allende remains a fairly remote destination by modern standards. However, despite the fact that it has no beaches, no 18-hole golf courses, and no Mayan ruins, San Miguel remains one of Mexico's top tourist destinations. Something else that sets the city apart from other Mexican tourist hotspots is the notable lack of mega resorts. If your idea of a perfect vacation is sitting by the pool all day and never leaving the hotel, this is probably not the place for you. Certainly, San Miguel has plenty of first-class accommodations to offer, including spas, fancy restaurants, and swimming pools. However, the essence of San Miguel is the city itself. The majority of hotels here draw on the city's colonial past, incorporating beautiful architecture, old world customs, and a uniquely Mexican ambiance to provide an experience that is culturally rich and lavishly enjoyable. Many hotels also take advantage of San Miguel's history of being a noted artist's colony by incorporating original art in their decorations. Because San Miguel has grown into such a popular tourist destination, there is plenty to choose from here.

Likewise, the nearby city of Guanajuato has also flourished in recent years, taking advantage of its rich colonial history. It is known as a prime destination within Mexico, and each year its extravagant festivals draw visitors from all over the world. Like San Miguel, Guanajuato is peppered with boutique hotels and bed and breakfasts converted from colonial mansions. Though each has a unique take on providing lodging, most tend to at least attempt to incorporate colonial atmosphere, with antique furnishings and gilded décor. Outside the city center you can find a few examples of large chain hotels, but for the most part hotels here tend to be small and unique.

With so many unique hotel options in such a small area, it is definitely worth your time to investigate several hotels to find the one that sounds most interesting to you. Most hotels maintain their own Web sites where you will find photographs and brief descriptions of amenities. You can also make reservations directly online, ensuring that everything is in order when you arrive. Smaller hotels may not have a Web site and will require you to call them directly for reservations. In instances such as this, you may be required to send a deposit to finalize your reservations. However, their staffs do not necessarily speak English, making phone conversations a complicated process if your Spanish is less than fluent. Getting a hotel on arrival is always an option, though it's not recommended, especially if your visit is during a festival.

Lodging in San Miguel tends to be more expensive than any other colonial city in this region of Mexico. Anything under $120 per night here would be considered inexpensive, while moderate prices run up to around $200 per night. Anything more than that should be considered expensive, even by San Miguel standards. By contrast, lodging in Guanajuato for around $90 per night or less would be inexpensive, though you can certainly find adequate lodging for $50 per night or less even at the city center, if you don't mind a no frills room. Moderate rates in Guanajuato run up to about $150 per night and anything over that should be considered expensive. Rates tend to go up a bit during the high tourist season of December 15 to April 1, when days are sunny and clear and nights are crisp and cool. However, during festivals such as Cerventino, *Semana Santa*, and the week after Christmas, prices go up rather dramatically. That said, the rates in this colonial enclave are still much more reasonable than you will find in Mexico City or in the resort towns on the Pacific.

GUANAJUATO

Lodging in Guanajuato is generally less expensive than what you will find in San Miguel de Allende. You can usually find inexpensive lodging for less than $90 per night, and it's certainly not unheard of to find adequate, no frills lodging for $50 per night or less. Moderate rates in Guanajuato run up to about $150 per night, and rates go up a bit during the high tourist season of December 15 to April 1. During festivals such as Cerventino, *Semana Santa*, and the week after Christmas, prices go up dramatically. Credit card acceptance policies are indicated below with AE (American Express), D (Discover), MC (Master Card), and V (Visa).

Because of where the city is located, you should be prepared to walk up a lot of stairs during your stay (and this is not just limited to your hotel). Most of the more interesting hotels are located in buildings that are at least a century old and do not have elevators (though larger hotels away from the city center do have elevators). Furthermore, the city is located on the side of a mountain and several of the hotels are actually built into the side of it. Though you'll undoubtedly see local women wearing them, this is not a town that has been constructed with high heels in mind. Be sure to pack some comfortable walking shoes.

LA ABADIA

Manager: Carmen Lara
473-734-1079
www.abadia.com.mx
San Javier #1, Guanajuato, Gto. 36000
Price: Inexpensive
Credit Cards: AE, MC, V
Special Features: Wireless Internet access
This is a very attractive hotel, particularly for its size. With 176 rooms and three restaurants, La Abadia manages to maintain a distinctly Mexican look and feel while providing all the amenities of a modern hotel. As with most hotels in Guanajuato, you should be prepared to walk up a lot of stairs. It features a disco with a full bar, a swimming pool, and several banquet halls that can accommodate up to two hundred people. Room service is also available. The hotel is located somewhat off the center of

town, but the hotel provides transportation service or you can take a taxi to downtown for around $3. The rooms here are not luxurious but they are comfortable. Standard rooms are carpeted and are furnished with two double beds. There are also two suites and a small villa available.

LA CASA AZUL

Manager: Paulina Herrera
473-731-2288
www.lacasaazul.com.mx
Calle Carcamanes #57, Guanajuato, Gto. 36000
Price: Moderate
Credit Cards: MC, V
Special Features: Good location, rooftop terrace, on-site cantina

This attractive boutique hotel is located in a quiet neighborhood just a few blocks north of the town center. It features three large rooms with sitting areas. They are decorated in a sparse Mexican hacienda style that is both warm and inviting. The rest of the hotel is as simple and lovely as the rooms and has an atmosphere that takes you back to Guanajuato's colonial days. There is a small garden area with a stone fountain just in front of a small chapel. There is also a cantina with bare brick walls, dim lighting, and rustic wooden furniture. Sitting here, you almost get the feeling that you should've brought your six-shooter. However, you may find yourself spending the most time on the hotel's rooftop terrace, which has plenty of shade and a beautiful panoramic view of the city.

CASA COLORADA

Manager: David Castillo Sagahon
473-734-1151
www.hotelesrefugio.com
Cerro de San Miguel #13, Guanajuato, Gto. 36000
Price: Moderate
Credit Cards: AE, MC, V
Special Features: Wireless Internet access business center, on-site restaurant.

This elegant hotel was built in the 1970s as a center for economic and social studies but in the 1980s was converted into the private retreat of a former Mexican president. In 2002, the Refugio Tourist Group acquired the property and converted it into the elegant boutique hotel it is today. It is located in the hills above Guanajuato behind the famous Pipila statue that overlooks the city. It features six tastefully decorated suites with panoramic views of the city below. The Refugio Casa Colorada Restaurant serves gourmet haute cuisine and fine wines, and also provides a wonderful view of the city. For business meetings and other social events, the hotel has two executive suites with a capacity for 10 to 20 people, audiovisual equipment, wireless Internet access, and meal service.

CASTILLO DE SANTA CECILIA

Manager: Lupita Marquez
473-732-0485
Camino a la Valenciana Km. 1, Colonia San Javier, Guanajuato 36000
Price: Moderate to Expensive
Credit Cards: MC, V
Special Features: Room service, business area

The hotel Castillo de Santa Cecilia is located high above the city just outside of town, on the way to Dolores Hidalgo. It occupies an imposing medieval-style castle constructed in the 17th century and has been a hotel since 1939. However, its interior is much more warm and inviting than the exterior appearance. It offers 66 standard rooms, 15 junior suites, and seven master suites. Rooms are decorated in an old-world style with stone walls and wrought iron beds and generally have very good views of the city. They are furnished with either a king-size bed or two double beds. Master suites have a combination of king-size beds and double beds. All suites have separate sitting rooms. Rates for suites here tend to be quite a bit more than for standard rooms and can vary greatly by season. The property features a heated outdoor swimming pool as well as expansive lawns and gardens, and the remnants of a 17th-century silver mine. La Cava restaurant is located here, serving up traditional Mexican cuisine and providing room service. It is open daily from 7 AM to 10 PM. Communication can be a problem here if you don't speak Spanish.

GRAN PLAZA

Manager: Ana Peñaranda
473-733-1990
www.hotelgranplaza.com
Carretera Guanajuato Juventino Rosa Km. 6, Guanajuato, Gto. 36000
Price: Inexpensive
Credit Cards: AE, MC, V
Special Features: Restaurant/bar, room service, business center

Located just northeast of Guanajuato, this hotel offers 107 air-conditioned rooms. Most are furnished with two doubles, though there are a few with one king-size bed. Rooms are generally what you'd expect to find at a decent chain hotel north of the border. They are simply decorated in a generic style, but comfortable. This hotel has facilities that would make it an option for anyone planning a large event such as a wedding or a reunion. Its La Hacienda Restaurant is open from 7 AM to 11 PM serving a variety of local dishes as well as several favorites from north of the border. The Cazadores Bar is open from 2 PM to 11 PM. Room service is also available. The hotel also features a resort-style pool that makes a nice place to relax and have a drink.

HACIENDA DEL MARQUES

Manager: Edmundo Almanza Moreno
473-102-4367
www.elmarqueshacienda.com
Carretera Libre Guanajuato-Irapuato Km. 11, Guanajuato, Gto. 36000

Price: Inexpensive
Credit Cards: AE, MC, V
Special Features: Conference rooms, tennis courts, swimming pool

Located about 9 miles outside of town, this hotel is a bit out of the way. However, this inconvenience is made up for by a long list of amenities that come at a price that can't be beat. The history of this hotel dates back to the 16th century when Luis de Velazco, the second viceroy of Spain, gave this property to Pedro Muñoz Maese de Roa for the establishment of a large hacienda. Today, it is a sprawling hotel with well-manicured gardens, and trees hundreds of years old. It offers 28 guest rooms and four cabin suites that are fairly spacious and decorated in an interesting colonial style. Other amenities include five conference rooms, tennis courts, and a soccer field. The hotel also offers banquet service, making it an option for weddings and other large get-togethers. Additionally, recreational activities such as mountain biking and horseback riding on the property are also available.

HOLIDAY INN EXPRESS GUANAJUATO

Manager: Jorge Cruz
473-735-2000
Euquerio Guerrero #120, Burocrat, Guanajuato 36000
Price: Moderate
Credit Cards: AE, D, MC, V
Special Features: Business center, indoor pool, gym, babysitting service

This hotel is large and actually quite beautiful. It has 165 standard rooms and six suites that are furnished with either single or double beds. Yes, it's a Holiday Inn, so the rooms come with the standard Holiday Inn décor but they are fairly good-size rooms and quite comfortable. The hotel itself is located a couple miles from the center of the city so you'll have to catch a taxi or have your own transportation. However, the hotel has plenty of amenities including a lovely indoor pool area, a playground, and a gym. Babysitting is also available. The hotel also provides plenty of business services including wireless Internet access, fax, and copying service; a computer is available to guests as well. There are also four conference rooms equipped with full audiovisual equipment.

LUNA GUANAJUATO

Manager: José Fausto Castillo Lule
473-732-9725
Jardín de la Union #6, Guanajuato, Gto.
36000
Price: Moderate
Credit Cards: MC, V
Special Features: Central location, patio restaurant on the main square, airport pickup
This hotel is located in a 19th-century building right at the center of the historic downtown district and has been operating for more than 100 years. In fact, it provided accommodations for Porfirio Diaz, the Mexican president, when he came to Guanajuato in 1903 to inaugurate Teatro Juárez. It offers 19 rooms and two suites; they are comfortable and elegant, even if they are somewhat small. They can also be very noisy if there is a lot of action in the Jardín. Some rooms have a balcony with views of the Jardín de la Union, but you might want to resist the urge to take one of these rooms if you are in town during a busy weekend and, instead, request a room away from the square to avoid the noise. Breakfast is included with each night's stay at the Conde Rul Restaurant, which is located on the hotel's ground floor facing the Jardín. The hotel also offers complimentary service to and from the León airport. Not having to worry about arranging an early morning taxi will put your mind at ease and allow you to enjoy the beautiful surroundings.

MANSION DEL CANTADOR

Manager: Guacinto Garcia
473-732-6888
Calle Cantador #19, Guanajuato, Gto.
36000
Price: Inexpensive
Credit Cards: None
Special Features: On-site restaurant, small conference hall
This hotel is located at the southwest edge of the city's historical center across the street from the Jardín del Cantador, a serene park that is a great place for a walk. It is close to the Mercado Hidalgo and the Museo de Alhóndiga, and most of the town's other attractions are within walking distance, though the walk is a bit brisk. It offers 40 rooms and two junior suites colorfully decorated in a Mexican art deco style. The hotel also offers a small conference room that has a 40-person capacity and is fully equipped with audiovisual equipment. The on-site Balcones del Cantador Restaurant offers up traditional Mexican food. It is open daily from 7:30 AM to 9 PM. Breakfast at the restaurant is included in the room rate for each night's stay. If you are making reservations, keep in mind that this hotel will only accept bank deposits for the first night's payment.

MESÓN DE LOS POETAS

Manager: Maria de Lourdes Enriquez Velazquez
473-732-6657
Positos #35, Esquina con Juan Valle, Guanajuato 36000
Price: Moderate
Credit Cards: AE, MC, V
Special Features: Laundry service, Internet access, continental breakfast
This charming hotel is one of the best-known hotels in Guanajuato. It is conveniently located just a couple blocks away from all the action in Guanajuato, yet provides a calm and inviting atmosphere that is perfect for relaxing and getting away from it all. Located in a cavernous house built into a hillside just down the street from the Diego Rivera Museum, it offers 30

rooms that are uniquely decorated, each dedicated to poets from Walt Whitman to Pablo Neruda. They all feature original paintings and Mexican décor. Rooms are furnished with two double beds or a double and a twin, and suites have king-size beds. They are also equipped with a kitchenette and a sitting area. The hotel's position against a hillside keeps the rooms quiet unless there is an antsy woman in high heels situated in the room above you (as happened to me one morning). Be prepared to walk a lot of stairs if you stay here because there are plenty of them. A continental breakfast is provided with each night's stay.

MESÓN DEL ROSARIO

Manager: Maria Mendoza
473-732-0666
Avenida Juárez #31, Guanajuato, Gto. 36000
Price: Inexpensive
Credit Cards: MC, V
Special Features: Central location
No frills here. Just a standard room with a television on the wall that gets a few Spanish language channels. However, if you are a budget traveler looking for a place to stay in Guanajuato, you can spend a lot more and do much worse than the Mesón del Rosario (and I have). Originally built to house miners, there is something cavernous about this hotel. Entering it, you are greeted by an old suit of armor that stands guard over a small sitting area, but what is most striking is the stairway that crisscrosses the interior courtyard, thus leading to the rooms that are located on several levels. Yes, getting to your room can be like a Stairmaster workout. But the rooms are comfortable, even if they are a bit sparse. Save the occasional group of college students in town for the weekend, this is a quiet hotel. Sign are posted everywhere warning guests against being noisy after 10 PM. However, if you've come to Guanajuato to see the sights, you can't beat the location.

Several good bars are just doors away, the Plaza de La Paz is right up the street, and all of the major sites of the historic center are within quick walking distance.

EL MINERO

Manager: Tomás Saldaña
473-732-4739
Alhóndiga #12-A, Guanajuato, Gto. 36000
Price: Inexpensive
Credit Cards: MC, V
Special Features: On-site restaurant
Another decent option for budget travelers, this hotel offers 20 comfortable rooms that are actually pretty roomy—especially for the price. It is located in a four-floor building, so be prepared to walk some stairs, especially if you are situated on the top floor. The rooms are well-tiled, nicely decorated, and clean, even if they are a bit dark. Most are furnished with a double bed and a single bed. The hotel is located 3 blocks from the Museo de Alhóndiga, so it is certainly not located at the center of the action but it is within walking distance. The hotel restaurant offers up good Mexican fare in the afternoon and evenings, but you will have to hike it for breakfast. Open daily from 1 PM to 10 PM.

MISIÓN GUANAJUATO

Manager: Antonio Tovar
473-732-3980
Camino Antiguo a Marfil Km. 2.5, Guanajuato, Gto. 36050
Price: Moderate
Credit Cards: MC, V
Special Features: Game room, business center, laundry service, babysitting, heated pool
This hotel, which is set on a relatively large property at the city's edge, was converted from a 17th-century hacienda. It offers 156 rooms, three junior suites, and a presidential suite. These rooms are decorated in a traditional Mexican style and are fairly roomy. Although the hotel's location is a

Mesón del Rosario

probably a bit out of the way for travelers looking to experience all that the historic center has to offer, it does have the feel of old Mexico and offers many services on site. Additionally, guests are provided with complimentary transportation to and from town as well as airport transportation. The hotel features the La Mancha Restaurant, open Monday through Saturday from 8 AM to 8 PM with international, traditional Mexican, and regional cuisines, and the El Callejón Bar. There is also a covered pool, a tennis court, and even a smoke shop. The hotel also features several fully equipped event halls for groups of 70 to 350 people, making it a good option for anyone planning a large get-together.

PASEO DE LA PRESA

Manager: Florencio Quiroz

473-731-0775

www.hotelesrealdeminas.com.mx/paseodelapresa

Carretera Panorámica Tramo Pípila, Guanajuato, Gto. 36000

Price: Inexpensive to Moderate

Credit Cards: MC, V

Special Features: Satellite TV, panoramic views

This 58-room hotel is located on a hill above the center of Guanajuato and provides a beautiful panoramic view of the city. The hotel itself looks a bit like a giant green Mexican hacienda that has somehow outgrown itself. Rooms are furnished with two double beds and are decorated in standard hotel room décor with factory furniture and a small television sitting on the dresser. Standard room rates are inexpensive and are set for double occupancy. There is an additional charge of around $10 for each additional occupant. Junior suites are also available. Its La Cascada Restaurant offers a nice view of the hotel grounds and serves mostly traditional Mexican food. In the lobby, you will find the El Jardin Bar, which is a nice place to relax and have a drink.

The hotel does have an attractive pool area as well as tennis courts, and several large rooms for banquets and special events with the capacity to serve groups of between 10 and 300 people.

PARADOR SAN JAVIER GUANAJUATO

Manager: Eduardo Aredondo

473-732-0650

Plaza Aldama #92, Guanajuato, Gto. 36000

Price: Moderate

Credit Cards: MC, V

Special Features: Wireless Internet access, on-site disco, conference halls

Located in a converted silver-mining hacienda, this hotel features 116 rooms and suites on six floors (and yes, there is an elevator). Standard rooms are large, well lit—many with vaulted brick ceilings—and furnished with two double beds. They are decorated in a sparse but colorful Mexican colonial style. Suites are much larger, with separate well-furnished sitting rooms, and king-size beds. The hotel itself is located in a walled compound 5 blocks above the Museo Alhóndiga. It has a nice swimming pool area as well as an indoor children's pool. A natural spring is located on the property in a cave just below the hotel bar, The Well, open Monday through Saturday from 5 PM until midnight. This hotel also has a restaurant that features many Mexican favorites. It is open daily from 7 AM to 10 PM.

POSADA SANTA FE

Manager: Gerardo Herrera

473-732-0084

www.posadasantafe.com

Jardín de la Union #12, Guanajuato, Gto. 36000

Price: Moderate

Credit Cards: MC, V

Special Features: Central location, streetside dining, features high-valued original artwork

This hotel is located right on the Jardín, so it's a great place for those who like to be in

Location, Location, Location

Both San Miguel de Allende and Guanajuato are places where the points of interest are gathered around a central location, and they are also places where having a car can be impractical. For those reasons, you will probably want to find a hotel close to the center of things when planning your trip. However, there are other factors you should consider when picking out a hotel.

Both towns have hotels located right on the central plaza. In San Miguel, the Posada de San Francisco is located right on the Jardín Principal and in Guanajuato the Hotel San Diego, the Posada Santa Fe, and the Luna Guanajuato are all located on the Jardín de la Union. These are all inviting hotels with attractive restaurants with plaza views that are great for people watching. And it's true that it is great to have the convenience of having a place that's all your own just steps away from the action, rather than having to walk several blocks every time you need to stop in at your room. However, this convenience can come with some pretty serious drawbacks.

If you are visiting during the peak tourist season or during one of the region's many festivals, you should be aware that noisy crowds will fill up the main plazas, sometimes late into the night. These crowds tend to create traffic jams near the entrances of hotels located on the plaza, sometimes actually making it harder to get to your room than if it was located on a nearby back street. What's worse is that these crowds can create quite a ruckus. If your room has a window that opens onto the street, it will catch all that noise, making your room sound like a frat party.

Therefore, sometimes it makes sense to consider finding a hotel that is a few blocks away from the action. What you give up in convenience you will get back several times over in a good night's sleep. Even if you plan on being part of the late-night party, it's always good to have a nice quiet place to relax just in case. However, if you insist on staying at one of these hotels with the impeccable location, keep in mind that the hotel staff will probably not warn you that you should expect to endure blaring noise at 4 o'clock in the morning. Be sure to take the initiative and request a room in the interior of the building away from the street.

Central plazas can be bustling places during festivals.

the middle of the action. Anyone looking to wind down in a quiet room at the end of the day will probably do well to look elsewhere. This hotel has been around since the 1860s and is probably the oldest hotel in Guanajuato. Having survived all that history, it is also one of the most attractive hotels in the city. It has on display an admirable collection of works from the local artist and historian Manuel Leal. The lobby is impressive, with chandeliers hanging from a high beamed ceiling, and antique chairs below giant paintings. Off the lobby is the hotel restaurant and lounge—a great place to have a drink and take in the atmosphere. The hotel's 40 rooms and 9 suites are located up a winding staircase. Standard rooms tend to be small but they are well maintained and comfortable. The suites have fancier furniture and exterior views of the Jardín. Breakfast is included in the room rate for each night's stay.

QUINTA LAS ACACIAS

Manager: Ana Perez Ordaz
473- 731-1517
www.quintalasacacias.com
Paseo de la Presa #168, Guanajuato, Gto. 36000
Price: Expensive
Credit Cards: MC, V
Special Features: Satellite TV, Jacuzzi
This boutique hotel is in a restored 19th-century French-style mansion right off Florencio Antillón Park. It is filled with European-style furniture and a combination of French and Mexican sensibilities. It is definitely worth at least a walk through. It offers seven rooms and three suites, each one individually decorated with a distinctly European flair. The décor is sure to please anyone who appreciates antiques. The gorgeous restaurant space takes you back a century, serving meals from their international menu daily from 7:30 AM to 11 PM. If you need an excuse to pass the time in interesting surroundings, the hotel also has

an attractive sitting room that provides an elegant atmosphere, as well as several terraces, including one with a Jacuzzi.

QUINTA LAS ALONDRAS HOTEL

Manager: Rodrigo Paniagua Anda
473-733-3030
www.quintalasalondras.com.mx
Autopista Guanajuato Silao Km. 1, Guanajuato, Gto. 36000
Price: Moderate
Credit Cards: AE, MC, V
Special Features: Pool, spa center, gourmet restaurant
This 51-room hotel offers friendly service and a luxury atmosphere. Rooms are fairly spacious and decorated in a simple but elegant manner that takes advantage of natural light and cool colors. If you're cramped from the trip, book an appointment at the in-house spa, which provides facials, massages, and other services. The hotel restaurant offers a rather extensive and diverse menu; it is open daily from 7 AM to 10:30 PM. The hotel also has a fairly large swimming pool, as well as several rooms for banquets and other special events. The hotel is located a short walk from the bus terminal but quite a distance from anything else. If you want to get into the historical center, you will have to hire a cab. The cab ride into town runs around $4.

REAL DE MINAS GUANAJUATO

Manager: Esperanza Gonzalez
473-732-1460
www.hotelesrealdeminas.com.mx
Nejayote #17, Guanajuato, Gto. 36000
Price: Moderate
Credit Cards: AE, MC, V
Special Features: On-site restaurant, pool, several banquet halls
This large hotel is located just outside of Guanajuato's historical center. It features 25 suites and 135 regular rooms. Rooms are relatively spacious and have a fairly interesting décor for this type of hotel. They have

carpeted floors with air conditioning and modern Mexican furnishings. Suites are equipped with Jacuzzi bathtubs. The hotel grounds have a terrace bar, a ladies' bar, and a small but attractive pool area. The hotel also has 10 conference halls for special occasions of all sizes. The big drawback is that the hotel is not really within walking distance of the town's historic center. To get to Guanajuato's main attractions, you'll have to hire a taxi, which will run you around $4.

HOTEL SAN DIEGO

Manager: Ricardo H. Muñoz
473-732-1300
www.hotelsandiego.com.mx
Jardín de la Unión #1, Guanajuato, Gto. 36000
Price: Moderate
Credit Cards: AE, MC, V
Special Features: Convenient location, wireless Internet access in lobby

This is an old and historic hotel, as can been seen in the murals right off the lobby, which depict the building during its colonial days. Located right on the main square, you certainly can't beat the location of the Hotel San Diego, which offers 43 comfortably appointed suites—though there is nothing particularly special about the décor of the rooms. They range from singles to quadruples to junior suites. However, before you get excited about the prospects of a convenient location, it's important to remember that Guanajuato is a college town that loves to stay up late. If you're there for the weekend or during a festival, you may notice that the noise coming from the street is quite loud just as you get ready to turn in for the night. This is particularly true if you're unfortunate enough to get stuck with a room facing Alonso, the street that runs along the back of the hotel. Something about the acoustics in these rooms seems to amplify the sounds of cars driving by, night club music from down the street, and the rambunctious partyers as they laugh and yell to each other at all hours of the night. When those clubs let out at five in the morning, you may think with some relief that you can finally get some shut-eye after a hellish night of tossing and turning. However, you just may find yourself lying there an hour later listening to those partyers who have posted themselves at the street corner and who continue to play loud music and laugh even louder. By then, you will have realized that you could've saved yourself a hundred bucks and slept on a park bench in the Jardín and gotten the same experience.

The Hotel San Diego

VILLA MARIA CRISTINA

Manager: Ismael Guevara
473-731-2182 or 1-866-424-6868 (U.S.)
www.villamariacristina.com.mx/guanajuato/
Paseo de la Presa de la Olla #76A,
Guanajuato, Gto. 36000
Price: Expensive
Credit Cards: AE, MC, V
Special Features: Roman-style spa, Jacuzzi,
swimming pool, gym
Located in a 19th-century neoclassical
townhouse, this beautiful boutique hotel
offers 13 suites designed for privacy and
comfort. They feature high ceilings, wood
floors, dark wood furniture, and marble
bathrooms with whirlpool tubs. The hotel
has a Roman-style spa with a large sunken
pool and several treatment rooms where you
can be pampered with various treatments
and facials. If that doesn't provide enough
relaxation, try out the Swiss shower and
steam bath, or work out in the on-site gym.
There is also a terrace with a large Jacuzzi
that is a great place for kicking back and
taking it all in. For dinner, try the gourmet
cuisine and fine wines found at the on-site
restaurant. The hotel also provides private
limousine service to the airport in Leon or
even as far away as Mexico City.

SAN MIGUEL DE ALLENDE

As stated above, lodging in San Miguel
tends to be more expensive than any other
colonial city in this region of Mexico.
Anything under $120 per night here would
be considered inexpensive, while moderate
prices run up to around $200 per night.
Anything more than that should be considered expensive, even by San Miguel standards. Hotels here have become
accustomed to dealing with foreign visitors
so you can expect your hosts to speak
English, particularly in the higher end
hotels. It is not uncommon for hotels to be
run by expatriate Americans, in which case
language will not be a problem at all. Also,
major credit cards are widely accepted
here. Credit card acceptance policies are
indicated below with AE (American
Express), D (Discover), MC (Master Card),
and V (Visa).

EL ALCÁZAR HOTEL

Manager: José Luis Devesa
415-152-0354
Cuna de Allende #13, San Miguel de
Allende, Gto. 37700
Price: Moderate
Credit Cards: MC, V
Special Features: Good location, on-site
coffee shop, rooftop terrace
This beautifully rustic hotel has the kind of
stone architecture you come to San Miguel
to see. Located just one block from the
Jardín Principal, this boutique hotel offers
six rooms within quick walking distance of
shops, restaurants, and other important
points on your itinerary. Breakfast is
included with each night's stay. The relatively spacious rooms feature bathrooms
decked out in colorful Mexican tile. The
rooms are clean and appointed in brightly
colored Mexican blankets and traditional
folk art. They are also surprisingly quiet,
considering the hotel's central location.
The hotel's rooftop terrace offers an ideal
place to relax with a drink and watch dusk
fall over the city. The coffee shop is open
from 7 AM to 10 PM.

ANTIGUA VILLA SANTA MÓNICA

Manager: Sergio Reyes Retana
415-152-0427
www.antiguavillasantamonica.com
Fray José Guadalupe Mojica #22, San Miguel
de Allende, Gto. 37700
Price: Expensive
Credit Cards: AE, MC, V
Special Features: On-site gourmet
Mexican/International restaurant, garden
courtyards
One of San Miguel's longest continuously

running hotels, the Antigua Villa Santa Mónica is located in an 18th-century hacienda originally owned by a Spanish silver baron. It opened its doors as a hotel in 1940 and continues to offer luxury service and colonial charm. Its 14 rooms feature handmade tile and wood-beamed ceilings, and they are furnished with romantic wrought iron four-poster beds shrouded with linens. They also feature brightly colored Mexican earthenware called *talavera* and regional rugs to create a distinctly Mexican ambiance. The on-site restaurant is open from Tuesday through Sunday and features an extensive menu and wine list. Breakfast is served from 7:30 AM to noon and lunch from 1 PM to 5:30 PM. This is a great place for a romantic getaway but not for a family vacation. Children under eight are not allowed.

ARCADA HOTEL

Manager: Carlos Beltrán
415-152-8940
Calzada de la Estación #185, San Miguel de Allende, Gto. 37700
Price: Very Inexpensive
Credit Cards: AE, MC, V
Special Features: Private parking, cable T.V., Restaurant/Bar, gym, on-site restaurant
This 22-room hotel is located on the western edge of San Miguel de Allende. It is a bit of a walk to where the action is, but the hotel offers guests transportation service. Guests are also offered laundry service for a nominal fee. It features a billiards room, a small gym, and a restaurant/bar that is open daily from 7 AM to 10 PM. Room service is available. The hotel also has a spa that offers massages for around $27. Rooms are not large but they're adequate and come furnished with either a queen-size bed or two doubles. At the price, it's a good value and a buffet breakfast is included with each night's stay.

ATOTONÍLCO EL VIEJO HOTEL RESORT & SPA

Manager: Javier Giráldez
415-185-2133
www.atotonilcoelviejo.com
Carretera Santuario, San Miguel de Allende, Gto. 37700
Price: Moderate to Expensive
Credit Cards: MC, V
Special Features: Resort accommodations, guided horseback and bicycle tours, room service, palapa bar
Located just outside the village of Atotonilco, about 8 miles from San Miguel de Allende, this is one of the relatively few hotels in the area to offer resort-style lodging. This is curious, considering the nearby church for which it is named is a sanctuary and place of atonement for the poor and decrepit. The hotel itself is located in a gated compound surrounded by facilities that offer a wide variety of amenities. These include two pools (indoor and outdoor), golf course, tennis courts, game room, spa, and banquet halls for special events. The on-site spa offers all kinds of services, including body exfoliation, clay wraps, and chakra therapy. The restaurant, located just off the main pool, offers indoor or outdoor service, as well as service at the palapa bar. Rooms are spacious and feature woven *bóveda* (arched) ceilings, intricately carved wooden headboards and nightstands, handmade tile floors, private balconies or terraces, and Jacuzzi bathtubs. They are furnished with one king-size bed or two matrimonial beds.

CASA DE AVES

Manager: Janet DiBenedetto
415-155-9610 or 1-866-406-4771 (U.S.)
www.casadeaves.com
Rancho los Fresnos, Corridora #1, San Miguel de Allende, Gto. 37700
Price: Expensive
Credit Cards: AE, V, MC
Special Features: Spa service, swim-up bar, outdoor adventures

This retreat boutique hotel is located several minutes' drive from the city center. It features eight elegantly furnished private villas, each with a large bedroom, dining room, sitting area, and kitchen. These rooms are not overly decorated but are instead laid out with comfort in mind. Each of these villas is also furnished with a rooftop Jacuzzi and patio for your private enjoyment. The property is replete with amenities, and constructed in a way that makes it blend with the natural environment. Amenities include a pool with swim-up bar, a gym with yoga area, and a conference room equipped with a movie theatre. There is also an on-site spa that offers facials, massages, and other services to help you unwind and take it all in. Visitors can enjoy the surrounding area by taking a bird-watching hike or a ride on the mountain bikes that are provided by the hotel. For dinner, enjoy the Mexican fusion cuisine from the hotel's restaurant, open daily from 7 AM to 10 PM. No need to worry about getting into town for some sight-seeing either, as the hotel offers complimentary transportation service into town.

CASA LINDA

Manager: Linda McLaughlin
415-154-4007
www.hotelcasalinda.com
Mesones 101, Colonia Centro, San Miguel de Allende, 37700
Price: Expensive
Credit Cards: AE, MC, V
Special Features: Indoor lap pool, Jacuzzi, steam room, gym, laundry service
Located just a block off the main square, this luxury hotel combines the charm of a rustic colonial with modern amenities. There are 10 suites appointed with original Mexican art and *artesenia* as well as private fireplaces and kitchenettes. Each room is individually decorated with handmade furniture and colorful additions such as hand-stitched pillows and colorfully woven placemats. These rooms are relatively spacious and beautifully decorated with hardwood or tiled floors and elegant antique furnishings. After a long day of trudging up and down San Miguel's cobblestone streets, you'll be happy to take advantage of the in-room spa service that is available. If you are not a guest of the hotel, you can always pay a visit to the on-site day spa that is open to the public by appointment. The hotel's restaurant, Nirvana, serves breakfast, lunch, and dinner daily from 8:30 AM to 10 PM. This is a great place to sit on the patio and take in the gorgeous colonial surroundings on a warm day. Additionally, the hotel offers room service from several of the nearby restaurants, for weary travelers or those just wanting a romantic evening alone.

CASA PUESTA DEL SOL

Owners: Daniel and Gabriela Scher
415-152-0220
www.casapuestadelsol.com
Fuentes #12, San Miguel de Allende, Gto. 37700
Price: Moderate
Credit Cards: AE, V, MC
Special Features: Country club privileges (golf, tennis, swimming), computer, and Internet access
This lush colonial bed and breakfast is located on a hillside above San Miguel de Allende in a brick red villa with vine-covered terraces that overlook the city. This space provides a magnificent view of the city and the valley beyond. Every room of this hotel has been painstakingly painted in natural colors and decorated with a wide variety of local art, including stained glass windows and thick, colorful cotton blankets. It features four standard rooms and two suites, all decorated in an old-world Mexican style that is rich and colorful. The grounds of the hotel are beautifully landscaped with gardens, ponds, and a waterfall. Whatever they pay their gardener is

A Few Words About Bathrooms and Toilet Paper

One of the less delicate issues that you will quickly face when you are traveling in Mexico, particularly in less tourist-centered areas, is the difference in bathroom etiquette. Toilet paper tends to clog most Mexican plumbing and septic systems to the point where it sometimes even requires digging up the pipes to clear them. Therefore, it is necessary to deposit used paper into the wastebasket that is invariably placed next to the toilet. Many moderate and expensive hotels understand that this is more than a minor culture shock to their American guests and have gone to the trouble to equip rooms with plumbing that can handle toilet paper. However, you shouldn't assume this is the case unless there is a sign posted in the bathroom directing you to flush toilet paper. Still, part of the draw of San Miguel and Guanajuato is the architecture, and many of these old buildings simply have not been brought up to the standards that you are used to. Quite often, there will be a sign explicitly asking you NOT to flush your used toilet paper. Also, women should never flush feminine products. You may find this unpleasant but it's better than dealing with a room with a stopped-up toilet.

There are other differences that you are likely to run into when you are out and about and discover that you need to use the public restroom. First of all, janitorial work is largely considered "women's work" in Central Mexico. Therefore, it is always possible that men may be surprised by an elderly female janitor entering the restroom while they are taking care of their business. If this happens, do your best to maintain a blasé attitude, remembering that you're not doing anything she hasn't dealt with before. You will likely find well-stocked facilities in high-end establishments that cater to tourists. However, you cannot always count on this. More often, public restrooms will cost a few pesos and an attendant will hand you a few squares of toilet paper when you enter. There are still other places where you will find no toilet paper at all, and perhaps even the toilet seats will be missing. It's best to be well prepared, especially if you are traveling with children, who seem to have the habit of having to go at the worst possible times. Be sure to pack a roll of toilet paper or—even better—a travel pack of baby wipes before you leave your hotel for the day. It is also a very good idea to pack a small bottle of disinfectant lotion, which you can pick up at any drugstore or pharmacy. This will go a long way toward making sure you don't pick up any of those nasty digestion problems that Mexico is so famous for.

probably not enough because every inch of the property seems to be manicured with great care. Guests of the hotel receive golf, swimming, tennis, and other privileges at a nearby country club. Other services include in-room salon services and tours of the city and surrounding area. Standard room rates are inexpensive to moderate while suites go for quite a bit more.

CASA CALDERONI

Owners: Ben and Mary Calderoni
415-154-6005
www.casacalderoni.com
Callejón del Pueblito #4-A, San Miguel de Allende, Gto. 37700

Price: Inexpensive
Credit Cards: MC, V
Special Features: Concierge service, wireless Internet access, free calls to the United States and Canada

This intimate hotel is a great value. It enjoys a great location just 3 blocks off the town square. It features nine rooms, each one dedicated to and named after a different artist. The rooms are not the largest in town but they are comfortably appointed in an elegant colonial or southwestern style with tiled bathrooms, solid wood furniture, and wrought iron bed frames. They are decorated in a tasteful manner that is warm but not busy, with handmade tile floors and wrought iron headboards. The higher end suites are much roomier and feature sofa beds. This hotel also features a rooftop terrace with an outstanding view of the city. Pets and children under 14 are not allowed. The standard room and junior suite rates are inexpensive and full suite rates are not much more than that.

CASA DE LA CUESTA

Owners: Bill and Heidi Le Vasseur
415-154-4324
www.casadelacuesta.com
Cuesta de San José #32, San Miguel de Allende, Gto. 37700
Price: Moderate
Credit Cards: MC, V
Special Features: Plenty of traditional art, colonial feel

Located just above the *Mercado de Artesenias*, this elegant bed and breakfast offers six individually appointed rooms with private fireplaces and access to a terrace that overlooks San Miguel and the nearby mountains. They open onto a central patio with a tiled stone fountain, providing the atmosphere of an authentic Mexican villa. Throughout the property are numerous Mexican-style arched doorways, and the walls are covered with traditional art. Each room is furnished with one king-size bed that can be converted to two singles. The floors are beautifully tiled and decorated in a colonial style. The common dining room is tiled, with an attractive fireplace and a high beamed ceiling, decorated in a way that makes you feel right at home (though children under 16 are not allowed). A full Mexican breakfast is complimentary with every night's stay.

CASA DIANA

Owner: Carmen Gutiérrez
415-152-0885
www.casa-diana.com
Recreo #48, San Miguel de Allende, Gto. 37700
Price: Inexpensive
Credit Cards: MC, V
Special Features: On-site art gallery, complimentary gourmet breakfasts

This bed and breakfast boutique hotel offers three rooms in a restored colonial house just 2 1/2 blocks from the Jardín Principal. It was restored by surrealist artist Pedro Friedeberg. The first floor of the house is a gallery featuring the work of several artists while the second floor houses the guest rooms, though the entire house is uniquely decorated. For example, you will find the original work of Friedeberg throughout the house. This sitting area is adorned with a lion-face chimney and the second floor terrace has a miniature-size Indian temple. A gourmet breakfast is included with the price of your room. Breakfast is served either on the second-floor terrace or in the gallery area.

CASA DE LÍZA

Owner: Liza Kisber
415-152-0352
http://casaliza.com
Bajada del Chorro #7, San Miguel de Allende, Gto. 37700
Price: Moderate to Expensive
Credit Cards: MC, V
Special Features: Laundry service, private parking, concierge service

This bed and breakfast is located in a 17th-century colonial estate. Its American owner purchased the estate in the 1980s and set about creating a distinctive guesthouse designed to provide a unique experience. The hotel features eight unique accommodation options ranging from luxury suites to casitas, or small houses complete with full kitchens. You will be greeted with fresh flowers grown in the hotel's private greenhouse. Rooms boast features such as fireplaces, elegantly carved French doors, and Jacuzzi bathtubs. Some rooms have king-size beds while others have two twins that can be pushed together to create one

The Casa Rosada courtyard Courtesy of Casa Rosada

queen-size bed. A gourmet breakfast of eggs, cereals, and seasonal fresh fruit is provided when and where you want, even if that happens to be in bed. Appetizers are also served around the heated pool in the late afternoon. All rooms have cable television and Internet access. Additional on-site salon services such as manicure/pedicure, hair styling, and massage therapy are also available by appointment. Suite rates are moderate while casitas are a bit more expensive.

CASA QUETZAL HOTEL
Owner: Cynthia Price
415-152-0501; 800-624-4548 or 1-206-315-9804 ext. 101 (U.S.)
www.casaquetzalhotel.com
Hospicio #34, San Miguel de Allende, Gto. 37700

Price: Moderate to Expensive
Credit Cards: MC, V
Special Features: Wireless Internet, private parking, cable TV with DVD
Located just around the corner from the Jardín Principal, this boutique hotel offers seven suites and four standard rooms in a restored colonial residence. Each room is uniquely decorated in a range of styles from elegant Asian to modern Mexican art deco. Each room features a private terrace area. Most rooms are furnished with kitchenettes, microwaves, and mini-refrigerators. The common-area terrace with a Jacuzzi is a nice place for relaxing and having a drink. Other services offered to guests of this hotel include in-room spa service, airport transportation, and (believe it or not) plastic surgery recovery service. Standard room rates are moderate while suites are a bit more expensive.

The Casa Sierra Nevada, pool area Courtesy of Sierra Nevada Hotels

CASA ROSADA

Manager: José Ignacio López
415-152-8123
www.casarosadahotel.com
Cuna de Allende #12, San Miguel de
Allende, Gto. 37700
Price: Expensive
Credit Cards: AE, MC, V
Special Features: Good location, wireless
Internet access, laundry service, private
parking
This hotel is located in an 18th-century
residence just 1 block off the main square.
Rooms are sparsely decorated with neutral
colors and a combination of Mexican,
Hindu, and Moroccan art. Casa Rosada
offers seven standard rooms, three junior
suites, and three master suites. Master
suites include a living room and a private
terrace, and junior suites have a balcony or
a small terrace. The standard rooms are
fairly roomy and are certainly comfortable
and attractive. The rooms are simply and
tastefully appointed and include cable television and wireless Internet access. Some
rooms also have air conditioning, which
can be a big plus in the summertime.
Standard room rates are on the high side of
moderate while master suites are quite a bit
more expensive. The on-site Xipal restaurant offers elegant Mexican cuisine and is
open daily from 7 PM to 10 PM.

CASA SCHUCK BOUTIQUE HOTEL

Owner: Nancy Cordelli
415-152-0657
www.casaschuck.com
Bajada de la Garita #3, San Miguel de
Allende, Gto. 37700
Price: Moderate to Expensive
Credit Cards: None
Special Features: Garden pool, fireplaces,
rooftop sundeck
This gorgeous boutique bed and breakfast
is located in a large 18th-century colonial
villa on a hillside overlooking the city. It
was restored in the 1960s by a couple of
American expatriates and is now run by
their granddaughter. It offers 10 spacious
suites, each one uniquely decorated in
styles ranging from traditional Mexican to
art deco. Rooms feature private tiled bathrooms and either one king-size or two
twin-size beds, as well as high-beamed
ceilings and working fireplaces that are
perfect for setting a romantic mood. Darkly

colored wood and natural colors complete the effect. A full Mexican or American-style breakfast is provided. Casa Schuck also features an intimate garden swimming pool and a rooftop sundeck that provides breathtaking vistas. Just a few blocks off the town square, this hotel has a location that is hard to beat. This is an adults-only hotel, so leave the little ones at home if you plan on staying here. Weddings and special events can be done on the premises. Call or see their Web site for details. Room rates vary significantly, depending on the room.

A room at the Casa Sierra Nevada   Courtesy of Sierra Nevada Hotels

CASA DE SIERRA NEVADA HOTEL

Manager: Rafael Carpio
415-152-7040
www.casadesierranevada.com
Hospicio #42, Centro, San Miguel de Allende, Gto. 37700
Price: Expensive
Credit Cards: AE, MC, V
Special Features: On-site cooking school, day spa, event planner

This hotel is actually a collection of four houses within several blocks of one another offering 32 rooms and suites in all. Because of the hotel's unique circumstances, no two rooms are alike, though they are all decorated with richly colored art and antiques, with tiled bathrooms and Mexican furniture. Many have fireplaces while others have terraces opening onto the streets of San Miguel. Additionally, this hotel functions as a cooking school, offering classes in gourmet Mexican cooking. If you are planning a trip to San Miguel for a wedding or other event, this hotel has several venues on-site. Besides the facilities available in the hotel, the Casa de Sierra Nevada offers three event spaces for meetings, presentations, receptions, and banquets. No guests under the age of 16 are allowed.

DOÑA URRACA HOTEL

Manager: Lourdes Mora de Poirier
415-154-4481
www.donaurraca.com.mx
Hidalgo #69, San Miguel de Allende, Gto. 37700
Price: Moderate to Expensive
Credit Cards: AE, MC, V
Special Features: Wireless Internet access, spa services, Jacuzzi, heated pool, private parking

This spa hotel is located several blocks north of the city's main square. The architecture is colonial with modern touches, such as large windows and hardwood floors. It offers 32 rooms furnished with one king or queen bed or two double beds. Rooms are good size and moderately decorated with neutral colors, emphasizing the natural light. Rates for standard rooms are moderate while rates for master suites are quite a bit more expensive. This hotel also includes a lap pool at the back of the property, plus a small café featuring many Mexican favorites and a long wine list, which is open daily from 7:30 AM to 10 PM. The hotel spa offers facials, body massages, and other treatments. Check their Web site for special packages.

DOS CASAS

Manager: Jesús Ayala
415-152-4958
www.livingdoscasas.com
Quebrada #101, San Miguel de Allende, Gto. 37700
Price: Expensive
Credit Cards:
Special Features: In-room spa services, cooking classes, private parties, wireless Internet access

If you're looking for elegant charm near the heart of San Miguel de Allende, you won't go wrong with Dos Casas. This is a beautifully appointed boutique hotel located just 3 blocks from the town's main plaza. It is decorated with an interesting blend of modern and colonial decors. It offers six stylish suites with dark-stained high-beamed ceilings and handmade tile bathrooms. They are decorated in cool neutral colors and exposed-stone walls. Several have canopy beds for that added romantic touch. The property also has a rooftop terrace with full bar and light snacks, open daily from noon to 8 PM. There is an elegant wine bar on the property that is open Tuesday through Sunday from 1 PM to 10 PM. Guests are offered walking and bicycle tours of the city, as well as in-room spa services and cooking classes. Private parties are also available.

HACIENDA DE LAS FLORES

Owner: Alicia Franyutti de Cornish
415-152-1808
www.haciendadelasflores.com
Hospicio #16, San Miguel de Allende, Gto. 37700
Price: Inexpensive to Moderate

Credit Cards: MC, V
Special Features: Wireless Internet access, special events, pool, garden, conference room

This hotel is located on a lush property a good walk from the center of San Miguel. It offers 17 brightly appointed rooms that are arranged in a variety of accommodation configurations. There are special rates available for longer stays, and children under 12 stay for free. The hotel grounds are ideal for large groups as well as special events, such as weddings or reunions. The property has several nicely landscaped gardens and a good-size patio swimming pool. There is also a garden bar and a rooftop Jacuzzi. The restaurant serves up a menu of Mexican favorites. Breakfast is served daily from 8 AM to noon, and lunch and larger parties by appointment.

LA MANSIÓN DEL BOSQUE

Owner: Ruth Hyba
415-152-0277
Aldama #65, San Miguel de Allende, Gto. 37700
Price: Inexpensive
Credit Cards: None
Special Features: Private fireplaces, semiprivate terraces, pets allowed

This bed and breakfast is a warm and inviting hotel that is located off Juarez Park, 3 blocks from the city center. It offers 23 rooms, each with its own private fireplace and access to semiprivate terraces. They are comfortably appointed in a rustic Mexican style that quickly makes you feel at home. Guests are welcome to bring along small pets. However, be sure to mention this when you make your reservations. The owner, a published cookbook author, personally supervises the kitchen, designing a different menu from fresh local ingredients every day. After dinner, head to the outdoor patio and enjoy a drink from the hotel bar. It's a perfect way to end a long day of traveling.

LA MORADA HOTEL

Manager: Laura Torres-Septien Torres

415-152-1647

www.lamoradahotel.com

Correo #10, San Miguel de Allende, Gto. 37700

Credit Cards: AE, MC, V

Price: Moderate to Expensive

Special Features: Fireplaces, personal Jacuzzi, direct-line phone

This hotel is located 1/2 block off the Jardín Principal, offering a convenient location from which to experience San Miguel. It has 15 spacious rooms and suites featuring woven *bóveda* or high-beamed ceilings, finely tiled floors, and rustic wooden furniture. Each room is individually decorated with bright colors and Mexican designs, with handmade wrought iron bed frames. They feature dark wood wall units and handmade cotton blankets. Most are equipped with a sitting room, fireplace, and private Jacuzzi for relaxing after a long day of pounding the pavement. The master suite features a rooftop terrace with Jacuzzi for two, and a sitting area that overlooks the city. Room rates vary significantly by season. Check their Web site for special packages.

MISIÓN DE LOS ANGELES

Manager: Victor Piscil

415-152-2099

www.hotelmisiondelosangeles.com.mx

Carretera San Miguel de Allende Km. 2, San Miguel de Allende, Gto. 37700

Price: Moderate

Credit Cards: AE, D, MC, V

Special Features: Domed ceilings, swimming pool, gym

This luxuriously appointed hotel offers 57 rooms and suites with domed brick ceilings, and most are equipped with kitchenettes and dining rooms. They are surprisingly spacious, particularly the suites, and have balconies opening onto the pool area. The hotel architecture is distinctly colonial, with more than three hundred arches to be found throughout the property. Two stone arches tower over the hotel pool and the bar just a few feet away, where you can get a drink and relax. Adjacent to the pool is a grass area that is ideal for outdoor banquet weddings and other special occasions. The hotel is also equipped with a small gym where you can work up a sweat if you have any energy left after touring the beautiful city of San Miguel all day. The location is a little out of the way, though a shuttle provides complimentary transport into San Miguel, or you can catch a taxi for about $5.

OASIS

Owner: Nancy Hooper

415-154-9850 or 1-210-745-1457 (U.S.)

www.oasissanmiguel.com

Chiquitos #1-A, San Miguel de Allende, Gto. 37700

Price: Expensive

Credit Cards: AE, M, V

Special Features: Concierge service, wine cellar, executive center

This Moroccan-themed bed and breakfast hotel is a converted 17th-century villa with four elegantly appointed suites. The Bedouin and Berber Suites feature a king-size bed, extra large shower, and French doors that open onto a private wall fountain and pond. The Sahara Suite features a king-size four-poster bed and shuttered windows with a nice view of San Miguel. The Nomad Suite features a king-size four-poster bed and a hand-carved Mudejar daybed. The room also has a Moroccan style bath with double vanities, and a water wall that stretches the length of the suite. As with all the suites, a gourmet breakfast is provided with each night's stay. Each suite has a private fireplace, wireless Internet, and flat screen TV. Additionally, the property has a rooftop terrace with a 360-degree view of the city.

PABLOS SUITES

Owner: Pablo Lavista
415-152-2916
www.pablosuites.com
Ancha de San Antonio #13-A, San Miguel
de Allende, Gto. 37700
Price: Inexpensive
Credit Cards: AE, MC, V
Special Features: Wireless Internet access
This Pablo-themed hotel is one of San
Miguel's more interesting hotels. It is
located 3 (long) blocks southwest of the
main square, just across the street from the
Arte School Instituto Allende. The hotel
takes its name from the owner, however
there are a couple dozen photos of other
famous Pablos (or Pauls) throughout the
hotel, including Newman, Neruda, and, of
course, Picasso. There are four suites, each
one named after a particular Pablo. They
are spacious and elegantly appointed in a
modern style with either one king-size bed
or two double beds and a living room area. A
continental breakfast is provided with each
night's stay. It certainly doesn't seem like a
budget hotel, but the rates here are inexpensive, making this hotel a great value.

POSADA DE LA ALDEA

Manager: Lena Codiga
415-152-1022
Calle Ancha de San Antonio, San Miguel de
Allende, Gto. 37700
Price: Inexpensive
Credit Cards: MC, V
Special Features: Swimming pool, tennis
courts
This relatively sprawling 66-room hotel is
located about a mile off the city center near
the Instituto Allende. This is an attractive
option for those who are traveling with kids
because it is fairly inexpensive and offers
plenty to do on-site. The rooms are a bit
small though nicely appointed with two
double beds. There is a spacious restaurant
on-site open daily from 8 AM to 5:30 PM,
serving up traditional Mexican fare as well

as several options that are favorites from
north of the border. There is also a swimming pool and two clay tennis courts, just
in case you did not get enough exercise
walking around San Miguel all day. Non-
guests are welcome to use these facilities
for a small fee. If you are a registered student at the Instituto, be sure to ask for the
student discount.

POSADA CARMINA

Manager: Francisco García
415-152-0458
www.posadacarmina.com
Cuna de Allende #37, San Miguel de
Allende, Gto. 37700
Price: Inexpensive
Credit Cards: MC, V
Special Features: On-site restaurant, wireless Internet access
This hotel is located in an 18th-century
colonial villa just down the street from the
city center. It offers 24 elegantly appointed
rooms furnished with either one king-size
bed or two doubles. Rooms are not colorful
but instead put an emphasis on modera-
tion, with only a touch of Mexican tile here
and there. The rooms are built around an
attractive arch-filled cobblestone courtyard, a perfect place for relaxing and planning the day. The restaurant is a remodeled
stable and has an attractive fireplace,
wrought iron windows, and large stone arch
that almost take you back to the colonial
days of the 18th century. It offers indoor
and courtyard seating. There is wireless
Internet access in this area of the hotel.
This restaurant offers a traditional daily
comida or meal of the day. It is open daily
from 7:30 AM to 11 PM. Don't miss the two-
for-one happy hour Monday through Friday
from 5 PM to 8 PM.

POSADA CORAZÓN

Owner: Cesar Arias
415-152-0182
www.posadacorazon.com.mx

Lodging for Students of Spanish Schools

In the years following World War II, San Miguel became a popular destination for war vets looking to study art and live off the money they received from the G.I. Bill. This has given rise to a small industry of Spanish schools in San Miguel and Guanajuato. Today, these cities are among the most popular destinations in Mexico for foreign tourists looking to study Spanish. Every year, hundreds of language students come here for periods ranging from a few days to a few months. Over the years, the area's language schools have come up with a variety of options for lodging that they offer to their students.

If you are traveling to Guanajuato or San Miguel to study Spanish, be sure to investigate several schools to find out what they can offer in terms of accommodations as well as their curriculum. The majority of these schools prefer their students to take lodging with local families to facilitate Spanish immersion. Rates for these types of accommodations usually cover several home-cooked meals with your host family every day. This can save you money and will certainly give you plenty of exposure to everyday Mexican culture. However, with so many great restaurants nearby, you may find yourself skipping a few of those family meals. Some schools work with local hotels to offer students discounted rates. If you plan on going with this type of arrangement, make sure you investigate the hotels that are offered so that you know exactly what to expect when you arrive. Still other schools maintain nearby apartments and small houses that they rent out to their students. Because most Spanish schools are located at or near the center of town, these residences tend to have very convenient locations. This is important since you will only be in class for a few hours a day. The rest of your time will likely be spent out exploring and hanging out in cafes and bars with your classmates. Additionally, since the schools tend to offer these personal residences at ridiculously low rates, this can be a very attractive option.

Aldama #9, San Miguel de Allende, Gto. 37700
Price: Moderate
Credit Cards: D, MC, V
Special Features: Organic breakfast, private parking, wireless Internet access
This bed and breakfast inn is located just a block south of the Jardín Principal, offering a convenient location from which to explore San Miguel. It features six rooms diversely decorated that open onto a central garden courtyard. The rooms are simple but elegant, with touches like carved marble headboards and handmade sitting chairs. One suite features a private patio pool. The main house itself is decorated with a nice blend of rustic and modern appointments such as exposed stone walls and a small library. There is also a comfortable living room containing a small library, and a stone patio that is a nice place for just relaxing. The property is equipped with wireless Internet access and private parking. An organic breakfast is included with each night's stay. Additionally, private massages and gourmet coffee drinks are also available on site.

POSADA DE LAS MONJAS

Manager: Manolo Garcia
415-152-0171
www.posadalasmonjas.com
Canal #37, San Miguel de Allende, Gto. 37700
Price: Very Inexpensive
Credit Cards: MC, V
Special Features: Laundry service
This 64-room hotel is conveniently located just 3 blocks west of the Jardín Principal. It is a charming hotel with architecture similar to a small castle. Despite the fact that it shows its age, it provides clean accommodations. Guests are offered laundry service for a nominal fee. The reception area has a

Enjoying a relaxing afternoon at the Posada de San Francisco hotel

nice fireplace and is an inviting place to relax and have a conversation. The rooms are not fancy or particularly spacious. However, the beds are surprisingly soft and comfortable. Plus, if you can get a room on the top floor, your room will not only be quiet but you will have a nice view of the city as well. Be warned, however, there is no elevator and it can be quite a workout. If you're traveling on a budget, you could do much worse. Triple occupancy rooms are available.

POSADA DE SAN FRANCISCO

Manager: Georgina Bautista López
415-152-7213
www.posadadesanfrancisco.com
Plaza Principal #2, San Miguel de Allende, Gto. 37700
Price: Inexpensive to Moderate
Credit Cards: AE, MC, V

Special Features: Satellite TV, convenient location

This impressive hotel is located right on the city's central plaza, offering guests the ability to step out the front door and right into the middle of things. It features 46 rooms and suites decorated in a simple but comfortable Mexican style. The walls are not overburdened with art, but there's something about it that tells you you're in Mexico. Standard rooms are fairly small and are furnished with a queen-size bed. Suites are furnished with two queen-size beds and have a living room area. However, the main attraction here is the location and the hotel itself. There is bar and food service in the interior courtyard and the restaurant has large arches that open onto the street, making it a great place for people watching.

LA PUERTECITA BOUTIQUE HOTEL

Manager: Donato Ortega
415-152-5011
www.lapuertecita.com
Santo Domingo #75, San Miguel de Allende, Gto. 37700
Price: Expensive
Credit Cards: AE, MC, V
Special Features: Outdoor pool, restaurant, gym, wireless Internet access

Located a brisk walk from the city center, this hotel offers luxury accommodations with a colonial feel. The grounds of the hotel are lush and well manicured with crawling vines next to close-cropped hedges. Spa service is offered poolside, with facials and body massages. The hotel also has an elegant restaurant serving breakfast daily from 8 AM to 11:30 AM, lunch from 1 PM to 4 PM, and dinner from 7 PM to 9 PM. With 32 rooms, including 12 suites and junior suites, this is one of San Miguel's larger hotels. Rooms are furnished with either one king-size bed or two queen-size beds and are appointed with a rather modern Mexican décor. This hotel caters to groups such as wedding parties or business retreats. In any case, ask for special deals when making your reservation, as the hotel does offer them.

RANCHO EL ATASCADERO

Manager: Carlos A. Maycotte
415-152 0206
www.hotelatascadero.com
Prolongación Santo Domingo, San Miguel de Allende, Gto. 37700
Price: Inexpensive to Moderate
Credit Cards: AE, MC, V
Special Features: Private fireplace, private parking, massage room, sauna, baby sitter

This colonial resort is located on a converted 18th-century hacienda about a mile off the city center. Guests are provided with courtesy transportation to and from the city center from 8 AM to 3 PM. The hotel offers four family suites and 48 rooms, each with its own fireplace. Family suites accommodate up to five people. The hotel grounds are extensive and well manicured, with rows of stone arches and secluded cobblestone patios. This is an attractive option for anyone planning an event or get-together. They feature several gardens and sitting areas as well as a pool, Jacuzzi, and tennis court. There is also a restaurant with full bar that is open daily from 7:30 AM to 10:30 PM. It would be an ideal place for a wedding or other special event.

REAL DE MINAS SAN MIGUEL DE ALLENDE

Manager: Marcelo Castro Vera
415-152-2626
www.realdeminas.com
Calle Ancha de San Antonio, San Miguel de Allende, Gto. 37700
Price: Moderate to Expensive
Credit Cards: AE, MC, V
Special Features: Kids area, laundry service, billiards, helicopter pad, activities, car rental desk

This spacious, colorful hotel offers its guests a long list of amenities and services to fill up their days, just in case they run out of things to do and see in town. On-site features include a tennis court, gift shop, game room, helicopter pad, and even a bull ring, just to name a few. There is also a conference center for business meetings and special events, as well as a restaurant with a full bar that is open daily from 7:30 AM to 10 PM. This makes the hotel an ideal option for anyone planning a special event. It has 215 rooms and suites, making it one of San Miguel's larger hotels. Standard rooms are simply decorated in white and furnished with two double beds, and suites have king-size beds. If you are looking to experience the authentic colonial feel of the city, this may not be the hotel for you, though rooms are fairly spacious and competently appointed.

SUSURRO

Owner: Robert Waters
415-152-1065
www.susurro.com.mx
Recreo #78, San Miguel de Allende, Gto.
37700
Price: Moderate
Credit Cards: MC, V
Special Features: Laundry service, fireplace, wireless Internet, purified water throughout property

Roughly translated as "whisper," Susurro earns its name with quiet elegance. Located just 3 blocks off the Jardín Principal, this bed and breakfast hotel is actually an 18th-century colonial mansion with lush gardens, tiled patios, and a pool. The property was purchased in 2001 by its American expatriate owner, and restored to its current elegant condition. It retains a colonial feel with beamed ceilings and arched doorways. A gourmet breakfast is included with each night's stay, served either in the dining room, the garden courtyard, or on your private terrace. With only four suites, this hotel provides very intimate accommodations. Rooms feature private tiled bathrooms, hand-carved fireplaces, and king- or queen-size beds, or two twin-size beds.

LAS TERRAZAS SAN MIGUEL

Owners: Greg Johnson and Murray Friedman
415-152-5028; (U.S.) 707-534-1833
www.terrazassanmiguel.com
Santo Domingo #3, San Miguel de Allende, Gto. 37700
Price: Inexpensive to Moderate
Credit Cards: MC, V
Special Features: Wireless Internet, continental breakfast, cable TV

This bed and breakfast is actually a compound of four private casitas, or small houses, on a hillside overlooking San Miguel de Allende. These accommodations range from a studio to a one-bedroom, to a couple of two-bedroom casitas, all furnished with queen-size beds. They are decorated in a variety of styles, combining Mexican traditions with pieces from elsewhere, such as a baboon-head fountain and bamboo chairs. While this hotel doesn't have the old-world feel of some of the other bed and breakfasts in town, the rooms are comfortably appointed and there are plenty of amenities, such as wireless high speed Internet access, cable television, and landscaped patios. Guests are greeted with fresh flowers and a bottle of wine, as well as a gourmet breakfast each morning. Rates are set with a three-night minimum stay.

VILLA JACARANDA

Owners: Don and Gloria Fenton
415-152-1015
www.villajacaranda.com
Calle Aldama #53, San Miguel de Allende, Gto. 37700
Price: Moderate
Credit Cards: MC, V
Special Features: Sheltered parking, on-site fine dining restaurant

This quiet converted mansion is located on a tranquil cobblestone street 3 blocks from the town center. The aim at this establishment is to provide guests with a relaxing, quiet atmosphere, as well as service with a personal touch. This hotel is ideal for anyone wanting to enjoy the sights and sounds of San Miguel and then have a place to come back to at the end of the day and take it easy. It offers 18 nicely appointed rooms and suites and one studio. The décor is more reminiscent of north of the border with touches such as pastel flower-print blankets, but it's warm and comfortable nonetheless. Room rates go up significantly during holidays. Children under 12 stay for free. The restaurant has a full bar as well as inside and outside dining. It is open daily from 7:30 AM to 10:30 PM.

VILLA MIRASOL HOTEL

Owner: Carmen Avery

415-152-8057

Pila Seca #35, San Miguel de Allende, Gto.
37700

Price: Inexpensive to Moderate

Credit Cards: AE, MC, V

Special Features: Country club access, complimentary tea time

This beautiful hotel is located in a two-story mansion in downtown San Miguel. It offers 10 suites that are fairly spacious and decorated in a simple manner that draws on natural light, making you feel right at home. Rooms are furnished with either one king-size bed, one queen-size bed, or two twin beds, and feature private patio areas. All in all, this is a very comfortable hotel. Breakfast is included with each night's stay and there is a complimentary tea time service between 5 PM and 6 PM. Just in case you want to shake up your itinerary, guests of the hotel also receive access to the local country club for swimming, tennis, and golf.

VILLA RIVERA HOTEL

Manager: Jesús Calvo García

415-152-0742

www.villarivera.com

Cuadrante #3, San Miguel de Allende, Gto.
37700

Price: Expensive

Credit Cards: MC, V

Special Features: Private fireplaces, outdoor pool, restaurant/bar

This is a comfortable and inviting hotel with a great location right in the heart of San Miguel. Its 12 rooms are decorated in a homey Mexican style, with wrought iron beds and fresh flowers. They are furnished in a variety of configurations. Most have either one king-size bed or one queen-size bed, though a couple are furnished with two doubles. Several rooms have private fireplaces. Many rooms also open onto a terrace that overlooks a patio pool below. There is also a spacious restaurant that has a full bar. It is open daily from 8 AM to 11 PM. Be sure to enjoy the live music and drink specials Thursdays and Saturdays from 7 PM to 10 PM.

VISTA REAL HOTEL

Manager: Laura Torres-Septien

415-152 3984

www.vistarealhotel.com

Callejón de Arial #4, San Miguel de Allende, Gto. 37700

Price: Moderate

Credit Cards: AE, MC, V

Special Features: Heated pool, conference room, wireless Internet service, valet parking

This attractive hotel is located a five-minute drive from the city center. If needed, there is transportation service provided every half hour between 9 AM and 10 PM. The hotel has 21 suites, most of which overlook the pool-dominated courtyard, and a beautiful view of the city beyond. Standard rooms are furnished with one queen-size bed and suites have two queen-size beds. The Restaurant La Vista is located in the main dining room and is open Tuesday through Sunday, serving breakfast 9 AM to noon, and lunch and dinner from 1 PM to 10 PM. Room service is also available. Be sure to check out happy hour Tuesdays and Wednesdays from 5 PM to 8 PM.

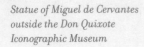

4

CULTURE

Both San Miguel de Allende and Guanajuato are first and foremost thought of as historic colonial cities. This is because they were built into gorgeous towns with stunning architecture during the colonial period of Mexico's history. And it is true that the remains of the 18th century alone would warrant a visit. However, this rich colonial history with matching architecture is not what most makes Guanajuato and San Miguel de Allende unique and inviting. Mexico is full of picturesque colonial towns that have moseyed into the 21st century surrounded by remnants of a more glorious past. What makes these two towns worth your while is the vibrant and creative life that is taking place in them today.

This vibrancy comes from distinct and even surprising sources. It is a common complaint about San Miguel that the culture here has somehow been watered down by the five thousand or so American and Canadian expatriates that now call this city home. First of all, it's not as if the city has really been overrun by foreigners. Expats are still a small minority of San Miguel de Allende's population. Secondly, it is not as though the last 60 years have seen this city descended upon by a multitude of retired accountants (not that I have anything against accountants, of course). By and large, these expatriates have been highly creative, daring people who have come to reinvent themselves by doing what they've always wanted to do. In the process, they have reinvented San Miguel de Allende, making it an active artist colony where just about anything seems possible. No, the town is not as traditional as it might otherwise be, but hey, if Spanish is not your strong suit, this may be the easiest town in Central Mexico for you to get along in. Guanajuato's lively energies come from a different source. The town's university has changed the course of its history. It was the university that took over the Teatro Principal after years of neglect. It was university students

A typical Guanajuato street performer entertains crowds in front of Teatro Juárez. Mary Delgado

The Parroquia of San Miguel de Allende is one of the most unique churches in all of Mexico.

who sowed the seeds that would eventually grow into the International Cerventino Festival. And it has been the presence of this young crowd that has made the city a popular weekend destination, despite the fact that there isn't a beach within miles of here. Young people are a constant feature here and they give the place a spirited atmosphere that is creative and intellectual. Combined with their close proximity, San Miguel de Allende and Guanajuato offer a modern, enlightened experience against the backdrop of old Mexico.

Some of San Miguel de Allende's architecture is in an extremely fragile state.

ARCHITECTURE

During the three centuries of Spanish rule, San Miguel and Guanajuato were basically constructed from the ground up following the path of Spanish architecture. Beginning with Gothic, then moving on to renaissance, followed by baroque and finally ending with neoclassical, the architecture of this region can be traced back to the preferences of Spanish architects. However, structures also display distinct local variations, such as the signature pastel-colored stucco of Guanajuato and the pale pink stone of San Miguel's churches, which infused the predominantly Spanish architecture with a markedly regional flair.

Without a doubt one of this region's most charming features—as well as a big reason why Guanajuato was designated a UNESCO World Heritage site in 1988, and the entire town as a national monument in 1926—is the beautiful colonial architecture that is found throughout the area. During the colonial period, San Miguel was home to one of the most prosperous populations in all of New Spain. Furthermore, when the region's silver-mining resources were first discovered in 1558, and the settlement that sprung up around these mines immediately began to flourish, it was during the period of transition between renaissance and baroque architecture. The Spanish had tapped what turned out to be one of the world's most productive silver veins, and it filled silver barons' pockets. This surge of wealth set off a boom in construction that provided both Guanajuato and San Miguel with the graceful mansions and arresting churches and plazas that continue to provide visitors and residents alike with enchanting public spaces.

The Renaissance was truly a period of rebirth of ancient cultural, artistic, and architectural ideals, as it drew from the Roman and Greek traditions. In Mexico, this movement generally manifested itself in the form of Plateresque. *Plata* being the Spanish word for silver, this branch of the renaissance style earned its name because it was particularly ornamental and thought to resemble decorative silverwork. Plateresque is predominantly

The Roman arch that marks the entrance to Plaza Reforma, Guanajuato

known for the sculpted stone of its façades and doorways, which are still considered important elements of architecture in San Miguel de Allende.

In the early 17th century, the baroque architectural style began to become fashionable in San Miguel. Where the renaissance style emphasized the balance of classic shapes like circles, squares, and triangles, the baroque style integrated elements like curves, contrasts of light and shadow, color, and elaborate decoration for a more dramatic impact. This movement also incorporated other artistic elements such as ornate and massive altar-pieces. Churrigueresque, a specific form of the baroque, peaked in Mexico between 1730 and 1780. Constructions from this period boast amazingly elaborate decoration. You can see quintessential examples of this in the façades of the Templo de San Francisco and La Campañia de Jesús in Guanajuato.

In the 18th century, the neoclassical period brought another change of tastes with a return to the simplicity, harmony, and sobriety of early Greek and Roman civilizations. Guanajuato's best example of this would probably be the plain blocklike structure of the Alhóndiga de Granaditas. It was also during this time that Zeferino Gutiérrez gave San Miguel's Parroquia its Gothic façade, which has come to symbolize the city itself.

Art Classes

For nearly a century now, art has been the cultural element that has made San Miguel de Allende thrive. Before it was known as an enclave for expatriates or restaurateurs, it was a burgeoning artist colony. In fact it was the opportunity this town presented, of learning from its artists, that resulted in such an international community. These opportunities still exist today in San Miguel de Allende. Of course, the two main schools of Bellas Artes and Instituto Allende are still in operation, offering classes on such diverse subjects as photography, ceramics, and dance. But there are also plenty of other outlets offering classes that are perhaps more personalized and less structured. Many of the graduates of San Miguel's great art schools have stayed in the city and set up schools of their own. If you plan on staying in town for an extended period, there is a wide range of options for whatever medium you are interested in. If you plan to be here for just a day, or even a few hours, there are certainly schools here to accommodate you.

BELLAS ARTES (EL NIGROMENTE)
Director: Francisco Vidargas
415-152-0289
E-mail: cceniba@prodigy.net.mx
Hernández Macías #75, San Miguel de Allende, Gto. 37700
Open: Hours vary
This school has a storied history, having its roots in the first school established by Felipe Cossío del Pomar in 1937. It is located 1 block off the Jardín Principal. It offers monthly classes on a wide variety of artistic mediums, including drawing, painting, sculpture, photography, and ceramics, as well as music, ballet, and dance. Classes begin on the first of the month and foreign student tuition is about $100 per month plus a lab fee, depending on the course. Children are admitted at half price.

Baile folklorico figures made of corn husks.

CLASSES UNLIMITED
Directors: Jo Brenzo and Gary Berkowitz
415-154-5366
www.classesunlimited.com
E-mail: acdphoto@acdphoto.com
Mesónes #57, Interior B, San Miguel de Allende, Gto. 37700
Open: Hours vary
Despite its name, instructors here keep class size limited, offering personalized instruction in a variety of subjects, including photography, writing, and fine arts, including drawing and painting for children age six and older. Prices vary by subject and coursework.

EDINA SAGERT STUDIO
Director: Edina Sagert
415-120-8088
www.edinasagert.com
E-mail: edinasagert@yahoo.com
Fábrica la Aurora, San Miguel de Allende, Gto. 37700
Open: Mon.–Fri. 10 AM–5:30 PM; Sat. 10 AM–2 PM
Edina Sagert is a German-born artist who has lived and traveled all over the world, including India, Southeast Asia, and the United States. She offers watercolor classes intermittently throughout the year in San Miguel de Allende. Classes are intensive but are

appropriate for both beginners and advanced students. These classes are generally three hours long and cost $20 a session.

INSTITUTO ALLENDE
Director: Héctor Ulloa
415-152-0190
www.instituto-allende.edu.mx
E-mail: iallende@instituto-allende.edu.mx
Ancha de San Antonio #22, San Miguel de Allende, Gto. 37700
Open: Mon.–Fri. 8 AM–5 PM; Sat. 9 AM–1 PM
Another one of San Miguel's historic art schools, this institution began offering classes in 1951. It is located in a large colonial building and offers courses in such subjects as painting, drawing, sculpture, ceramics, and art history. It also offers a Spanish program. This is an accredited institution offering academic credits and even MFA degrees. Many of its students have gone on to set up art studios here in San Miguel de Allende. Classes run year-round and prices vary depending on coursework.

KEITH KELLER'S LA ESCUELA
Director: Keith Keller
415-152-0637
www.casadesuenosmexico.com
E-mail: keithkellerart@yahoo.com
Ancha de San Antonio #27, San Miguel de Allende, Gto. 37700
Open: Mon., Wed., Fri. 10 AM–1 PM
Keith Keller is the primary instructor at this school, which he founded in 1985; he offers classes in drawing and painting. He provides students with personal instruction and unlimited access to two studios that open onto a garden courtyard. Beginners generally start by learning to draw simple forms then move on to figurative drawing. More experienced artists generally paint as they wish and receive critique, or learn techniques such as glazing. Registration is not required and materials can be purchased in Mexico. Tuition is $180 per month with a minimum payment of $100 for short-term students.

SILVER JEWELRY WORKSHOP
Director: Enrique López Larrea
415-152-1737
E-mail: joseantoniolopezm@hotmail.com
Calle San Pedro #27, San Miguel de Allende, Gto. 37700
Open: Mon.–Fri. 9 AM–12 PM and 2 PM–5 PM
Enrique López Larrea spent 49 years as the Instituto Allende's Professor of Silver Smithing, and over the years his work has been exhibited in many galleries. Today, the professor and his son Antonio offer year-round individual instruction to small classes on the art of jewelry making. Courses are arranged into 36 hour-long sessions over four weeks. Courses of shorter time periods may also be arranged.

Fresh produce is readily available in San Miguel de Allende.

COOKING CLASSES

Over the last 30 years, San Miguel de Allende's reputation as an international center of culture has grown to include the culinary arts. As local cooks have found a market in cooking classes and as international restaurateurs have settled here, cooking vacations have become a cottage industry. These knowledgeable chefs teach their students the time-honored techniques of classical Mexican cuisine. And best of all, when the class is over, you get to eat the results. These cooking classes are usually combined with cultural excursions in which you learn about the city and the surrounding environs. Often, this will include jaunts over to Guanajuato to take a look at the highlights over there. Moreover, these cooking vacations result in an experience that you can share with friends and family in a way that they will thank you for. What follows is just a few of the opportunities you will find in San Miguel de Allende.

HUGH CARPENTER COOKING SCHOOL

707-252-9773
www.hughcarpenter.com
3960 Hagen Road, Napa, CA 94558
Hugh Carpenter is the author of 16 cookbooks and has been teaching cooking for more than 30 years. While he is based in California, he offers weeklong cooking courses in San Miguel de Allende from January through March. Carpenter is well known for his laid-back and amiable personality, and his courses are composed of a full itinerary in which students learn the art of Mexican cuisine in a variety of venues and meet several of the local artists living in San Miguel. Activities include wine tasting, hands-on cooking, and cultural events. These camps cost around $1,920 per tour member.

LA COCINA COOKING SCHOOL

415-154-4825
www.mexicocooks.com
Jesús #23, San Miguel de Allende, Gto. 37700
Culinary Adventures of Mexico is run by Kris Rudolph, also the owner of El Buen Café. Rudolf is the author of three cookbooks and has been teaching cooking in San Miguel de Allende since 1996. She offers classes on a variety of topics including Naturally Healthy Mexican Cuisine, Modern Mexican Fusion, Market Tour, and Salsa Cooking. Most classes cost between $45 and $55 per person and run about three hours.

MEXICAN COOKING VACATION

415-152-5299
www.mexicancookingvacation.com
Callejon Atascadero #5, Barrio de San Jose, San Miguel de Allende, Gto. 37700
This cooking school is run out of the Arcos del Atascadero Bed and Breakfast and offers weeklong courses nearly year-round. Students are taught a variety of classic Mexican dishes, as well as cake decorating, and receive guided tours of sites such as the people's market, Guanajuato, and Dolores Hidalgo. Classes are taught by María Marquez, who has taught such celebrity chefs as Rick Bayless. Prices vary depending on room and package.

NANCY ZASLAVSKY COOKING TOUR OF SAN MIGUEL DE ALLENDE

310-440-8877
www.nancyzaslavsky.com
4061 Mandeville Canyon Road, Los Angeles, CA 90049
Nancy Zaslavsky is the author of two cookbooks and has been traveling throughout Mexico exploring its cuisine since 1970. She offers a weeklong tour of San Miguel de Allende in February, in which she guides foodies through the culinary highlights of San Miguel de Allende and Guanajuato. Tour members stay at a restored colonial bed and breakfast in the heart of downtown San Miguel and will take tours on such things as cheese and tequila making as well as several cooking classes. This tour runs around $2,300 per person, which includes your room and all museum entry fees.

TRADITIONAL MEXICAN COOKING SCHOOL

415 152-4376
www.traditionalmexicancooking.com.mx
Calle de La Luz # 12, San Miguel de Allende, Gto. 37700
The Traditional Mexican Cooking School is run by Marilau Ricaud, who belongs to a family that boasts several generations of Mexican cooks. She teaches students how to make traditional dishes from all over Mexico, including mole poblano, tamales, and pazole. Classes are Monday through Friday beginning at 10 AM and run approximately three hours. These classes cost around $55 per person for group classes and around $99 per person for private sessions.

GALLERIES

San Miguel de Allende is without a doubt one of North America's most significant artist colonies. For almost a century it has been a place where artists come to dedicate themselves to their art. Its rich colonial atmosphere has inspired these artists to go beyond themselves to create works they didn't know they were capable of. Consequently, the town is replete with galleries selling original works of art by local artists. These galleries range from the modest to the luxurious, and prices range just as much. You will find art here by unknown local indigenous artists, and established painters with works in galleries worldwide. Furthermore, works run the gamut from watercolors to hand-pounded copper pieces. What is wonderful is that you are free to evaluate and enjoy the work as you wish. Furthermore, more often than not, you will have the opportunity to interact with these amazing individuals that have put so much of themselves into their work. What follows is only a small sampling of what you will find here.

Some local artists sell their work right off the street.

GALERÍA ARTE SACRO

415-152-3292
www.galeriasartesacro.com.mx
E-mail: kusycraft@hotmail.com
San Francisco #10, San Miguel de Allende, Gto. 37700
Open: Mon.–Sat. 9 AM–5 PM
This art gallery specializes in portraits of Catholic saints. The portraits are painted in a style of painting that was popular in the colonial period and became widespread among native artists in Peru in the 17th century. The subjects are painted in the foreground, often wearing highly stylized costumes, usually with a scenic view of a landscape or a town in the background.

GALERÍA CARLOS MURO

415-154-8531
E-mail: CarlosMu_Ro@hotmail.com
Zacateros #81A, San Miguel de Allende, Gto. 37700
Open: Tues.–Sun. 10 AM–6 PM
This handsomely appointed gallery displays sculpture, paintings, and black and white photographs, as well as several very interesting vases of handwrought copper. The photographs and paintings are by Muro himself and the wrought copper art is made by local artisans who hammer them out in an ancient process.

GALERÍA PÉRGOLA

415-154-5595
www.galeriapergola.com
E-mail: info@galeriapergola.com
Ancha de San Antonio #20, San Miguel de Allende, Gto. 37700
Open: Mon.–Sat. 10 AM–6 PM
This gallery offers a large collection of works of various artists from throughout Mexico. A large variety of styles and mediums are available. It is located in a complex of the landmark school Instituto Allende, the summer home of the prominent 17th century Canal family, the patron family of San Miguel. This gallery opened here in 1951 as an exhibit space for Instituto Allende. The building has gone through renovation and now features vaulted ceilings and light-filled spaces that mix with colonial architecture. The work here is high quality and eclectic, and easily interesting enough to warrant a look even if you're not in the market for fine art.

HELENA MORENO FINE ARTS GALLERY

415-152-8815
www.helenamorenogallery.com
E-mail: gmenache@avantel.net
Jesus #10, San Miguel de Allende, Gto. 37700
Open: Mon.–Fri. 10 AM–6 PM
This fine art gallery features three exhibit halls with more than two hundred works of art. It primarily features work by three artists: Fernando M. Diaz, a Mexican painter who has exhibited his plastic work in countries around the world; Hugo Arquimedes, a Mexican sculptor who creates geometric and contructivist works and modern Latin-American Art; and Gabriela Espein, a Mexican painter who also works in plastic art.

JUAN EZCURDIA GALLERY

415-152-6539
www.ezcurdia.com
E-mail: jezcurdia@yahoo.com
Mesones #80, San Miguel de Allende, Gto. 37700
Open: Mon.–Sat. 9:30 AM–6:30 PM
This gallery features the work of highly acclaimed Mexican artist Juan Ezcurdia. He is a self-taught painter who paints colorful works with a fanciful flair. He won the National Illustration Prize in 1997 and now has works in private collections all over the world.

THE WILLIAM MARTIN GALLERY

415-152-5282
www.williammartingallery.com
williammartingallery@hotmail.com
San Francisco #37, San Miguel de Allende, Gto. 37700
Open: Mon.–Sat. 10 AM–7:30 PM
This gallery is located in an old colonial home in the heart of San Miguel. It features the work of a small number of artists. Their work runs from portraits and landscapes to abstract works. Private and semiprivate art classes with William Martin may also be arranged by contacting the gallery or by going to their Web site.

Many language schools offer programs for children.   Mary Delgado

LANGUAGE SCHOOLS

For various reasons, both San Miguel de Allende and Guanajuato are well equipped with institutions ready to teach foreigners Spanish. For San Miguel de Allende, the reason is obvious. The town has a large population of non-Spanish speakers who make their home there full time. This population has given rise to a large number of Spanish schools catering to local retirees, as well as to tourists that are in town for a couple of days or a couple of weeks. Paradoxically, however, because San Miguel has such a large population of expatriates from Canada and the United States, the need to speak Spanish is probably less there than anywhere else in Central Mexico. In Guanajuato, the university has drawn language students from other countries. Not only has the International Cerventino Festival, which was started by university students, given the city exposure to a worldwide group of travelers, but the university also has hosted study-abroad programs that have drawn international students as well. Some former university professors have seen the market for language schools and have struck out on their own, establishing schools here that cater to cultural vacationers looking to expand their horizons. You can find classes in each city for all levels of proficiency, as well as classes for children. Most students stay with local families to increase their language immersion. However, some schools offer special rates from certain hotels, or they might even maintain nearby flats to rent out. This kind of accommodation may be your best bet since you get your own place at a highly reduced rate.

Guanajuato

ACADAMIA FALCON

Director: Jorge Barroso

473-731-0745

www.academiafalcon.com

E-mail: academiafalcon@hotmail.com

Paseo de la Presa #80, Guanajuato, Gto. 36000

This school is located just outside the center of town, in the neighborhood of La Presa named after the nearby Presa de la Olla. It occupies the houses and gardens of a former private estate and provides a relaxed learning environment for students. The classroom and dormitory building have nice views of the surrounding mountains. This school breaks the learning of language into four categories: reading, speaking, writing, and listening. With this in mind, they use a variety of teaching methods to hone these skills. Classes start every Monday and the program teaches total immersion Spanish. There is also a kid's program for all levels of learners. If you like, the school will also set you up with a host family. Tuition ranges from $65 to $120 per week, depending on how many sessions you have a day. One-on-one classes are also available at a slightly higher rate.

ESCUELA MEXICANA

Director: Torsten Rufer

473-732-5005

www.escuelamexicana.com

E-mail: escuelamexicana@hotmail.com

Potrero #12, Guanajuato, Gto. 36000

This school is located in a cavernous house just up the street from the Museo Iconográfico del Quixote. They offer classes year-round at all skill levels. When you arrive, you will be given a placement exam to determine at which level you should be studying. Courses cover all facets of Mexican culture including literature, legends, politics, and dance. There is also a children's program available. These classes tend to fill up quickly over spring break and the summertime. There is a one-time registration fee of $35 and tuition ranges from $60 to $115 per week, depending on how many classes you take during the day. Private classes are also available at a slightly higher rate. The school will also set you up with a host family or rent you a nearby casita.

San Miguel de Allende

ACADEMIA HISPANO AMERICANA

Director: Paulina Hawkins Masip

415-152-0349

www.ahaspeakspanish.com

Mesones #4, San Miguel de Allende, Gto. 37700

This Spanish school has been operating in San Miguel since 1959. They offer a comprehensive Spanish immersion program, as well as a semi-intensive program and one-on-one courses. The school's courses are divided into 12 four-week sessions that roughly correspond with the months of the year. There are no classes in late December or early January, or in late March or early April. Prices start at $190 a week. This school prefers that you stay with a local family during your stay. They will arrange this when you enroll. However, if you choose to stay elsewhere, you must make your own arrangements. Check their Web site for specific dates. Open Monday through Friday 8 AM to 7 PM.

CENTRO BILINGUE
Director: Sara Hernández
415-152-5400
www.geocities.com/centrobilingue
Correo #46, San Miguel de Allende, Gto. 37700
This school offers intensive or conversation-level Spanish courses for business professionals or just those who would like to learn another language. The faculty of the school will evaluate you upon arrival to determine your level of proficiency and course needs. They will also help to arrange for you to stay with local families during your stay in San Miguel. There are special seasonal courses for children during the winter, spring break, and summer seasons. Classes run from $70 to $400 per week depending on intensity level and class length. Private lessons can also be arranged for $20 per hour. Open Monday through Friday 7:30 AM to 2 PM and 4 PM to 7 PM. Weekend hours are also available.

CENTRO MEXICANO DE LENGUA Y CULTURA DE SAN MIGUEL
Director: Josefina Hernández
415-152-0763
www.infosma.com/centromexicano
Orizaba #15, San Miguel de Allende, Gto. 37700
This school offers Spanish classes at varying levels of proficiency, from the very basic to the very intensive. As part of their curriculum, they go out into the community to introduce their students to different aspects of San Miguel that ordinary tourists usually don't see, such as hospitals, churches, and factories. They will help you make arrangements for accommodations, though they recommend that you stay with a local family. They also offer private sessions, as well as a special program for children. This program is geared toward children between the ages of three and 12 and involves weekday classes of four-hour sessions.

INSTITUTO DE HABAL HISPANA
Director: Attilio Tonelli
415-152-0713
www.mexicospanish.com
Calzada de la Luz #25, San Miguel de Allende, Gto. 37700
This school focuses on intensive immersion Spanish classes for adult learners. These classes include learning songs, taking walks through San Miguel, and even Mexican cooking lessons. They take students with beginner through advanced Spanish skills, with courses that run up to four weeks. See their Web site for specific dates. They will help you make arrangements for staying with a local family or at a hotel, and they can also help you with renting an apartment. Tuition begins at $120 a week. One-on-one private lessons are $12 an hour and private classes with two or more students are $8 an hour.

WARREN HARDY SPANISH SCHOOL
Director: Warren Hardy
415-154-4017

www.warrenhardy.com
San Rafael #6, San Miguel de Allende, Gto. 37700
This school specializes in teaching adult language learners with beginning to proficient
level Spanish needs. They also offer a complete series of books and CDs for their learn-at-
home program. The on-site courses in San Miguel are two and a half weeks long, with
classes meeting for three hours per day, three days per week. These courses are designed
to teach you to speak Spanish in the Mexican dialect, with an emphasis on Mexican culture.
Classes rotate throughout the year, with many focusing on different aspects of Spanish
conjugation and tenses. See their Web site for the schedule of classes.

MONUMENTS

The most obvious monuments of this region are the magnificent churches, which are covered in the next chapter. However, you will come to know many others during your time
here. Some have deep cultural significance and almost define their city, such as the giant
Pípila statue towering over Guanajuato. Still others are hidden away and easy to miss, such
as the tiny but picturesque El Campanero Bridge. However, they all have fascinating stories
behind them and are worth the effort of a look.

Dolores Hidalgo

The relaxed character of present-day Dolores Hidalgo is a far cry from the frenzied,
chaotic atmosphere that must have prevailed here on the morning of September 16, 1810,
when Miguel Hidalgo made what has become known as *El Grito de Dolores* (the Cry of
Dolores). It was a call to insurrection against the Spanish powers that ruled Mexico. In the
early morning hours, Father Hidalgo ordered the church bells to be rung to gather the people of Dolores. From the balcony of his residence he addressed the crowd, and legend has
it that he ended his speech by calling out, *"¡Viva la Virgen de Guadalupe! ¡Viva Fernando VII!
¡Mexicanos, viva México!"* (Long live Our Lady of Guadalupe! Long live Fernando VII!
Mexicans, long live Mexico!) After this speech, he and Ignacio Allende gathered their rag-
tag forces and headed for San Miguel de Allende. It is from this that Dolores Hidalgo has
become known throughout Mexico as the "Cradle of Independence" and Miguel Hidalgo is
revered as the father of Mexican independence.

Every year on the night of September 15, thousands of people crowd Mexico City's giant
Zócalo square, the seat of Mexican government and one-time center of the Aztec Empire.
At 11 PM, the country's president steps onto the balcony of the national palace overlooking
the square and rings the actual bell that Father Hidalgo rang in the predawn hours in 1810.
The ceremony reaches its conclusion at midnight with the president repeating Hidalgo's
speech, calling out *"Viva"* with the names of people who were vital to the independence, as
well as *"¡Viva la independencia!"* With each call by the president, all of the voices of the
crowd call back, *"¡Viva!"* The Grito culminates with a high point of *"¡Viva México!"* At that
point, the sky lights up with fireworks. Moreover, every six years this ceremony is held in
the tiny town where Hidalgo actually made the call for independence, cramming Dolores
Hidalgo's main plaza with thousands of people and attracting such dignitaries as the first
President Bush in the 1990s.

Obviously, the town of Dolores Hidalgo takes great pride in its role in Mexico's independence. The city's many monuments and museums are a reminder of this. The main

CITY OF DOLORES HIDALGO

1. Museo de la Independencia Nacional
2. Palacio Municipal
3. Parroquia de Nuestra Señora de los Dolores
4. Monumento a Miguel Hidalgo
5. Casa de las Visitas
6. Museo Casa de Hidalgo
7. Hospital General Dolores Hidalgo
8. Hospital Civil Ignacio Allende
9. Jardin de los Compositores Dolorenses
10. Templo de la Tercera Orden
11. Parroquia de la Asuncion
12. Casa de Jose Alfredo Jimenez
13. Monumento a la Bandera

0   1/4 mile
0   250 meters

plaza is wide open with a bandstand toward the south end, a monument to Hidalgo at its center, and a beautiful church at its north end. Near the bandstand along the corner of Calle Michoacán and Calle Hidalgo, you will find a row of ice cream vendors selling flavors that you will never find at Baskin Robbins. Your trip to Dolores Hidalgo is not complete until you've sampled some flavors.

The Mausoleum of José Alfredo Jiménez

HOUSE OF ABASOLO
Half a block north of Plaza Principal off San Luis Potosí, Dolores Hidalgo, Gto. 37800
Open: Mon.–Fri. 8:30 AM–5 PM
Admission: Free
This was the house of Mariano Abasolo, another hero of Mexican independence.
Abasolo was born in Dolores and rose to the rank of major general during his partici-
pation in the insurgency. He was eventually captured by the Spanish and was sentenced
to 10 years imprisonment in Cádiz, Spain, where he died in 1819. In 1906, the city gov-
ernment acquired this house and converted it into the mayor's office. Inside, there is a
replica of the bell rang by Miguel Hidalgo when he called for an insurgency against the
Spanish.

JOSÉ ALFREDO JIMÉNEZ MAUSOLEUM
Municipal Cemetary, Calle Aldama, Dolores Hidalgo, Gto. 37800
Open: Daily 9 AM–7 PM
Admission: Free
José Alfredo Jiménez is considered the most important composer of Mexican *rancheria*
music. He was born in Dolores Hidalgo in 1926, the son of a pharmacist. However, when
his father's business went bankrupt eight years later, the family moved to Mexico City.
Despite leaving at such a young age, the connection that Jiménez felt to the land of
Guanajuato was reflected in many of his songs. He composed more than a thousand songs

despite a lack of any formal musical training. He died in 1976, a musical icon throughout the Spanish-speaking world. The tomb itself used to be a simple white stone bust of Jiménez. However, in 1998 this was replaced by a sprawling mausoleum that stands in stark contrast to the simple white headstones that surround it. This mausoleum is shaped like a giant sombrero wrapped in a colorful, flowing *serape* (a traditional Mexican garment that looks something like a blanket with a hole in the middle). On the stripes of this serape are the titles of many of Jiménez's favorite songs. To this day, every year hundreds of music lovers make the pilgrimage to see it.

MONUMENT TO THE HEROES OF THE INDEPENDENCE
Intersection of Calle Aldama and Calle Abasolo, Dolores Hidalgo, Gto. 37800
Open: Daily 24 hours
Admission: Free
This towering monument at the entrance to the city was built to commemorate the heroes of the Independence: Miguel Hidalgo, Ignacio Allende, cavalry captain Juan Aldama, and priest and rebel leader José Morelos. It was designed by sculptor Jorge Gonzalez and architect Carlos Obregon Santacilla.

MONUMENT TO MIGUEL HIDALGO
Center of the Plaza Principal, Dolores Hidalgo, Gto. 37800
Open: Daily 24 hours
Admission: Free
In the center of the main plaza in Dolores Hidalgo stands a bronze statue of Hidalgo, which was erected in 1891 by the artist Miguel Noreña. It is an impressive sculpture all by itself but is made all the more beautiful with the backdrop of the parish of Nuestra Señora de los Dolores.

VISITORS HOUSE
West side of the Plaza Principal, Dolores Hidalgo, Gto. 37800
Open: Mon.–Fri. 8:30 AM–5 PM
Admission: Free
This house was built in 1786 as a residence for the subdelegate of the Spanish government. Its façade consists of six arches that support carved stone balconies. In 1940, the Guanajuato state government acquired the house and converted it into a residence for visiting dignitaries. Now every Mexican president comes to Dolores Hidalgo in the fifth year of his government to hold the official Mexican Independence Day celebration, in which he stands on the balcony of this building where he performs *El Grito* to cheering crowds. If you go to the front gate of this residence and tell the guard you want to see inside, he will let you into the inner courtyard.

Guanajuato
Guanajuato is a city revered throughout Mexico for its beauty and cultural importance. Groups of schoolchildren commonly wander its streets on cultural field trips from nearby towns, gazing up at El Pípila towering above the city, and lunching on the steps of the square in front of the Alhóndiga Museum. The thing that is striking about this relatively small colonial city is the dense wealth of impressive churches, plazas, museums, and colonial architecture. However, it's only when you begin to dig deeper, by learning the stories

The Visitor's House in Dolores Hidalgo

behind the city's beauty, that you really begin to appreciate Guanajuato. From the heroic bravery behind El Pípila to the tragic love of Callejón del Beso, this city will never cease to grab your interest and amaze you.

Callejón del Beso

CALLEJÓN DEL BESO

Off Callejón del Patrocinio, Guanajuato, Gto. 36000
Open: Daily 24 hours
Admission: Free
At this corner of Guanajuato, you will find a narrow alley with two balconies that hang just
27 inches apart. Known as "The Alley of the Kiss," it has become famous for a tragic inci-

dent that supposedly occurred here. Legend has it that the home on the left was once home to Doña Carmen, the only daughter of a violent and obstinate man. After discovering her being courted at church by a young man by the name of Don Luis, Carmen's father locked her in her room. He had plans to marry her off to a rich man in Spain to restore his dwindling fortune. Hearing this news, Luis became desperate to see his love and purchased the home across the alley, knowing that the window in her home gave onto the balcony, where he could get close enough to touch her. One night, as the two sweethearts stood at the balconies holding hands, Carmen's father burst into the room and plunged a dagger in her heart. Stunned, Luis could only place a kiss on Carmen's lifeless hand before letting go. Okay, it's a depressing story without the subtlety and grandeur of a Shakespearean sonnet, but it's still worth a look. To get here, go to Plazuela de los Ángeles off Avenida Juárez, and walk about 50 yards up Callejón del Patrocinio on the right side of the plaza. Callejón del Beso is on the left. There is no charge to enter but this is a popular spot, so you may have to wait several minutes to get in.

EL CAMPANERO BRIDGE

Calle Cantarranas and Subida del Tecolote, Guanajuato, Gto. 36000
Open: Daily 24 hours
Admission: Free

This short, picturesque *cantera* (quarry) stone bridge was built in 1778 to provide street access to a house on Subida del Tecolote that belonged to a wealthy resident. The house originally had its entrance on the street level. However, because the street was lowered on two separate occasions to allow carriages to pass through, the bridge became necessary. The house itself also had to be modified, as a window was converted into the primary entrance, and stairs were added in the foyer of the house

El Campanero Bridge

next door. The name *El Campanero*, or "bell ringer," comes from the fact that men would stand on this bridge in the 19th century and ring a bell to announce the arrival and departure of carriages. Today, the bridge is used as the patio for the Santo Café, kind of a dark, bohemian coffee shop.

EL PÍPILA

Carreterra Panorámica, Guanajuato, Gto. 36000
Open: Daily 24 hours
Admission: Free

High above the town is the towering rose-colored monument known as El Pípila. As the story goes, José de los Reyes Martínez, who went by the nickname of *El Pípila*, was a native of San Miguel de Allende working in the mines of Guanajuato in September of 1810, when

El Pípila

Miguel Hidalgo arrived with his band of insurgents. *El Pípila* quickly took up with Hidalgo, whose goal in Guanajuato was to take the Granaditas Corn Exchange (the present-day site of the Alhóndiga del Granaditas Museum). Guanajuato's provincial governor, Juan Antonio de Riaño y Barcena, had taken up position in this building with the soldiers of the garrison, where they guarded a treasure of some three million pesos in silver ingots and cash from the Royal Tax Office, as well as military equipment and food supplies. A bloody battle ensued in which *El Pípila* put a large piece of flagstone on his back to protect him from the Spanish gunfire and crawled to the door of the corn exchange with a torch in his hand. He set fire to the door, eventually allowing the insurgents to take the building. This monument was erected in 1939 to honor José de los Reyes Martínez's bravery and commitment to Mexican independence. The statue is in a plaza paved with cobblestones and ringed by a balustrade, and a door to a staircase at the back of the monument takes you to the top. Besides being an amazing statue, there are stone bleachers at its feet that face out toward the city and provide a spectacular panoramic view day and night of Jardín de la Unión and the rest of this colorful town. To get here, walk south on Calle Sopena from Jardín de la Unión and turn right up Callejón del Calvario. Follow the signs to El Pípila. The monument is about a 10 minute walk uphill along this alley and along Subida de San Miguel, so be sure to wear comfortable shoes. If the walk is too brisk for you, hop on a city bus marked El Pípila. The ride will cost 3 pesos, or about a quarter.

UNIVERSIDAD AUTÓNIMO DE GUANAJUATO

Lascuráin de Retana #5, Guanajuato, Gto. 36000
Open: Daily 24 hours
Admission: Free
This site was first developed as a hospice by Jesuit missionaries with the help of Doña Josefa Teresa de Busto y Moya, the wife of a wealthy mine owner. She and several of her wealthy friends donated the money to establish the first school in what was then a sleepy mining village. In 1744, the Spanish crown granted the Jesuits in Guanajuato a license to operate their hospice as a college. They called it the College of the Holy Trinity and offered courses in arts and letters. The Jesuits began construction of the Church of la Compañía de Jesús in 1747, and the adjacent building, which would eventually house the college as it exists today, began in 1759. However, the Jesuits were expelled from New Spain eight years

Universidad Autónimo de Guanajuato

later due to political conflict between the Spanish crown and the papacy in Rome. As a result, the college remained unfinished, with only one floor having been built. Later, in 1796, a new boarding college was established on the site, offering courses in art, rhetoric, and philosophy, and continued to operate through the turbulent years of the Mexican struggle for independence. In 1828, the state government took ownership of the college

and turned it into a public institution by the name of the College of the Immaculate
Conception, offering courses in mining and law. In 1867, after many chaotic years, the
name changed once again to the National College of Guanajuato. However, it wasn't until
1945, when it gained university status, that the current institution was born. It was at this
time that the main building was remodeled and expanded to the grandiose edifice that
exists today. This impressive neoclassical building houses the rector's office, administrative and academic offices, as well as a number of the university's schools and faculties.
This institution is largely responsible for the vivacious atmosphere that permeates the city
of Guanajuato today. Its students are a constant complement to the Jardín de la Unión and
they have created a nightlife that is like no other this side of Mexico City. They also com-
prise the bulk of the city's street performers, such as the wandering minstrels and the
clowns that entertain daily in front of Teatro Juárez. To get to the University from Plaza de
la Paz, walk north on Calle de Estudiante from the north side of the Basilica. You can also
walk east on Calle Positos and continue along Lascuráin de Retana when you cross Calle
Juan Valle.

VALENCIANA MINE
Highway 30, Guanajuato, Gto. 36000
Open: Daily 7 AM–2 PM
Admission: $5

At one time this mine was by far the most important silver mine in the world, producing
fully two-thirds of the silver that packed Spanish coffers during the colonial period. It was
discovered in 1548 and reached its peak in 1760, when miner Antonio de Ordoñez
unearthed a silver deposit of incalculable value. The mine continues to be in operation
today, with a main tunnel that is more than 1700 feet deep. There are two nearby shafts–El
Nopál and San Ramón–that are used as show mines for tourists. These tours have trained
guides and accident insurance.

The tour of the Valenciana mine takes you through a series of rooms in an old building
filled with artifacts that tell the history of the mine. Displays of old black and white photos
show the owners and workers that have lived and died here over the years. And many did
die. In fact, a miner's life expectancy was about 10 years from the first time he stepped foot
in the mine. Needless to say, the miners working here, made up mostly of young indigenous men, were savagely exploited. You learn what it was all for in the final room, where
you will find a series of cases filled with gleaming silver plates, pitchers, and jewelry made
from that shiny metal dug out of the earth below. At this point of the tour, you begin a
descent into the narrow mineshaft. As you walk down the twisting stairwell, it is hard to
imagine how workers managed to get their equipment down to where they would need it.

Located next to the mine is the Temple of la Valenciana. It is also known as San
Cayetano and is an imposing 18th-century church with an intricate churrigueresque façade
of pink stone. This church was built by Antonio de Ordoñez, as a gesture of gratitude to
God for the incredible riches he found here. Completed in 1778, the magnificent oil paintings inside, as well as the gold laminated altar and altarpieces, stand as a testament to the
wealth the Valenciana Mine has produced. Several shops near the church sell artesenia
such as clay pots, jewelry, and other craft work. Feel free to negotiate with these vendors.

Las Estudiantinas: The Pied Pipers of Guanajuato

In 1962, a group of enthusiastic university students became interested in *estudiantina*, a type of traditional Spanish minstrel music played by small instrumental groups. They would get together to sing it
and, within a year, they had formed Guanajuato's first *estudiantina* group with the backing of the university. They were known as La Estudiantina de la Universidad de Guanajuato, and they made their
debut on the town's cobblestone streets on April 13, 1963. Today, Guanajuato has several student
minstrel groups that perform through the city's streets serenading and staging sketches. When night
falls over the city, the sound of these groups and accompanying laughter echo through the narrow
alleys as they lead crowds of people through the town's winding boulevards.

They gather at dusk in front of Templo de San Diego. They're easy to spot in their distinctive costumes that mimic the fashions of 17th-century Spain. This costume is usually comprised of a black velvet
vest with bright yellow piping, over a shiny black and red striped shirt. Many of them also carry guitars or
lutes. To begin, they warm up the crowd with short skits and dancing. At this time, a member of the
group will wander through the crowd soliciting onlookers to join the group on a *callejoneada*, or a walking tour of Guanajuato. This will cost a few dollars and you will receive a cup that they repeatedly fill
with libations along the way before making a series of rambunctious toasts. It is also fairly common for
people just to follow along with the crowd. As the tour begins, the group of *estudiantinas* leads the
crowd up stairs and through narrow alleys. It's important to step carefully, particularly since it can be
dark. Usually there is a member of the group whose sole job is to manage the crowd, pointing out haz-
ardous spots and directing traffic. Along the way, they continuously play music and tell jokes. If you
don't speak Spanish, much of this will be lost on you, though the happy atmosphere that is created is
definitely contagious, no matter what language you speak. The tour usually ends at the Callejón del
Beso, where a young boy always seems to be present, ready to recite the legend.

Estudiantina performers lead a group of people through the streets of Guanajuato.

MUSEUMS

This region seems to have a museum to appeal to just about everybody. Quite obviously, anybody who is interested in Mexico's history will have their hands full, visiting the museums throughout the area that tell the story of how these tiny towns prompted a nation to seek independence. However, being a university town, Guanajuato has been blessed with an array of other museums dedicated to other fields of study. From the grand Alhóndiga Museum with its pre-Hispanic archaeological artifacts to the highly specialized Mineral Museum with its impressive geological collection, Guanajuato is rich with exhibits devoted to academic inquiry. Furthermore, thanks to the fact that this city has been home to several noted 20th-century Mexican artists, there are also world-class collections of fine art to be found at the Diego Rivera Museum and the museums sponsored by José Chavez Morado and Olga Costa. And, of course, who could forget that Guanajuato is home to the Mummy Museum, a collection of unfortunate souls who failed to pay their taxes. Whatever your interests, there is sure to be something here to fascinate you.

Dolores Hidalgo

MUSEO CASA DE DON MIGUEL HIDALGO
418-182-0723
Calle Morélos #1, Dolores Hidalgo, Gto. 37800
Open: Tues.–Sat. 10 AM–5:45 PM; Sun. 10 AM–4:30 PM
Admission: General $2; Children under 13 free; Sunday general admission free

A small statue of Miguel Hidalgo in his former residence

This 18th-century house was the home of Miguel Hidalgo. Several of the rooms have been preserved to authentically re-create the atmosphere of the time of the War of Independence. While many of the items are not originals, many of the items here did belong to Hidalgo, including furniture, garments, and other personal effects. Farther into the house, you will find several shrines and other testaments to Hidalgo and the other heroes of the independence.

MUSEO DE LA INDEPENDÉNCIA NACIONAL
418-182-0193
Calle Zacatecas #10, Dolores Hidalgo, Gto. 37800
Open: Fri.–Wed. 9 AM–5 PM
Admission: General $1

This 18th-century building was originally used as a prison. However, on September 16, 1810, Miguel Hidalgo set the inmates free and bade them to join his crusade for independence. The museum displays several historical and patriotic objects from that time as well as several paintings, photographs, and other works of fine art. There is also a display dedicated to José Alfredo Jiménez, the world-famous Mexican folk music composer who was born here.

Guanajuato

CASA DE DIEGO RIVERA (DIEGO RIVERA MUSEUM)

473-732-1197
E-mail: culture@rcdes.int.com.mx
Positos #47, Guanajuato, Gto. 36000
Open: Tues.–Sat. 10 AM–7 PM, Sun. 10 AM–3 PM. Closed Mon.
Admission: General $1.50; students $0.50

This museum is located in the large 19th-century neoclassical house in which the famous muralist Diego Rivera was born and lived. Even if this house did not have this distinction, it would be worth the price of admission just to walk through and see how the residents of Guanajuato have laid out their homes on multiple floors. Diego Rivera was a world-renowned painter famous for his leftist views and politically provocative murals, as well as for being the husband of Frida Kahlo. In the early to mid-20th century, Rivera painted murals in places as remote as San Francisco, Detroit, and New York. Today, his work is

Ground floor of the Diego Rivera Museum

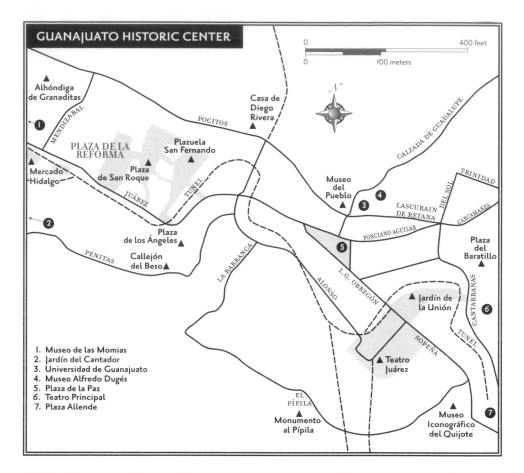

displayed in many of the world's most prominent museums. This museum opened in 1975, after several years of restoration. The ground floor of the museum has a small gift shop and showcases the original furniture that belonged to the Rivera family at the end of the 19th century. The upper floors display approximately one hundred works by Rivera, comprising a collection that is considered one of the most important in Mexico. As you make your way to the upper floors, you will see that this wonderful collection of works is representative of the different stages of his artistic career, including a variety of techniques and mediums such as oil paints, pencil, ink, lithography, and watercolor. The museum also presents temporary exhibitions of different works of the plastic arts, as well as cultural events on Tuesday through Sunday from 10 AM to 1:15 PM and from 4 PM to 6:30 PM.

MUSEO ALFREDO DUGÉS (ALFREDO DUGÉS NATURAL HISTORY MUSEUM)

473-732-0096
www.ugto.mx/duges
E-mail: duges@quijote.ugto.mx
Lascuráin de Retana #5, Guanajuato, Gto. 36000
Open: Mon.–Fri. 10 AM–6 PM. Closed Sat. and Sun.
Admission: General $0.70; Students $0.20
This natural history museum is located in the main building on the campus of the

University of Guanajuato. It was founded in December 1941 in honor of Alfredo Dugés, a French scientist who was a professor here during the years it was a state college in the 19th century. Dugés specialized in amphibians and reptiles, but this collection exhibits a wide variety of samples of local plants, animals, and fossils. It also houses a collection of water-colors and drawings of flora and fauna made by Dugés during his study of the region.

MUSEO DE LA ALHÓNDIGA DE GRANADITAS
473-734-1062
www.inah.gob.mx
E-mail: alhondiga@int.com.mx
Mendizábal #6, Guanajuato, Gto. 36000
Open: Tues.–Sat. 10 AM–1:30 PM and 4 PM–5:30 PM, Sun. 10 AM–2:30 PM
Admission: $3

Looking at this worn, square building, you might not guess that it's actually one of the most important edifices in this architecturally rich city. However, when you think about it, the Alhóndiga does wear its history for all to see. Though today it houses great art, this build-ing was originally built to store grain. In the opening days of the Mexican War for Independence, however, fate took over. This was the site of a storied battle in which the insurgent forces, led by the now-famous *El Pípila*, seized this strategically important building. However, afterwards a slaughter ensued, one that convinced many people who were considering joining the move for independence to remain loyal to Spain. Later the

Murals by José Chávez Morado adorn the stairway of the Alhóndiga Museum.

Spanish forces retook Guanajuato, and to dissuade residents from further insurrection, they hung the heads of the insurgent leaders Hidalgo, Allende, Aldama, and Jiménez from the four corners of this building, where they remained for a decade. Even after that, the Alhóndiga was just about as far away from being a museum as you could imagine. In 1864, the building was converted into the state penitentiary of Guanajuato. Finally, in 1949 renovation began to turn the interior of this neglected neoclassical building into a regional museum that would display an impressive collection that spanned the pre-Hispanic era right through the colonial days of Mexico's past. The collection, which is located on the second floor surrounding the interior courtyard, is divided into four major themes. The first is the ethnographic, which includes an assortment of regional crafts. The second is the archaeological, which is comprised of more than five thousand pieces of indigenous artwork from pre-Hispanic Mexico. Prominent pieces among this collection include an assortment of ancient stamping tools. The third section is historical, with objects dealing with Mexico's struggle for independence. Much of this collection was donated by the artists Olga Costa and José Chavez Morado. The final section is a fine art collection with paintings from artists such as Hermenegildo Bustos. However, perhaps the museum's most impressive display is the mural by José Chávez Morado on the walls of the stairway that depicts Mexico's revolutionary wars and folk tradition. Located 1 block north of the Mercado Hidalgo and 2 blocks west of the Diego Rivera Museum, the Alhóndiga is probably the farthest from the center of town of Guanajuato's major sights that still manages to be within walking distance.

The figure of Diego Rivera at the Guanajuato Wax Museum

MUSEO DE CERA GUANAJUATO (GUANAJUATO WAX MUSEUM)

551-395-9107
www.museodeceradeguanajuato.com.mx
E-mail: yanezhugo@yahoo.com
Calle 28 de Septiembre, Guanajuato, Gto. 36000
Open: Tues.–Sat. 10 AM–1:30 PM and 4 PM–5:30 PM, Sun. 10 AM–2:30 PM
Admission: $3

Okay, so this museum does not have the historical significance of the Alhóndiga, or indigenous artwork that has been around for hundreds of years. But where else are you going to find a creepy sculpture of Tom Cruise in the next room from Jesus Christ? This museum does seem to have a little bit for everybody. If you're interested in heroic figures that shaped the history of Mexico, you'll find them in the first room to the right, where the bloody decapitated heads of Hidalgo, Allende, Aldama, and Jiménez sit in bird cages, preserved for eternity exactly how the Spanish displayed them 200 years ago just across the street at the Alhóndiga. If you're looking for religious figures, yes, you can stand in the same room with Jesus and Pope John Paul II. Or, if you're just in the mood for inexplicable life-size wax sculptures of movie stars, Tom Cruise and Sean Connery are here for you, too. Rumor has it that Robert de Niro and Bruce Willis are soon to join them. All in all, this museum is fun for a quick excursion and since it's right across

Museo Ex-Hacienda San Gabriel de Barrera courtyard   Mary Delgado

the street from the Alhóndiga Museum, it's not all that far out of the way either. The tour ends with a horror-filled room of zombies and disemboweled wax corpses that might be too much for young children, but mostly it's a good time.

MUSEO EX-HACIENDA SAN GABRIEL DE BARRERA

473-732-0619
Carretera Guanajuato-Marfil Km. 25, Guanajuato, Gto. 36000
Open: Daily 9 AM—6:30 PM
Admission: Adults $2, children and students $1.50
In the late 17th century, Captain Gabriel de la Barrera became a wealthy mine owner and established a series of haciendas and ore-concentrating mills throughout the area that carried his name, including Hacienda de Barrera Grande, Hacienda de Barrera en Medio, Hacienda de San Antonio de Barrera, Hacienda de Dolores, and Hacienda de Sacramento. This hacienda, originally known as Hacienda de Barrera Grande, was without a doubt the most important in the area, as well as one of the most beautiful. After many changes in ownership throughout the centuries, it was acquired by the Guanajuato state government in the mid-1970s, and opened to the public as a museum in 1979. It offers visitors the chance to stroll along its beautiful grounds and get a sense of what life on a Mexican hacienda was really like. This 237,000 square foot estate is divided into three parts. The first is the main house, which contains the museum offices and many impressive rooms filled with 18th-century paintings, furniture, and tapestries. The second part is a small

Outside the Museo Ex-Hacienda San Gabriel de Barrera. Mary Delgado

chapel featuring a 15th-century Spanish altarpiece where the Barreras' personal religious services were held. The third and final section is a work area that features the location where the precious ore was extracted, now converted into 17 unique gardens, including courtyards that are wonderful for relaxing and enjoying a beautiful day. Here you will also find the storage rooms, aqueducts, water wheels, tanks, and horse stables that housed the horses necessary for mining silver ore.

MUSEO ICONOGRÁFICO DEL QUIJOTE (DON QUIXOTE ICONOGRAPHIC MUSEUM)

473-732-3376
http:/museoiconografico.guanajuato.gob.mx
E-mail: mquijote@guanajuato.gob.mx
Manuel Doblado #2, Guanajuato, Gto. 36000
Open: Tues.–Sat. 10 AM–6 PM, Sun. 10 AM–3 PM
Admission: Free

This museum demonstrates why the UNESCO Center of Castilla–La Mancha in Spain conferred upon the city of Guanajuato the title of Cervantine Capital of the Americas, during the 400-year anniversary celebration of the novel *Don Quixote de la Mancha*. The museum came to fruition thanks to the donation of Eulalio Ferrer, a Spanish refugee and Quixote enthusiast who adopted Mexico as his second home country. The museum was inaugurated in 1987 in a ceremony that marked the 15th International Festival of Cervantes. In attendance was the Mexican president, Miguel de la Madrid, as well as the prime minister of Spain, Felipe Gonzalez. It contains an extensive collection of paintings, scultures, drawings, tapestries, and other artwork dedicated to Don Quixote—the sad, chivalrous figure—and his loyal squire Sancho Panza, characters created by Miguel de Cervantes in what is considered the world's first novel. Some of the works of art are true masterpieces, including pieces by Mario Orózco Rivera, Salvador Dali, and Pablo Picasso.

MUSEO DE MINERALOGÍA (MINERALOGY MUSEUM)

473-732-2291
Lascuráin de Retana, Guanajuato, Gto. 36000
Open: Mon.– Fri. 10 AM–6 PM
Admission: General $0.70; Students $0.20
This museum located inside the Faculty of Mining on the campus of the University of Guanajuato features nearly twenty-five thousand examples of minerals from all over the world. All minerals are identified in Spanish. However, if you can remember your chemical formulas, you should be okay. Most are encased in glass, though several larger specimens, such as a giant geode, are out in the open. It's not for everybody, but if you're a fan of geology, this might be an interesting place to spend an hour or two.

MUSEO DE LAS MOMIAS (MUMMY MUSEUM)

473-732-0639
Calzada del Panteón, Guanajuato, Gto. 36000
Open: Daily 9 AM–6 PM
Admission: $3
Mexicans have a running joke in which they will tell you they have a relative in Guanajuato. The punch line comes when they tell you that this relative resides at the Museo de las Momias. This museum is widely regarded as one of Guanajuato's biggest attractions. In fact, anyone who knows Guanajuato will likely ask you if you visited this museum. However, the exhibits at this macabre museum are not likely to satisfy anyone's anthropological interests, being that the bodies on display here are not mummies at all, in the traditional sense, but are instead just a collection of unfortunate corpses. What you are likely to bring away from this place is a deeper appreciation of the cultural differences in the way with which Mexicans deal with death, and quite possibly you will leave feeling a little sick.

Between the late 19th century and the 1950s, local law required relatives of deceased persons to pay a grave tax. If the family failed to pay the tax, the body was exhumed. It was quickly discovered that the mineral-rich earth and dry climate of the area seemed to mummify anything buried in it. In the early 1900s, these strangely preserved bodies began attracting tourists, and cemetery workers quickly discovered that they could charge people viewing fees, and the museum was established. However, interest in this gruesome spectacle really took off in 1970 with the release of the popular movie *Santo Versus the Mummies of Guanajuato*, which starred the masked wrestler Rodolfo Guzmán Huerta.

Today, the mummy museum displays 119 bodies exhumed during the years that the grave tax was enforced. Perhaps their most interesting aspect is their tattered clothing, some of which dates to the late 19th century. Other than this minor fascination, this museum seems to have the effect of making visitors ponder their own fates. The drying process has contorted the faces of these poor people so that they all seem to be frozen in a permanent state of agony. Sadly, several of the subjects have not only met an unpeaceful end, but an undignified one as well. Clumps of matted hair cling to exposed skulls, toes poke through deteriorated boots, and torn clothing reveals dehydrated genitals. However,

Some of the gruesome faces to be seen at the Mummy Museum.

perhaps the museum's most disturbing exhibit is its finale: a mother and child who both died in the act of childbirth. The woman still displays the long scar from the attempted cesarean section and the emaciated child is propped upright and labeled *"La momia más pequeña del mundo"* (The smallest mummy in the world). Needless to say, this museum is not for everybody. And when asked if you visited it, you can always say you lost track of time over at Diego Rivera's house instead.

MUSEO DE ARTE OLGA COSTA–JOSÉ CHAVEZ MORADO

473-731-0977
E-mail: museoolgacosta@guanajuato.gob.mx
Pastita #158, Guanajuato, Gto. 36000
Open: Thurs.–Sat. 9:30 AM–4 PM, Sun. 9:30 AM–3:30 PM
Admission: General $1.50; Students $0.50; Children free
This museum is located in the 17th-century tower at the Hacienda de Guadalupe. In 1966, a pair of painters–Olga Costa and José Chavez Morado–acquired this estate to convert it into a home and studio for Costa. In 1990, the artists opened the tower to the public as a museum that bore both of their names. In 1993, shortly before the death of Costa, they donated the museum along with the collection within to the state government of Guanajuato. The collection is comprised of approximately five hundred pieces, including furniture, works of contemporary art, and original work by the couple.

Cultural Differences

You will find the Mexican people to be, by and large, warm and vivacious. However, it is important to keep in mind that theirs is a different culture with certain aspects that are different from your own. The more familiar you are of these differences, the better you will be at navigating through Mexican culture. For example, Mexicans consider the exchange of proper greetings to be very important. Handshakes are exchanged between men and a cheek-to-cheek embrace is customary between women, and between men and women, often even if you've just met. Also, it is customary to greet all members of a group individually. A single collective greeting to a group is viewed as both lazy and rude. And even if your Spanish is incredibly poor, Mexicans greatly appreciate any effort that you make to speak the language. A quick "Buenas dias" will go a long way to earn you respect in the eyes of local residents. Always remember that family and religion are central to Mexican culture, so avoid making derogatory or critical comments about either. It is also considered in poor taste to end a conversation by stating that you soon need to be somewhere else. And keep in mind that siesta falls between 2 PM and 5 PM every day. You'll notice that during this time, many businesses shut down and the town seems to clear out a bit.

In Guanajuato and San Miguel de Allende, many locals can speak English proficiently. However, they will likely be confused by certain aspects of your colloquial English. When conversing in English with locals, try to speak in grammatically correct sentences and avoid using slang. However, don't speak unnecessarily slowly or in disjointed sentences. This can understandably come across as insulting.

Among the things that you may find odd and uncomfortable, Mexicans tend to operate with much less personal space than is customary north of the border. Try to keep this in mind if you find your personal space being encroached upon in casual conversation. Also, Mexicans can be more overtly flirtatious than you may be used to. If you are a woman traveling alone, be prepared for the occasional whistle and teasing comment. Ignore this and avoid getting confrontational, as it is likely to get you nowhere.

MUSEO DEL PUEBLO DE GUANAJUATO (PEOPLE'S MUSEUM OF GUANAJUATO)

473-732-2990
Positos #7, Guanajuato, Gto. 36000
Open: Tues.–Sat. 10 AM–2 PM and 4 PM–7 PM, Sun. 10 AM–2 PM
Admission: $2
This museum houses a collection of 18th- and 19th-century art donated to the people of Guanajuato in 1979 by the artists José Chavez Morado and Olga Costa. The museum also holds temporary exhibitions. It is located in a 17th-century building with a churrigueresque chapel built in 1776 that serves as the Olga Costa Auditorium, with murals and decorated with furniture that was once owned by Morado himself. Unfortunately, this chapel was defaced, probably some time during the 19th century.

San Miguel de Allende

MUSEO HISTÓRICO DE SAN MIGUEL DE ALLENDE

415-152-2499
Cuna de Allende #1, San Miguel de Allende, Gto. 37700
Open: Tues.–Sun. 10 AM–4 PM
Admission: $3.50
On the west side of the Parroquia (parish church), you will find this museum in a

two-story colonial house that was once owned by the city's prominent de Allende and Unzaga families. This museum is dedicated to Ignacio de Allende, who fought and died for Mexican independence, and the man for whom the city is partially named. It features a historic collection of weapons, documents, and other objects either belonging to the leader or pertaining to the Mexican War for Independence. It also has a few pieces of contemporary art. In one corner of the museum you will find a sculpture of Allende. A plaque in the façade says, *"Aqui nacio el conocida en todas partes,"* (roughly translated as "Born here, known everywhere").

NIGHTLIFE

When it comes to nightlife, both Guanajuato and San Miguel de Allende offer a wide variety of choices to suit all ages and tastes. However, it's safe to say that each scene is dominated by their respective unique cultures. San Miguel de Allende has a bit of a reputation for being rather a quiet town full of old retirees. Nothing could be further from the truth. San Miguel is a place where people know how to have a good time. Certainly, the scene here is a bit older than in Guanajuato, but it is a place where you can always find live music and dancing going on. Many of the downtown bars tend to cater to the artist and expatriate crowds. There are a few nightclubs here, but you won't find any shortage of lounges or sports bars. In Guanajuato, the weekends belong to the university students, who can be found congregating on the steps of Teatro Juárez until the wee hours of the morning. Throughout the historic center (and especially just south of the university), you will find loud bars packed with young people dancing or lounging about having a good time. There are also a few dance clubs in town that stay open (and packed) until around 4:30 AM, just in case you didn't wear yourself out at the museums earlier in the day. Guanajuato has become a popular weekend destination for American students studying abroad in other cities. This is particularly true during festivals, when bars pack to the rafters. At these times, expect to pay a cover charge. Having said all this, Guanajuato certainly has plenty of nightlife options for an older crowd as well, particularly in the bars around Jardín de la Unión. Here there are several relaxed bars with live music every night. Some of these musicians are very good, and if you find one you like, you might consider finding out where his next set is so you can walk over to that bar when he finishes playing at the one you're at.

Guanajuato

ALKATRAZ
473-732-0870
Allende #15, Guanajuato, Gto. 36000
Open: Daily 4 PM–2 AM
This bar booms with lively music, making it popular with the young and beautiful set—with emphasis on the word "young." It's sometimes hard to get used to the fact that the drinking age here is 18, but some of the kids here look as though their high school field trip took a wrong detour. That said, the atmosphere here is animated and enjoyable with all kinds of drink specials. Some of the drinks you will recognize (sex on the beach, tequila sunrise) some you might not (michilada, vampiro). Located on the north side of the Jardín de la Unión toward the University, window seats also provide good people watching.

APPLE

473-732-6200
Alonso #26, Guanajuato, Gto. 36000
Open: Tues.–Sun. 4 PM–2 AM
This is another bar that is popular with the young local crowd. It plays a lot of electronic music and has a small dance floor. The bar offers plenty of drink specials during the week but not so much on the weekend, when it tends to be crowded.

B LOUNGE

473-732-0662
Juan Valle #10, Guanajuato, Gto. 36000
Open: Tues.–Sun. 6 PM–3 AM
This downstairs bar at the corner of Juárez has lots of art deco furniture and bright fluorescent lighting. There are pool tables here and several television screens that play incomprehensible videos, while loud techno music blares in the background. It does seem to be a popular place on some nights, while on others there's not much going on here.

BAR FLY

473-732-5719
Sostenes Roca #30, Guanajuato, Gto. 36000
Open: Daily 5 PM–2 AM
This bar is popular with travelers and locals alike. The crowd is fairly international, definitely bohemian, and fairly young, though not postpubescent as is the case at some of the other bars in town. And occasionally you'll find some funky 30-somethings hanging out here as well. They play a lot of reggae music and have a rooftop patio that is great for just hanging out. The décor is interesting, with brightly painted walls and surfboards hanging from the ceiling. There is also a stage where they have live music on the weekends.

BAR OCHO

473-732-7179
Constancia #8, Guanajuato, Gto. 36000
Open: Daily 3 PM–2 AM
This bar, located behind the Templo de San Diego, attracts a young, hip, university crowd. Its name, a play on the word *borracho*, which means drunk, tells you that this isn't the place to come for a quiet cocktail. It is a fun bar that is popular with university and international students. It has a small candlelit patio, a pool table, good food, and a welcoming atmosphere. Come, hang out, and maybe by around 3 AM you just might be *borracho* enough to join in singing songs you don't know the words to.

BORA BORA MICHELADAS & FOOD

473-732-1269
Constancia #9B, Guanajuato, Gto. 36000
Open: Mon.–Sat. 12 PM–12 AM
This lounge bar located behind Teatro Juárez specializes in micheladas, a type of drink that mixes beer, lemon juice, and hot sauce in a salted glass. However, they offer a variety of low alcohol mixed drinks and wine spritzers. There are several cushioned stools placed around low tables where you can kick back and have a quiet conversation.

La Botellita is a popular cantina-grill.

LA BOTELLITA

473-732-7424
Jardín de la Unión #2, Guanajuato, Gto. 36000
Open: Tues.–Sun. 12 PM–12 AM
This colorful cantina-grill is a fun place to hang out in a TGI Friday's sort of way. To be fair, the décor here is very eye-catching and interesting, creating a stylish feel. Inside you will find a large bar and several rooms of tables with plenty of space for larger parties, unless it's already packed. Located right at the entrance of the Jardín de la Unión, window seats provide great opportunities for people watching. The menu here offers all types of drinks as well as appetizers and full entrees, including a large selection of the type of Mexican food that any gringo will be right at home with. There are also happy hour specials daily from 3 PM until 7 PM. During festivals and busy weekends this place fills to the rafters and you may have a hard time getting in.

CAPITOLIO

473-732-0810
Plaza de la Paz #62, Guanajuato, Gto. 36000
Open: Daily 10 PM–4:30 AM
Located in the heart of the city right at the tip of Plaza de la Paz, this disco is a favorite among locals and tourists alike. On weekends, this club is always packed with university students. It plays a mix of techno, dance, house, and traditional Mexican music. The club has a large main room in the front and a smaller room in the back that plays principally hip-hop music. The club also has two full bars offering all types of drinks and drink specials.

CORONDU

473-732-0445
Allende #13, Guanajuato, Gto. 36000
Open: Tues.–Sun. 3 PM–12 AM
This is a narrow nook of a billiards hall. Located right next to Alkatraz and across from the University bookstore, this bar fills up with students on weekend nights.

DE WALLEN

473-732-0655
Jardín de la Unión #1, Guanajuato, Gto. 36000
Open: Tues.–Sun. 3 PM–2 AM
You have to pay attention to find this bar since there is no sign directing you here. The entrance is a stairwell on Obregón, on the side of the Hotel San Diego. Follow your ears. The interior is wonderful, with exposed stone walls and a large arch right in front of the bar, giving you the feel that you're in some medieval tavern. However, they play the contemporary rock music loud here, so it's hardly a place to sit and have a quiet beer. That said, there aren't a lot of bars like this one in town.

GUANAJUATO GRILL

473-732-0285
www.guanajuatogrill.com.mx
Calle Constancia s/n, Guanajuato, Gto. 36000

Open: Daily 10 PM–4:30 AM
This two-level disco is the largest club in Guanajuato, located in a colonial building that is typical of the historic center. It is always packed on the weekend with the university crowd as well as with many 30-somethings. The interior design may be its most impressive feature, seeming at once modern with a traditional sensibility. It plays a variety of music ranging from techno to *norteño* and offers many drink specials.

LUNA BAR

473-732-5054
Jardín de la Unión #10, Guanajuato, Gto. 36000
Open: Daily 12 PM–2 AM
This bar at the Hotel Luna has enclosed patio seating right on Jardín de la Unión. Always a good place for people watching, this bar attracts locals and travelers alike. Often on weekends, mariachi bands will set up shop right off the patio area and sing traditional songs that everyone seems to know but the gringos. Good food combines with a fun atmosphere to make this bar a good place to begin the night.

LAS MUSAS

473-732-7186
Avenida Juárez #10, Guanajuato, Gto. 36000
Open: Tues.–Sat. 5 PM–2 AM.; Sun. 5 PM–1 AM
This intimate upstairs bar is located in one of Guanajuato's old houses. It has a very relaxed atmosphere that attracts a bohemian crowd. The drink list is extensive, including many fine whiskeys and tequilas. There is a bar area that's great for hanging out with larger parties. Farther inside, there is a long, narrow stage area filled with tables and chairs. Here is where musicians begin playing mostly acoustic rock music around 7 PM each night. There are windows here that look out onto Juárez, and you can hear the music down the street.

PUERTA DEL SOL

473-732-8856
Sopeña #12, Guanajuato, Gto. 36000
Open: Daily 5 PM–2 AM
This is a low-lit bar with a relaxed atmosphere. Generally speaking, the crowd here is in their mid-20s and older, making this a nice option for couples looking to avoid the university crowds. A classic cantina bar, there are several tables situated around a stage at the front where local musicians play regularly and visiting musicians play scheduled tour dates. Live music events are held every day but Monday.

EL RINCÓN DEL BESO

473-732-5912
Alhóndiga #84, Guanajuato, Gto. 36000
Open: Tues.–Sat. 4 PM–1 AM; Sun. 4 PM–11 PM
With a name meaning "kissing corner," how could this not be a small and intimate place to have a drink. It has a romantic environment with several small tables and a couch in the corner, as well as a small stage where acoustic folk music, poetry, and word art is performed.

VAN GOGH

473-732-6903
Jardín de la Unión #4, Guanajuato, Gto. 36000
Open: Daily 12 PM –2 AM
This is a fun place to hang out and have some drinks and eats just to get the night rolling. Located on a patio right on the Jardín de la Unión, it's right in the center of the action and always full of people enjoying themselves. The proprietors often put up a large screen television during big soccer matches, making this corner of the Jardín a gathering place for cheering fans. This bar also features live music every night. Usually the performers hired by Van Gogh take turns performing with the mariachis parked outside of Luna Bar just over the railing. However, sometimes the mariachis don't play nice and they sing over one another, turning both performances into just a lot of noise. But mostly the atmosphere here is fun loving. Follow the stairs to the second floor and you will find the Vicent lounge bar with a beautiful view of the Jardín de la Unión.

WHY NOT?

473-732-2600
Alsonso #34, Guanajuato, Gto. 36000
Open: Daily 5 PM–2 AM
This bar is a good option if you're looking for an informal setting. It is a great place to relax and listen to various types of alternative international music such as cka, hip-hop, surfing, reggae, and rock. There are several pool tables here as well.

ZILCH

473-734-0755
Plazuela del Baratillo #16, Guanajuato, Gto. 36000
Open: Tues.–Sun. 5 PM–3 AM
This bar is located in a narrow nook back toward the university. It has a small menu of drinks and appetizers and attracts a young and hip crowd. Most nights, it also features live music.

San Miguel de Allende

BAR LEONARDO

415-152-2063
Umarán #8, San Miguel de Allende, Gto. 37700
Open: Daily 9 PM–3 AM
This is a small bar located in Mama Mía restaurant. It caters mainly to a young crowd, but not exclusively so. The walls are painted adobe red, with faithful re-creations of famous drawings by Leonardo da Vinci. The drinks are good and strong. Try the Margarita Cadillac if you're looking for something with an extra kick. During big sporting events, crowds gather here to watch their teams play. On other nights it is flooded with young 20-somethings. Don't be surprised if the girl next to you gets spontaneous and dances atop the horseshoe-shaped bar.

BERLIN

415-154-9432
Umarán #19, San Miguel de Allende, Gto. 37700

Try a local concoction such as a vampiro or a michilada.

Open: Mon.–Sat. 12 PM–1 AM
This bar is a favorite among the local expatriate crowd, comprised mostly of artsy Americans. It has a retractable roof and two fireplaces, so it is particularly comfortable no matter what time of the year it is. It also has a calm atmosphere and features good drinks and German food, making it a great place to start the night.

CANTINA LA CORONELA

415-154-2746
San Francisco #2, San Miguel de Allende, Gto. 37700
Open: Daily 12 PM –1 AM
This is an old-style Mexican cantina that caters to locals and travelers alike. It has a great relaxed atmosphere and traditional décor that seems right at home in this colonial city. The walls are covered with pictures of movie stars from Mexico's golden age of cinema.

EL CAPORAL

415-152-5937
Mesones #97, San Miguel de Allende, Gto. 37700
Open: Daily 8 PM–4 AM
This is a great place to come if you're looking for an authentic Mexican atmosphere. Here, live musicians play traditional ranchero songs as the crowd of locals of all ages sings along. This is a cozy, inviting place that reminds you that you're in the heart of old Mexico.

LA CAVA DE LA PRINCESA

415-152-14403
Recreo #3, San Miguel de Allende, Gto. 37700
Open: Tues.–Sun. 1 PM–2 AM
This is a popular spot for the 40-something crowd. This bar features daily live music and a small dance floor, as well as karaoke on Tuesday nights.

LA CUCARACHA

415-152-0196
Zacateros #22, San Miguel de Allende, Gto. 37700
Open: Daily 9 PM–3 AM
This is one of those bars you have to look for since there is no sign. However, usually it's not a problem since this is a boisterous cantina where the drinks flow easily. Popular among the locals, this is a good bar to end the night with.

LIMERICK PUB

415-154-8642
Umarán #24, San Miguel de Allende, Gto. 37700
Open: Daily 1 PM–1 AM
This casual Irish pub has a good mix of local and international people of all ages. There are no dartboards here, but there are free pool tables. Some nights they have live music. Other nights, DJs play a varied list of music. One thing that sets this place apart from most bars in town is that they have a good selection of imported beers. Guinness on draft never tasted so amazing.

MANOLO'S SPORTS BAR

415-152-7277
Zacateros #26, San Miguel de Allende, Gto. 37700
Open: Mon.–Sat. 1 PM–11 PM; Sun. 11 AM–11 PM
This is a good option if you happen to be in San Miguel during a big sporting event. It features five television sets hooked up to Direct TV, Sky, and cable. They offer draft and beer in the bottle as well as mixed drinks and a short wine list.

MECHICANO'S

415-152-0216
Canal #16, San Miguel de Allende, Gto. 37700
Open: Daily 12 PM–1 AM
This is a hip club with a glitzy, modern décor. It features two bars on the main floor as well as a spectacular terrace bar upstairs. These bars offer a variety of drink specials. Occasionally, this bar stays open late on the weekend. They have live music after 8 PM or the DJ spins an assortment of dance music.

EL PETIT BAR

415-154-8642
Hernández Macías #95, San Miguel de Allende, Gto. 37700
Open: Daily 1 PM–1 AM

This French-style establishment is a cozy wine bar. It has several small tables on one side and sofas situated around a fireplace on the other. This is a nice place for a quiet drink.

EL RING

415-152-1998
Hidalgo #27, San Miguel de Allende, Gto. 37700
Open: Wed.–Sat. 8 PM–3 AM
This former cockfighting ring is now a large interesting club. In addition to a large dance floor on the main level, there are also two tiers where a young, lively crowd parties late.

TAPAS Y TINIS

415-154-6276
Umarán #36, San Miguel de Allende, Gto. 37700
Open: Mon.–Sat. 3 PM–11 PM
This is a very intimate establishment with couches and small nooks decorated with bull-fighting art and old ranch implements. Overall, it has a very quiet atmosphere and is a great place to relax and have a conversation. As the name suggests, they have a menu of Spanish tapas and martinis. On Friday and Saturday nights they have live music.

PLAZAS AND PARKS

These cities were built to be experienced by pedestrians and with that in mind, their plazas are really what ties them together. These spaces function as a social center in many ways. Popular street-side cafes line their sidewalks, and they are always the gathering points for

School kids gather in the Plaza Principal in Dolores Hidalgo when class lets out.

Balloon vendor in the Plaza Principal, Dolores Hidalgo

community events. However, more often they are just a place to hang out and enjoy a beautiful day. As such, they become the iconic symbol of their respective cities and will surely be the first thing you think of when recalling your visit.

Dolores Hidalgo

PLAZA PRINCIPAL

INTERSECTION OF MICHOACÁN AND HIDALGO; SAN LUIS POTOSÍ AND ZACATECAS

Dolores Hidalgo is known as the Cradle of Mexican Independence, and this is where it all took place. And for this, the main plaza in Dolores Hidalgo has been given the attention it deserves. Despite the fact that this is a remote village of barely sixty thousand residents, this town has a *zócalo* (principal plaza) that is one of the most beautiful in Mexico. At its center, you will find a tall bronze statue of Miguel Hidalgo holding aloft the standard of the Virgin Mary in his left hand while extending his right hand as if imploring the onlooker to revolution. This statue is surrounded with

The Plaza Principal in Dolores Hidalgo is a relaxing place from a bygone era.

The state band plays for the enjoyment of residents and tourists in the Jardín de la Unión.

a circular walkway lined with benches shaded by various types of trees. Over Hidalgo's shoulder, the city's main church, Parroquia de Nuestra Señora de los Dolores, looms tall. It is quite a sight. This plaza is the social and actual center of town and you can find people here enjoying the plaza day and night. However, in the afternoons and on Sundays, this plaza fills with a heterogeneous mix of townspeople, old and young, who congregate here to sit in the shade, eat ice cream, and have long conversations. Looking at them, you may be tempted to say to yourself, "When in Rome. . . . "

Guanajuato

JARDÍN DE LA UNIÓN

CALLE OBREGÓN AND CALLE SOPEÑA

This beautiful triangular plaza is the social heart of Guanajuato. In colonial times (before there was a Mexican union), this plaza was called the Plaza de San Diego, because it served mainly as the front courtyard of the Templo de San Diego. At that time it was bare of trees and it doubled as an outdoor market and, at times, even a bullfighting ring. In 1836 a row of trees was planted, but the plaza as it is today did not start to take shape until the 1860s, when the main gardens were planted, benches were installed, and cobblestone walkways were laid around the perimeter. At this time it was rechristened Jardín de la Unión. Today, locals and visitors alike gather here to enjoy the shade of its manicured Indian laurel trees and listen to the music of the

Jardín de la Unión is a wedge-shaped plaza in the heart of Guanajuato.

mariachis or the *estudiantina* minstrels. The west side of the triangle is lined with shaded outdoor restaurants, while the east side has a variety of shops. At the south end, the Templo de San Diego and Teatro Juárez are popular staging grounds for street theatre and display areas for local artists. This is also a popular gathering place for students, who come with their laptops to take advantage of the WiFi of the nearby hotels. On Thursdays and Sundays at around 7 PM the plaza's central bandstand comes alive with the music of the state band.

PLAZA DE LA PAZ

AVENIDA JUÁREZ AND CALLE OBREGÓN

Walking west up Calle Obregón, you will come to another triangular-shaped plaza. This is Plaza de la Paz, and in colonial times it was the principal plaza of Guanajuato. Flanked on

The bronze and marble Monument to the Peace in Plaza de la Paz

one side by the Basilica of Guanajuato and lined with outdoor cafes and shops on the other, this was where aristocrats and wealthy silver lords once made their homes. Located in the center of a garden in front of the Basilica is the Monumento de la Paz (Monument to the Peace). This bronze and marble statue of a female was sculpted by the artist Jesús Contreras and added to the plaza in 1898. During festivals vendors set up handicraft and food stands here and the plaza fills to capacity, particularly along Obregón, where the crowd creates a bottleneck of people between Plaza de la Paz and Jardín de la Unión.

PLAZA DE LOS ÁNGELES

Between Avenida Juárez and Callejón del Patrocinio

Following Avenida Juárez west and south, you will find Plaza de los Ángeles on your right. This plaza is best known for being near the famed Callejón del Beso, but by itself, it is a beautiful little square. There are occasionally musical performances or demonstrations of street theatre here. It is also a popular gathering place for local students and you will often find children here playing near the fountain as their parents sit idly by.

PLAZA DE LA REFORMA

Avenida Juárez and Callejón Cañetos

Farther down Avenida Juárez, you will find a Roman arch flanked by a series of columns. This is the entrance to Plaza de la Reforma, which was built on the grounds of an old corral. It was constructed in 1861 by the architect José Noriega, to serve as a marketplace for Guanajuato residents. However, the city's population experienced growth in the late 19th century and in 1910, the Mercado Hidalgo opened and most of the city's merchants relocated there. In 1923 the Jardín Reforma was renovated, with gardens, a central fountain, and eucalyptus and cypress trees. In the center of the plaza is a dried-up *cantera* stone fountain surrounded by a series of gardens. There are a few quiet outdoor cafes here and it is a popular place for local families to spend a lazy afternoon, but it is not as well maintained as nearby Plazuela San Fernando.

Plazuela San Fernando is often the setting for cultural events.   Mary Delgado

PLAZA DE SAN ROQUE

AVENIDA JUÁREZ AND CALLEJÓN SAN ROQUE

Follow the cobblestone path up the northeast side of Plaza de la Reforma, and you will come to the Plaza de San Roque. In this plaza you will find a baroque church of the same name. There is also a stage here where theatrical performances are staged, particularly during the Cerventino Festival.

PLAZUELA SAN FERNANDO

AVENIDA JUÁREZ AND CALLEJÓN CANTAVITOS

Follow the short alley south out of Plaza de San Roque and you will come to Plazuela San Fernando, a pretty little square that tends to get better the more time you spend there. It is a lively open place surrounded by many outdoor cafes. Because it is more enclosed than either Jardín de la Unión or Plaza de la Paz, it has a very cozy atmosphere. And whereas many of the restaurants in Jardín de la Unión could theoretically have one kitchen hidden away serving them all because their menus are so similar, the restaurants of this plaza are much more diverse. The center of this plaza is often used for university events such as cultural exhibits and music concerts. This is a lovely place to relax with a coffee in the morning as you plan the day's itinerary.

The Florentine fountain at the center of Plaza del Baratillo

PLAZA DEL BARATILLO

CALLE CANTARRANAS

You will find this tiny plaza hidden away one block northeast of Jardín de la Unión or, perhaps more likely, you will just happen upon it as you make your way along the twisting alleys near the university. It is surrounded by colorful colonial buildings, and in the center of the plaza is a beautiful Florentine fountain adorned with sculpted fish at the base. This fountain was a royal gift from a French princess and at one time sat in the Plaza de la Paz but was transferred here in 1893 to make room for the Monumento a la Paz. However, this plaza does not take its name from anything so regal as the fountain. In the 19th century there was a market here where vendors would yell *"barato!"* assuring prospective customers that their wares were cheap. Hence, residents took to calling it *baratillo* and the name stuck.

The giant bronze statues of Don Quixote and Sancho Panza in Plaza Allende

PLAZA ALLENDE

CALLE PADRE BELAUZARÁN

If you follow Calle Sopeña east from Jardín de la Unión and continue past the Templo de San Francisco and El Campanero Bridge, you will end up at the Plaza Allende. This small plaza fronts Teatro Cervantes and is dominated by towering statues of Don Quixote and Sancho Panza. Usually this space is fairly empty, save for the occasional young couple looking for a quiet spot to hang out. However, during the International Cerventino Festival, this is a busy venue for cultural events.

JARDÍN EL CANTADOR

CALLE CANTADOR

Located west of Mercado Hidalgo on Calle Cantador, this park is located just outside of Guanajuato's central district. It is enclosed with a wrought iron fence and pink stone columns and is filled with grassy gardens crisscrossed by a series of walking paths leading to the center of the park. This is a strolling park, good for when you want a few quiet moments outside the crowded city center.

PRESA DE LA OLLA

PASEO DE LA PRESA AND MARQUES DE RAYAS

In the mid-18th century Guanajuato suffered from a water shortage, and thus the town

The gazebo in the Jardín Principal, San Miguel de Allende

council decided to dam an arroyo on the outskirts of the city to help alleviate that problem. They chose a ranch called *La Olla*, or "The Pot," as the site for this dam. The name stuck and the Presa de la Olla opened in 1749, supplying Guanajuato with a constant source of fresh water. Half the cost of the dam was covered by a wealthy mine owner. In 1795, Guanajuato's provincial governor, Juan Antonio de Riaño—who would later take refuge in the Alhóndiga in the battle that made *El Pípila* famous—took note of the beauty around this dam and commissioned a park to be constructed around it. The dam itself continued to provide water to the town and its neighbors until 1895. Today, it is the site of the June festivals of San Juan and the Festival of Presa de la Olla. It is also a beautiful place to spend an afternoon strolling along the Florencio Antillón Park, which features more than 1,000 square feet of gardens criss-crossed by symmetrical paths. At the center of the park, you will find a 17-foot statue of Father Hidalgo, designed in Rome by the artist Guis Trabachi. There is also a local legend that says, at twilight, from the Presa de la Olla, you can make out the profile of a bearded man on the side of the city's Bufa Mountain. According to tradition, this is said to be the profile of Jesus Christ. To get here from the southeast side of town, take Calle Sangre de Cristo from Plaza Allende to Paseo Madero, and then bear left onto Paseo de la Presa. From the northwest side of town, take the Tunel de los Ángeles and take a left when it lets out at Calle Nelayote. At the Monumento a Cervantes roundabout, bear left onto Boulevard Guanajuato and merge onto Carretera Panorámica.

Plaza Cívica is a nice place that is much smaller and quieter than the Jardín Principal.

San Miguel de Allende

JARDÍN PRINCIPAL

INTERSECTION OF CUNA DE ALLENDE AND PRINCIPAL DE CORREO

This large plaza is located at the cultural and historical heart of San Miguel de Allende. It is a lovely city square with manicured gardens of rose bushes and laurels, all surrounded by beautiful buildings and archways from the colonial era. The center of the plaza is a verdant garden known as Jardín Allende. Its lawns are crisscrossed by cobblestone paths on the circumference that also cut through the center. You will find a shaded gazebo here, and the perimeter of the square is lined by sculpted trees. On the north side of the square an 18th-century building houses the municipal government, flanked by several small businesses and restaurants. On the south side, a line of park benches faces the city's most famous church, the Parroquia de San Miguel. This is a great place to sit under the shade of the trees and relax for a half hour or so. Here you're sure to find plenty of American retirees lounging away the afternoon, and artists with their easels and brushes out, doing their thing. On Saturday evenings, the traditional promenade of young people circles the square to the sounds of mariachis and other live musicians. Boys walk the perimeter of the Jardín in one direction and the girls circle in the other direction, while parents watch from the park benches.

PLAZA CIVICA (CIVIC SQUARE)

CALLE MESONES AND CALLE COLEGIO

This square was constructed in honor of Don Ignacio Allende. In the center of the square is an equestrian statue of Allende astride his horse, with his saber heroically held aloft in his right hand. This square is bordered by the building that was the prestigious school of San Francisco de Sales in the 18th century, as well as the Iglesia de Nuestra Señora de la Salud (Church of Our Lady of Health). It is a quiet place with few vendors or shops. If you are traveling with small children, this would be a good place to bring them to run around or bounce a ball if you have some time to kill.

PARQUE JUÁREZ

CALLE HERMANOS ALDAMA AND CALLE DIEZMO

This is a large, well-kept park (though there is a bit of a graffiti problem). It is located 3 blocks south of the Plaza Principal along Calle Hermanos Aldama. There is a playground here with old-style metal equipment that would not pass the kind of safety standards we have come to expect north of the border. However, it is often filled with healthy kids having a good time. There are also picnic tables and charcoal grills here, as well as basketball courts that tend to fill up when school lets out.

SEASONAL EVENTS

The high season for traveling in Guanajuato and San Miguel de Allende is really determined by their festivals. The first tourist bump of the year comes a couple weeks before Easter and lasts until the week after Easter. During this time, festivals and cultural events fall one on top of the other, with crowds first jamming the streets of Guanajuato that

Seasonal fiestas draw large crowds from the countryside and around Mexico.

Thursday for *Día de las Flores* (Flower Day) and Friday of Sorrows the next day. The next week during *Semana Santa* (Holy Week), vacation season gets under way throughout Mexico and San Miguel de Allende is among the country's most popular destinations for Easter festivities. In the fall, this region sees another spike in tourism with Independence Day celebrations in mid-September, and of course the International Cerventino Festival, which lasts nearly the entire month of October. For Guanajuato, this is by far the busiest time of the year. Finally, the region is highly visited again at the end of the year with Christmas celebrations. San Miguel de Allende in particular is known for its beautiful and joyful Christmas festivities.

CORONA RALLY MÉXICO
León
February
This road race was started in 1979 by the two largest auto clubs in Mexico. It was originally held in the state of Mexico, but in 1998 it was moved to León, Guanajuato. Today this is an annual event in León, where it has an extremely compact route and attracts crews from around the world. The dirt roads in the mountainous region north of the city are perfect for sending cars flying over bumps and sliding around corners. The city's modern Poliforum Expo Center at Boulevard Adolfo López Mateos and Boulevard Francisco Villa hosts the rally headquarters and service park, where fans can examine the cars close up and meet the drivers and crews. There are also fiesta ceremonies held in the city of Guanajuato. For more information, call 477-771-2530 or visit the Web site at www.rallymexico.com.

An estudiantina troupe entertains a crowd in front of the Templo de San Diego.

FIESTA DEL SEÑOR DE LA CONQUISTA (LORD OF THE CONQUEST FEAST)

San Miguel de Allende

First Friday in March

This solemn celebration is in honor of the Holy Christ of the Conquest, a figure that was presented to the town of San Miguel by the King of Spain and brought by Franciscan monks in the 16th century from the town of Pátzcuaro, Michoacán, where it was carved. Today, this work of art can be found in one of the altars of the Párroquia de San Miguel. The Thursday before the feast, a parade of bulls decorated with flowers, fruits, and other items symbolizing fertility marches through town. This parade is accompanied by music, fireworks, and dancing. The next day, residents customarily attend mass followed by traditional dances in the Jardín Principal. Later in the afternoon, people

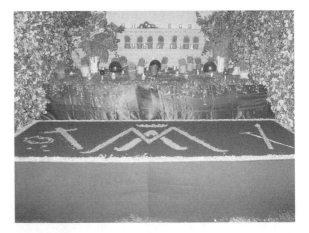

An ofrenda altar made of dried corn and beans

Children parade through the streets during Semana Santa. Mary Delgado

make offerings of bread and sugar, known as *parandes,* to the image of the Señor de la Conquista. In some parts of the city, the feast goes on through Saturday and Sunday.

VIERNES DE DOLORES (FRIDAY OF SORROWS)
Throughout Guanajuato
Weekend before Holy Week
In the days leading up to this celebration, residents set up altars for the Virgen Dolorosa (Sorrowful Virgin). These altars can be seen in churches, private homes, businesses, and even government buildings. The celebration itself is actually anything but sorrowful, except possibly for the person who has to clean up afterward. Thursday afternoon is devoted to cleaning and repairing public spaces in preparation for the coming festivities. On Thursday night, people crowd the streets partaking of fresh fruits and juices. In Guanajuato, people arrive from the countryside and set up shop in the Plaza de la Paz with stands selling flowers, handicrafts, and food. They work in shifts around the clock over the next couple of days, sleeping when they can right there on the street. Crowds of people jam the streets during this time doing the traditional *baile de las flores,* in which young men are expected to give flowers to their female friends. On Friday, many people attend solemn religious ceremonies, but festivities continue through the weekend.

SEMANA SANTA (HOLY WEEK)
San Miguel de Allende
Week of Easter
Throughout Mexico, the week of Easter and the week after *(Semana Pascua)* is the time of the year to take vacations, and Guanajuato is a very popular region to spend that vacation. For this reason, hotel rates throughout the area are significantly higher during this time. San Miguel de Allende is considered one of the best places in Mexico to come to experience two solid weeks of processions, parties, prayers, pageantry, and . . . well, there's no "p" word for fireworks. The most remarkable of these events takes place on Good Friday, with a huge procession organized by the town's churches. Roman centurions parade through town astride their horses, ahead of floats and effigies of biblical figures. Amazingly, this is followed by a man portraying Jesus who drags a heavy cross as blood drips from his forehead, which bears a real crown of thorns.

FIESTAS OF SAN JUAN AND PRESA DE LA OLLA
Guanajuato
End of June, beginning of July
On the days leading up to Saint's Feast Day, a large arts festival is held at the Presa de la Olla outside of town. There are all sorts of festivities, including music, dancing, and lots of food. On the actual day of the feast (June 24), people show up to picnic and enjoy a fireworks show. A couple weeks later, on the first Monday of July, the crowds return to Presa de la Olla to celebrate the annual opening of the floodgates. This celebration has been held since the dam was built, when the reservoir periodically had to be drained. Guanajuato's mayor and governor participate, signaling the opening of the floodgates, when a rushing waterfall pours out of the dam. There are hosts of festivities that go along with this event, including a traditional waltz performed by the state band, right at the moment the floodgates are opened.

INTERNATIONAL GUITAR FESTIVAL
San Miguel de Allende
July
This festival is a celebration of the guitar and the role this diverse instrument has played in different cultures. People come to San Miguel from all over the world to play all styles of guitar music, including classical, Spanish, jazz, and modern. In addition to these performances, musicians also host workshops, classes, and lectures on the art of guitar playing.

SAN ANTONIO DE PADUA
San Miguel de Allende
Sunday after July 13
This celebration is also known as the *fiesta de los locos y hortelanos*, or the fiesta of the insane and the farmers. It takes place in the crowded neighborhood of San Antonio. Tradition has it that this day of dancing is an offering to saints who have healed you or helped you out during the year. However, today the dancing is done purely for the pleasure of it, resulting in a crowd of insane people. People traverse the neighborhood in decorated carts, dressed in colorful or bizarre costumes.

DÍA DE LA CUEVA (CAVE DAY)
Guanajuato
July 31
This celebration is held in honor of Saint Ignatius of Loyola, founder of the Jesuit order; the Jesuits played a crucial role in the founding of the city of Guanajuato. The celebration takes place in a cave in the nearby hills of Cerro de los Picachos. Processions to the cave begin the night of July 30, when the hills become illuminated by flashlights and candles. Participants who do not go that evening, do so the next day. There are vendors and food sellers set up all along the way. Celebrations include a country fair, traditional dances, and fireworks.

FESTIVAL DE LA INDEPENDENCIA
Dolores Hidalgo
September
In the month of September, the town of Dolores Hidalgo stops to celebrate the vital role their town played in the independence of Mexico. This celebration is marked by a variety of cultural and artistic events. The most important of these takes place on the evening of September 15, when crowds gather in the town square for the traditional *grita de indepen-dencia* (cry for independence). Every five years Mexico's president comes to Dolores Hidalgo to perform this ceremony.

PAMPLONADA
San Miguel de Allende
Third Saturday in September
This is San Miguel de Allende's version of the Running of the Bulls in Pamplona, Spain. The bulls are released in front of La Parroquía and they run past the Templo de San Francisco, and return to the Jardín Principal. The entire route is barricaded to prevent any bulls from getting loose in the town. The event attracts a large crowd of mainly young peo ple and can be very dangerous.

FIESTAS DEL ARCÁNGEL SAN MIGUEL (FEAST OF SAINT MICHAEL THE ARCHANGEL)
San Miguel de Allende
Weekend after September 29
These festivities of the city's patron saint are the most important in San Miguel de Allende. They are also the most colorful and spectacular. The celebrations begin on Friday as people begin to pour in from the countryside. By nightfall, the Jardín Principal and the courtyard of La Parroquia are packed with people as mariachi bands play to the crowds. At 4 AM the next morning, tolling church bells ring in a fireworks display. This is traditionally supposed to be a very emotional event in honor of Saint Michael. Then, the bands that have gathered play *Las Mañanitas*, the song that is best known as the traditional Mexican birthday song. That morning, the celebrants have tamales and *atole* for breakfast as the sun comes up. In the afternoon, a procession of indigenous Mexicans make their way through the Jardín Principal to La Parroquia to make offerings of *xuchiles*, beautiful braids of marigolds and colored tortillas. The next day, a solemn mass is held in honor of Saint Michael, and the town pays homage to Friar San Miguel, founder of the city, with another parade.

A band of young musicians perform in front of the Don Quixote Iconographic Museum.

FESTIVAL INTERNACIONAL CERVENTINO
Guanajuato
Three weeks in October
This festival has come to be known as one of Latin America's most important cultural events. Certainly, it is the biggest thing to hit Guanajuato every year. During this celebration, thousands of fans of the 16th-century Spanish writer Miguel de Cervantes and his book *Don Quixote* make a pilgrimage to the city for three weeks of theatre, dance, music, and literary events. The festival had its humble beginnings in the 1950s when students from the university took to the streets with performances of short works written by Cervantes known as *entremeses*. In 1972, it became an international festival celebrated throughout Latin America. However, its epicenter remains in Guanajuato, with artists from more than 30 countries giving performances during the festival. The main venues for these events are the city's theatres, such as Teatro Juárez, Teatro Principal, and of course Teatro Cervantes. However, a constant stream of events also takes place in the city's churches, plazas, and in the streets as well.

INTERNATIONAL BALLOON FESTIVAL
León
End of November
Over the course of four days the skies above León are filled with dozens of colorful hot air balloons, as thousands of spectators gather to enjoy the events. Early in the morning in the city's Metropolitan Park these balloons begin their launch, filling the chilled air with the

sound of the enormous blazes that heat the balloons. This magnificent scene is repeated throughout the day as the skies fill with multicolored globes. At night, the flames are ignited once again, creating a spectacle of giant lanterns. However, the festival is about more than balloons. The four-day event is jam packed with other exhibitions, presentations, and performances including live music concerts, BMX bike exhibitions, and all kinds of diversions for the kids. For more information, visit their Web site at www.festivaldelglobo.com.mx.

LAS FIESTAS NAVIDEÑAS
Throughout Guanajuato
Last two weeks of December

Christmas is celebrated with two full weeks of celebrations and solemn religious ceremonies. The *posadas* are performed throughout the region, in which processions of people leave church and reenact the journey of Joseph and Mary as they tried to find a place to stay on the night of Christmas Eve. This is a lively tradition, especially for children. Finally, at designated locations shelter is given to the pilgrims, where they receive *buñuelo* (sweet bread) and *atole* (Mexican hot chocolate) and children break piñatas (decorated papier-mâché figure stuffed with candy). One of the most popular Christmas celebrations is held in San Miguel de Allende at the Nuestra Señora de Loreto next to the Templo del Oratorio. Here, ancient chants can be heard and an extended mass is offered.

Theatre opportunities abound in Guanajuato and San Miguel de Allende.   Mary Delgado

Teatro Cervantes is mainly used for cultural events during the Festival Cerventino.

THEATRE

In case you haven't figured it out yet, both San Miguel de Allende and Guanajuato have rich creative communities and vibrant art scenes. In San Miguel, there are artistic events open to the public nearly every day of the year, with everything from jazz concerts, to literary readings, to dramatic presentations. The Bellas Artes and Teatro Ángela Peralta are popular venues for these events, as is the Instituto Allende. Guanajuato's artistic scene is driven by the university, which is constantly sponsoring events at the Teatro Principal, including plays, lectures, and traditional Baile Folklórico performances. Teatro Juárez also has a full slate of events on its itinerary. Every day, you will also find street performers doing skits for indulgent crowds on the steps of Teatro Juárez. Of course, theatrical events get kicked into high gear during festivals, particularly during the International Cerventino Festival, when it seems that something is happening on every street corner.

Guanajuato

TEATRO CERVANTES

473-732-1169
Plazuela Allende, Guanajuato, Gto. 36000
Open: Varies
Admission: Varies by event
This theatre is a neoclassical building similar to the construction of the Alhóndiga. It has two floors and a capacity of 430 people. In 1979, it was converted into a theatre for the

Teatro Juárez is one of the most recognizable and impressive buildings in Guanajuato.

Festival Cerventino, with large statues of Don Quixote and his trusted squire Sancho just outside. This theatre is mainly used for cultural events during the Festival Cerventino.

TEATRO JUÁREZ

473-732-1542
Jardín de la Unión, Guanajuato, Gto. 36000
Open: Varies
Admission: General $6; with photography $12
This is considered one of the most beautiful theatres in Mexico. Inaugurated in 1903 by the dictator General Porfirio Diaz, it has a neoclassical façade crowned by bronze statues of the Greek muses. The wide steps of the theatre are flanked by two bronze lions and a *cantera* balustrade leading to a series of fluted Doric columns of green *cantera* stone. Inside the theatre, a Moorish-influenced lobby leads to five levels of seating that open to the auditorium, which is decorated throughout with intricate arabesque detail, and the curtain is adorned with a painting of Constantinople. It is reputed to be the only theatre in Mexico that has conserved its original furnishings. This theatre presents plays, ballet, and lectures, among other cultural activities.

TEATRO PRINCIPAL

473-732-1523
Cantarranas #1, Guanajuato, Gto. 36000
Open: Varies

Baile folklórico dances are the folk dances of Mexico.   Mary Delgado

Baile Folklórico

Baile folklórico, or "folk dance," is a traditional Latin American dance that emphasizes local folk culture. Though this type of dance is characterized by common heel-stomping steps, called *zapateadas*, every region of Mexico has its own particular brand of *baile folklórico*. Even the costumes are specific to each region, though they are always comprised of flamboyant outfits for the men and beautifully flowing, brightly colored dresses for the women, who also wear ribbons intricately woven into their hair. *Baile folklórico* dancers spend years learning the nuances of their region's distinct style of dance, often beginning early in their childhood. During performances, dancers are often paired off into couples as they dance in unison in routines that symbolize religious and social traditions of the local history. Performers create their interpretations through specific body positions, group formation, music, and scenery. Performances of *baile folklórico* often accompany festivals or other cultural events. These performances are lively and festive with members of the crowd periodically yelping out in approval.

The baile folklórico costumes are specific to each region of Mexico.   Mary Delgado

Admission: Varies by event

This theatre was originally built at the height of Guanajuato's mining heyday in 1788, to give the city a bit of culture. For more than a century it remained the town's only theatre, and over its more than 200 years it has had a rich but tumultuous history. It has entertained common people and prominent figures alike, and it has been abandoned and subsequently restored several times. In 1921, after being converted to a commercial cinema, it burned down. In 1955, it was rebuilt and has since been run by the Universidad de Guanajuato, all the while enjoying a successful cultural scene of theatre, ballet, and lectures, among other cultural activities.

San Miguel de Allende

TEATRO ÁNGELA PERALTA

415-152-7599

Hernandez Macias and Mesones

Open: Varies

Admission: Varies by event

In 1873, construction was completed on this neoclassical theatre that was meant to be a modest concert hall for the residents of San Miguel. Coincidentally, the famous soprano singer Ángela Peralta happened to be traveling through Guanajuato at the time. She accepted an invitation to come to San Miguel and was received with a grand procession. She gave several performances in the theatre, and in 1881 she returned to have the theatre re-inaugurated in her name. The theatre continues to be a center for art and performances. Today, the theatre hosts a variety of plays, ballets, and lectures, among other cultural activities.

Basílica Colegiata de Nuestra Señora de Guanajuato is the crown jewel of Guanajuato churches.

Sacred Sites

In case you haven't noticed, when it comes to the question of religion, Mexico—and particularly Central Mexico—is pretty solidly dominated by the Catholic Church. This is not to say the religious culture is monolithic. For example, in San Miguel de Allende you can find Jewish services, Mormon services, Jehovah's Witness services, and Unitarian services. However, other than the Anglican Church on Calle Calzada del Cardo, all of the other church structures in town are Catholic.

Of course, the Catholic Church has played a key role in the history of Mexico. Without the Catholic practice of conversion (as brutal as it was), it's likely that contemporary Mexico would lack its particular indigenous quality. For example, if the country had been settled by Calvinists, such as the pilgrims of the northeast United States, those settlers would have been far less likely to intermarry, thus creating the mestizo culture that later developed. However, change between the Catholic Church and Mexican culture has been a two-way street. Mexican Catholicism is extremely varied in practice. This is especially true in smaller rural communities, where folk religious practices evolved from the indigenous past are still practiced.

The Roman Catholic Church's role in Mexican history goes back to 1519 when Hernán Cortes landed on the coast of Veracruz. He was accompanied by Roman Catholic clergy, and all new Spanish territories were conquered in the name of the cross as well as the crown. The subsequent history of the relationship between church and state following independence involves a series of efforts on the part of the Mexican government to curtail the church's influence. Perhaps the most notable example of this was the law put into place during the 1920s that placed extensive restrictions on the Catholic Church. This paved the way for the bloody Cristero Rebellion from 1926 to 1929. Several of the battles of this rebellion were fought in the state of Guanajuato, including the destruction of the first statue of Cristo Rey, atop Cerro del Cubilete just west of Guanajuato.

Despite its tumultuous history here, the Catholic Church has peppered this region of Mexico with some of its most gorgeous monuments. The majority of the churches you find here are baroque works that were built during the 17th and 18th centuries. They have elaborately carved churrigueresque facades, though most of their altars are of the neoclassical period, dating back only to the late 18th and 19th centuries. The obvious exception to this, of course, is San Miguel de Allende's Gothic Parroquia. It was once a baroque church but had a major facelift in the 19th century by the indigenous architect Zeferino Gutiérrez, who was enamored of the churches of Europe that adorned postcards at the time.

Whether you are a devout Catholic or merely an admirer of architecture and artistic works, there is plenty in this region to catch your eye and take your breath away.

DOLORES HIDALGO

PARROQUIA DE NUESTRA SEÑORA DE LOS DOLORES

Plaza Principal, Dolores Hidalgo, Gto. 37800
Open: Daily 9 AM–7 PM
This magnificent baroque church of pink quarry stone towers over the town of Dolores
Hidalgo, facing out toward the Plaza Principal. It was built in 1778 and has been beautifully
preserved through all these years. In its extravagant churrigueresque are images of Jesus
Christ's arrest, trial, and crucifixion, commonly referred to as the Passion. The image of
the crucifixion finishes off the set at the cornice, on top of which sits a small clock tower.
On each side are columns supporting two bell towers, each containing three rows of
arches. These bells ring out each year on Mexico's Independence Day to commemorate the
town's most famous event, Hidalgo's call to independence. Inside, there is an altar covered
with gold leaf supporting a framed niche containing the image of the Virgin of Guadalupe.
On Sunday, masses are held at 10:30 AM and noon.

GUANAJUATO

BASILICA COLEGIATA DE NUESTRA SEÑORA DE GUANAJUATO

Plaza de La Paz #14, Guanajuato, Gto. 36000
Open: Daily 9 AM–7 PM
This gorgeous church sits in the heart of Guanajuato and is the main backdrop of the Plaza
de la Paz. Even from the Pípila, this edifice stands out among the town's many architectural
wonders. Many authorities consider the façade of this church to be the purest example of
baroque architecture in Mexico. Between 1691 and 1696, it was built with funds from
lucrative nearby mines to be the town's parish church. The Templo de los Hospitales was
previously the primary parish church in town. The Basilica is laid out in a Latin cross configuration that is nearly 200 feet long and nearly 30 feet wide. Amazingly, it is nearly 50
feet high in the vault and almost 100 feet high in the central dome, making it the largest
building in the city. It consists of two bell towers, a very large one on the north side and a
smaller one on the south, with a clock that was added in the late 18th century. In 1957, this
parish church rose to the rank of Basilica.

The church houses several early artifacts, including the much-revered statue of the
Virgin of Guanajuato, a carved wooden figure on a silver base that is believed to date back
to the 7th century. This statue was presented to the city by King Philip II of Spain, in 1557.
In fact, the need to provide a suitable home for this statue is partly what prompted the
town to build this church.

This church has three entryways. Each doorway has an intricate baroque facade of pink
stone. The atrium is neoclassical and was built between the 18th and 19th centuries. There
is also a neoclassical chapel near the baptistery. This section was also built in the late 19th
century. The Count of Valencia donated the body and blood of Saint Faustina to the Basilica
in 1826, and these remains were placed in a chapel altar, which was done by the architect
Edward Tresguerras. In 1907, to mark the canonical patronage of the Virgin of Guanajuato,
the remains of the saint were transferred to the upper altar. Sunday mass here is usually
standing room only. On Sunday, masses are held at 10 AM and noon.

Parroquia de Nuestra Señora de los Dolores towers over Dolores Hidalgo.

SANTUARIO DE MINERAL DE CATA
Carretera Panorámica (north of town), Guanajuato, Gto. 36000
Open: Daily 9 AM–7 PM
During the heyday of the silver boom, it was customary for successful miners to build
chapels at the work sites as a way of giving thanks and fulfilling their religious obligations.

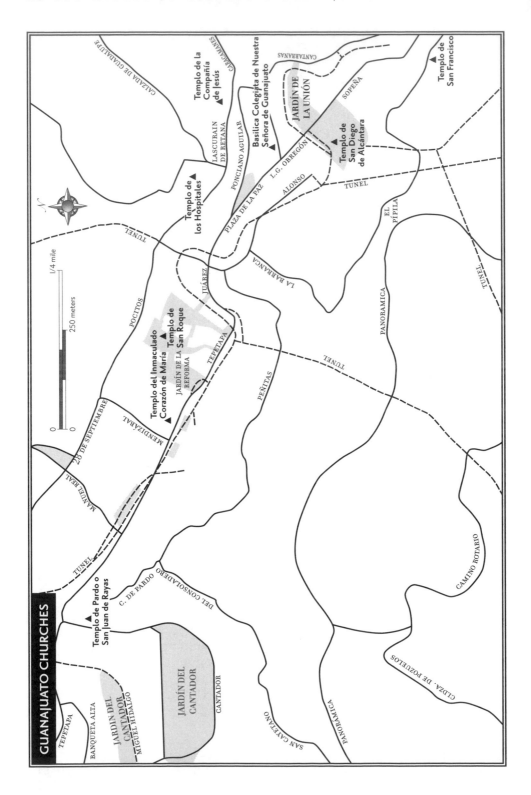

GUANAJUATO CHURCHES

N

1/4 mile

250 meters

TEPETAPA
BANQUETA ALTA
JARDÍN DEL CANTADOR
MIGUEL HIDALGO
JARDÍN DEL CANTADOR
CANTADOR
SAN CAYETANO
PANORAMICA
CLDZA. DE POZUELOS

Templo de Pardo o San Juan de Rayas

C. DE PARDO
DEL CONSOLADERO
CAMINO ROTARIO

MANTEL REAL
TUNEL
28 DE SEPTIEMBRE
MENDIZÁBAL
POCITOS

Templo del Inmaculado Corazón de María
Templo de San Roque
JARDÍN DE LA REFORMA

TEPETAPA
JUÁREZ
PEÑITAS
TUNEL

CALZADA DE GUADALUPE
LASCURAIN DE RETANA
PONCIANO AGUILAR

Templo de los Hospitales

Templo de la Compañía de Jesús

PLAZA DE LA PAZ
LA BARRANCA

Basílica Colegiata de Nuestra Señora de Guanajuato

CARCAMANES
CANTARRANAS
SOPEÑA
JARDÍN DE LA UNIÓN

Templo de San Francisco

L.G. OBREGÓN
ALONSO
TUNEL
Templo de San Diego de Alcántara

EL PÍPILA
PANORAMICA
TUNEL

The dome of the Templo de la Compañía de Jesús sat in ruins for much of the 19th century.

The baroque church at the Mineral de Cata mine is one such church. It has an impressive churrigueresque façade flanked by a single tower. It was commissioned by Alonso de Villaseca, a wealthy miner who owned mines throughout the region and had a hacienda nearby. It was actually built to house the statue of Christ, which you can see inside today. Construction on the church began in 1709 but, because of delays brought about by fluctuations in the mine's production, it wasn't finished until 80 years later. The Santuario de Mineral de Cata is now a destination of religious importance for worshipers throughout Mexico who come here to admire the Christ of Villaseca and ask for God's grace and good favors.

TEMPLO DE LA COMPAÑÍA DE JESÚS

Lascurain de Retana, Guanajuato, Gto. 36000
Open: Daily 9 AM–5 PM
Construction on this church began in 1746 and was concluded 20 years later under the direction of the friar José de la Cruz, a member of the Jesuit Order (Compañía de Jesus). He designed a façade with three churrigueresque doors, and niches for images of Jesuit saints. He was assisted by the Mexican architect Philip of Ureña, who probably only completed the tower. Much of this church is not original. The original dome collapsed in 1808 and, to preserve the church, it largely had to be reconstructed in the late 19th century by the architect Herculaneum Ramirez. The baroque altarpieces were replaced with neoclassical additions in the 19th century, as was much of the atrium. However, this church contains an important collection of Miguel Cabrera paintings from the 18th century.

TEMPLO DE LOS HOSPITALES

Callejón de los Hospitales, Guanajuato, Gto. 36000
Open: Rarely
Along the north side of the University, you will find the Templo de los Hospitales. In 1565, this church opened as the first church of Guanajuato. It was commissioned by the bishop of Michoacán, Vasco de Quiroga, and doubled as a hospital for the local indigenous population. It is the original parish church of Guanajuato and is known today simply as the Church of the Hospitals. Outside of a few improvements made to the church around 1940, its original interior has survived intact. Although today this church is usually closed, it is a historically and religiously important location for the town since it is the town's original church, as well as the place where the Virgen de Guanajuato statue was displayed for 130 years before the Basilica was built in 1696.

Domes of the Templo de San Diego de Alcántara

TEMPLO DE SAN DIEGO DE ALCÁNTARA

Jardín de la Unión, Guanajuato, Gto. 36000

Open: Daily 9 AM–7 PM

This church occupies the south end of the Jardín de la Unión. The first construction of a church on this site began in 1663. It was commissioned by friars of the Franciscan order of Dieguina, also known as the "Barefoot Franciscans." The church cemetery was once located on the site that Teatro Juárez now occupies. Nothing of that original construction exists today, due to destructive floods and reconstructions that took place in 1694 and 1780. This last construction resulted in the church that exists today. It has a churrigueresque façade of pink quarry stone embedded with intricate carvings. On the inside, you will find two chapels known as the Purísima Concepción and the Chapel of the Señor de Burgos. These chapels contain several 18th-century treasures including a painting that has survived several floods, and a series of paintings that depict the life of San Pedro de Alcántara, the founder of the order of Dieguina.

TEMPLO DE SAN FRANCISCO

Manuel Doblado #15, Guanajuato, Gto. 36000

Open: Daily 9:30 AM–6 PM

Less than a block south of the Museo Iconográfico del Quijote you will find this 18th-century orange baroque church. You will notice the entrance, elevated to protect against floods, is intricately carved churrigueresque stonework of plant motifs and niches containing images of Saint Peter and Saint Paul. Above it is a circular clock framed with green quarry stone. The façade is finished with bell towers on either side of the entrance, each containing double-level arches topped with small domes. In the interior, you will find images of the Virgin as well as Saint Francis of Assisi adorning the main altar. As with most of the churches in the city, the original baroque altar has been replaced by a later neoclassical model. On Sunday, masses are held at 10:30 AM.

Detail from the churrigueresque façade of the Templo de San Francisco in Guanajuato

TEMPLO DEL INMACULADO CORAZÓN DE MARÍA (BELÉN)

Calle Mendizábal and Avenida Juárez, Guanajuato, Gto. 36000

Open: Rarely

Right across the street from the Hidalgo Market, this baroque church appears cracked and faded but still imposing and beautiful. Its churrigueresque entrance rises from the ground all the way to the top of the church, containing niches with sculptures of Saint Anthony and Santo Domingo de Guzmán. The central niche is occupied by a statue of the

The neoclassical façade of the Templo de San Roque is much more plain than most churches in the region.

Virgin Mary; this aged façade dates back to the 1770s. The inside of the church is laid out in a Latin cross configuration. It has a neoclassical altar dating back to the 19th century. The left side of this altar is devoted to the Virgin of Guadalupe and on the right side is a large sculpture of the sacred heart of Jesus. The pulpit is renowned for its fine gold work.

TEMPLO DE SAN ROQUE

Callejón de San Roque, Guanajuato, Gto. 36000

Open: Daily 10 AM–7 PM

This church is located in the Plaza de San Roque, just off Plazuela San Fernando and Plaza de la Reforma and not far from the Diego Rivera Museum. It was constructed in 1726 and is one of the purely neoclassic churches in the region. One of the first things you will notice about it is that, unlike the more intricate churrigueresque churches in town, the façade of this church is sober, with straight lines and almost no decorative carvings. The door of the church is beautifully carved and forms a medium-size arch flanked by niches with religious statues. Above the door, the façade emphasizes a rectangular choral window flanked by fluted pilasters. Inside, the neoclassical altar has a niche with a statue of the Virgin of the Rosary. However, this church is perhaps best known as the backdrop for the *entremeses*, or short skits, performed in its plaza during the International Cerventino Festival. This plaza was chosen as the setting of the first *entremeses* performed in Guanajuato in February 1953, because it is said to resemble 16th-century Spain.

SAN MIGUEL DE ALLENDE

ORATORIO DE SAN FELIPE NERI

Insurgentes #12, San Miguel de Allende, Gto. 37700

Open: Daily 9 AM–7 PM

This chapel was built by the local indigenous population in the early 18th century and, physically speaking, it is best known for its many domes of different shapes and sizes. It was commissioned by the priest Juan Antonio Pérez de Espinoza from Pátzcuaro, Michoacán, who came to San Miguel for a short visit in 1712, and ended up staying. This is the most indigenous-influenced church in San Miguel de Allende. Although it has gone through several restorations, the original façade of pink stone is still present on the eastern side of the church, along with a small statue of Nuestra Señora de Soledad (Our Lady of Solitude). The southern exterior exhibits a much newer baroque façade. In the interior of the church are more than 30 oil paintings attributed to Miguel Cabrera that depict the life of San Felipe Neri, the Italian saint who founded the congregation of the Oratory.

There is also a rather strange local legend about this church. In 1910, when the Mexican Revolution was in full swing, many churches in the region were under constant threat by looters intent on stealing gold objects and other valuables. To hide their gold and religious artifacts, the priests bought a young bull from a local farmer. They slaughtered this bull and removed its organs, replacing them with their treasure. They then buried the bull underneath the altar of the Oratorio de San Felipe Neri. It is said that this bull is still buried there today, although there is no discernible evidence of this.

There is an adjoining chapel to the Oratorio de San Felipe Neri called Santa Casa de Loreto. This chapel was commissioned by the Canal family in 1736 and is a reproduction of the Santa Casa de Loreto in Loreto, Italy. To enter this chapel, go up the left aisle of the Oratorio to the front of the church and turn left. It has a small baroque nave covered with gold leaf and an altar dominated by a painting of the Virgen de Loreto.

LA PARROQUIA DE SAN MIGUEL ARCANGEL (THE PARISH OF ST. MICHAEL THE ARCHANGEL)

Principal del Correo, San Miguel de Allende, Gto. 37700
Open: Daily 9 AM–7 PM

The Parroquia de San Miguel, with its jutting vertical lines and intricately carved spires is one of the most distinctive churches in Mexico—and that is saying something. It has come to be the symbol of San Miguel and is dedicated to Friar Juan de San Miguel, the founder of the city. However, this distinctive work of architecture is not a cathedral, but rather a parish church. It was originally built in the 17th century with a baroque façade and three high towers. In the late 19th century, the indigenous Mexican architect Zeferino Gutiérrez radically changed the façade to the Gothic structure that you see today. Legend has it that he designed the church based on postcards of European cathedrals, drawing concepts in the sand to convey his ideas to his craftsmen. The result was the most unusual and distinctive church in the region. During special occasions, the church is lit up at night with colorful spotlights, giving it even more of an illusory appearance. A plaque in the entrance of the parish proclaims the attendance of a few former priests. It reads: *"Los curas Miguel and José Joaquin Hidalgo Ofrecieron misa en este templo. 1748."* (The priests Miguel and José Joaquin Hidalgo offered mass in this church. 1748.) The church also produces the loudest sound in the city, with church bells that are nearly 6 feet high and 8 1/2 inches thick.

The church's interior has been remodeled on more than one occasion over the years and presents a diverse example of objects and decorations from a variety of periods and styles. The neoclassical altars blend with murals by Federico Cantú that depict not only religious topics but make social commentary as well. These murals were considered so radical when they were completed that a parish priest tried to have them destroyed. To the left, you will find the chapel of the Señor de la Conquista with the figure of the Cristo de la Conquista. This highly revered 16th-century statue was sculpted by Indians in the city of Pátzcuaro, Michoacán, and is constructed of a paste of maize stalks, stuck together with a gum made from orchid tubers and coated with chalk. Other religious artwork within the parish includes the image of Saint Michael the Archangel on one of the altarpieces, as well as a statue of Christ in the vestry that was designed by the religious sculptor Fidias Elizondo. Former president Anastasio Bustamante is buried in the basement (though his heart is in Mexico City) in a crypt that is open to the public during *Día de los Muertos* (Day of the Dead). On Sunday, masses are held on the hour from 6 AM to 1 PM and again at 6 PM and 8:15 PM.

TEMPLO DE LA CONCEPCION (CHURCH OF THE IMMACULATE CONCEPTION)

Canal and Hernandez Macias, San Miguel de Allende, Gto. 37700
Open: Daily 10 AM–7 PM

This church is best known as "Templo de Las Monjas" (Church of the Nuns) because it originally belonged to the Order of the Immaculate Conception. Its size was considered excessive for the number of nuns that occupied it in the second half of the 18th century, which some historians have put at around eight. The funds for this church were put up by Josefa de la Canal, daughter of Don Manuel Tomás de la Canal, one of the city's great benefactors. Construction on this church was begun in 1755 by the architect Francisco Martinez Gudiño and, like La Parroquia, it was completed by Zeferino Gutierrez in the 19th century. In 1891, Gutierrez added a dome that was inspired by the Church of Saint-Louis des Invalides in Paris. This building also briefly housed an art school in the 1960s. The church's spacious atrium allows you to admire its enormous neoclassical interior, which is decorated with baroque sculptures that frame the doors, and a collection of paintings by famous artists such as Miguel Cabrera and Juan Rodriguez Juárez. Sunday masses are offered in English at 10 AM.

TEMPLO DE NUESTRA SEÑORA DE LA SALUD (CHURCH OF OUR LADY OF HEALTH)

Mesones and Plaza Civica, San Miguel de Allende, Gto. 37700
Open: Daily 7 AM–7 PM
This church, which faces Plaza Civica, dates back to the 18th century. It was commissioned by Father Luis Felipe Neri de Alfaro to be used as the chapel of the prestigious School of San Francisco de Sales. The interior is a Latin cross layout decorated with several oil paintings from prominent 18th-century artists, including several by Agapito Ping. This church features a dome covered with bright yellow and blue tile and an unfinished tower that houses the oldest bell in the city. It is also one of only six churches in Mexico with a concave entrance (*abocinada*), which is in the shape of a carved conch shell with a single eye inside a triangle. This symbolizes the omnipresence of God. However, there is also a local belief that this is actually because the church has the power to cure eye ailments.

TEMPLO DE SAN FRANCISCO

Calle San Francisco and Avenida Juárez, San Miguel de Allende, Gto. 37700
Open: Daily 7 AM–8 PM
Just northeast of the Jardín Principal, at the corner of Juárez and San Francisco, you will find a church that appears to be much more dated than La Parroquia. In fact it is, with a connected chapel (known as the Chapel of the Third Order) dating all the way back to 1713. The main building is the convent church of San Francisco, which was constructed with donations from wealthy families and funds from bullfights. Construction began in 1779, and it was finished 20 years later by the architect Francisco Eduardo Tresguerras. It has an

The bell tower of the Templo de San Francisco in San Miguel de Allende

The courtyard of the Templo de San Francisco in San Miguel de Allende

intricate churrigueresque façade with a lofty neoclassical tower. In front of the church is a small courtyard containing a monument to Christopher Columbus. Inside are nine altars and a neoclassical interior with paintings depicting the death of St. Francis. On Sunday, masses are held at 7:15 AM, 10:30 AM, noon, 6 PM, and 7:15 PM.

OTHER SITES

CRISTO REY DEL CUBILETE
Cerro del Cubilete
Open: Daily 6 AM–7 PM
At the highest point of the mountain
known as Cerro del Cubilete, nearly 8,500
feet above sea level, at a point that is pur-
ported to be the geographic center of
Mexico, you will find one of Mexico's
most important religious monuments.
Cristo Rey, or Christ the King, is a small
chapel topped by a giant, 65-foot bronze
art deco statue of Jesus that was built by
Nicolás Mariscal in 1944, at the site of a
similar but smaller statue that was
destroyed during the Cristero War. The
statue holds his arms open as two angels
kneel at his feet, presenting him with a
crown of thorns and a royal crown, repre-
senting martyrdom and glory. These figures rest upon a concrete hemisphere
that is meant to represent the universe. A
small chapel makes up the base of the
statue. Inside, the altar rests upon a circular platform and a large crown hangs
above, symbolizing the divine royalty of
Christ. The site also provides an exten-

This giant 65-foot bronze statue of Jesus is located at the geographic center of Mexico.

sive view of the entire region. This statue has become one of the most frequented religious
sites in Mexico, especially for the feast of Cristo Rey on November 21. The sculpture can be
accessed by a paved road that winds up the mountain until it comes to a roundabout
underneath the monument.

Cristo Rey is located about 30 minutes outside of Guanajuato, about halfway to Silao. To
get to Cristo Rey, you can sign up for the tour at the tourist office in Guanajuato. The tour
lasts about three hours and costs $10. However, if you'd rather go on your own, there are
buses that go up to the shrine from the Guanajuato bus station. These buses make the trip
about nine times a day between 6 and 6 during the week, and even more than that on the
weekend. Round trip bus fare costs about $4. To drive there, take Highway 110 southwest
toward Silao for about 10 miles and take the side road to the right, headed to La Valenciana.

SANTUARIO DE ATOTONÍLCO
Atotonílco, Gto.
Open: Daily 9 AM–7 PM
Seven miles northeast of San Miguel de Allende is the small but venerated sanctuary of
Atotonílco, meaning "place of the hot waters." This site was a hacienda when, in 1740, a
priest named Luis Felipe Neri de Alfaro acquired the land and began the construction of

The interior of the Atotonilco sanctuary is covered with murals by the indigenous artist Miguel Antonio Martínez de Pocasangre.

the church. Alfaro commissioned an indigenous artist named Miguel Antonio Martínez de Pocasangre to paint murals that have since made this church famous. Over the next 11 years, construction was completed on this impressive chapel. It contained an ornate altar of carved, gold-encrusted wood embellished with paintings on Venetian mirrors. Additionally, the lives of Catholic saints and martyrs and scenes of the Last Judgment are linked by ornate banners and colorful floral decoration. The church has been referred to as the "Sistine Chapel of the Americas," and almost every square inch of the walls and ceilings inside the sanctuary is covered with fresco paintings in a raucous expression of Mexican folk art. The murals also portray angels, archangels, saints, and demons amidst decorations of fanciful flowers and fruits. However, not all of this art is so jovial. There are many images of tortured, suffering souls as well as a 17th-century statue of Jesus bleeding horribly from his wounds. Years of neglect and environmental degradation have put all the artwork in this sanctuary in extremely fragile condition. In fact, the World Monuments Fund has put this church on its list of the world's hundred most endangered monuments.

However, the sanctuary of Atotonilco retains an honored place in Mexican religious culture. It has become a place where worshipers come to make atonement for their sins. Each year, thousands come to participate in such religious practices as sleeping on cold stone floors, crawling around the perimeter of the church on bare and bloodied knees, as well as wearing crowns of thorns and flagellating themselves with whips. In perhaps the most important annual event held at this shrine, large crowds of pilgrims walk in a solemn procession from the Atotonilco shrine to San Miguel de Allende. They carry the statue known as the Milagrosa Imagen del Señor de la Columna (the Miraculous Image of the Lord of the Column). It is highly venerated and has had several miracles attributed to it. In fact, the tradition of the procession began in the 18th century after San Miguel de Allende had been hit by an epidemic. A dying merchant asked for the statue to be brought to him in his final hours. As the story goes, once the statue was brought into his home, the man recovered and the epidemic broke.

The church is surrounded by a nearly deserted village of extremely poor residents, so a visit to this church is unlikely to be an uplifting experience. In fact, you are likely to be met by crippled beggars when you exit the shrine. However, you are unlikely to come away without being affected in some way. To get here, take Highway 51 north out of San Miguel de Allende or south out of Dolores Hidalgo. Turn west off the highway at Rancho Viejo.

Outdoor cafes are a great setting for relaxing with a cup of coffee.

6

Restaurants and Food Purveyors

When it comes to restaurants, San Miguel de Allende and Guanajuato are two completely different cities. Because of its unique history of drawing creative and ambitious people, San Miguel de Allende has a vibrant culinary scene with a wealth of fashionable restaurants. And although many are expensive by Mexican standards, they are generally far less expensive that what you would expect to pay north of the border. Furthermore, much of the cuisine is heavily influenced by the culinary traditions of the chefs that have come to settle here. You will find fine examples of French cuisine, Italian cuisine, South American cuisine, and Asian cuisine, among others. Of course, San Miguel de Allende also has plenty of fine Mexican restaurants that serve up traditional specialties. In fact, this city has become somewhat of a Mecca for chefs looking to learn a thing or two about Mexican cooking.

Guanajuato, on the other hand, has a culinary scene that is just beginning to flourish. There have been chefs that have come here and set up interesting restaurants, particularly in recent years, though not as many as in San Miguel de Allende. And if you spend an extended period of time in Guanajuato, you may find yourself quoting Chevy Chase from *The Three Amigos:* "Do you have anything besides Mexican food?" Guanajuato does have restaurants that serve up international cuisine and do it well. However, this is largely limited to a small number of Italian and French restaurants. The vast majority of Guanajuato's restaurants have menus that offer strictly Mexican food. Furthermore, these menus start to look the same after a while. That said, if Mexican food is your thing, you're bound to love Guanajuato. These restaurants range from tourist-oriented establishments to smaller places frequented by locals, which offer a much more home-cooked food atmosphere.

Most of these more traditional Mexican restaurants will offer a *menu del día* (also known as the *comida*), or menu of the day. This is a meal consisting of an appetizer, a soup, a traditional Mexican entree, a dessert, and a beverage. You will usually get your choice of two soups and two or three entrees (one of the choices is usually a type of enchilada). The drink is usually a pitcher of *agua fresca* (flavored water) such as *jamaica* (hibiscus) with unlimited refills, and the dessert can be anything from flan to a couple of slices of fruit. All this is served on traditional Mexican ceramic ware, which enhances the experience. These meals come at a fairly reduced price, usually not more than 5 or 6 dollars. If you go with the *menu del día*, don't expect large, Outback-sized portions. These meals, though they have several courses, are modest but satisfying. This is a great option if you're traveling on a budget or with kids (who aren't particularly picky eaters), or if you're just in the mood for something "authentic."

The menu del día is a great way to have an authentic Mexican meal.

Another wonderful feature about life here is the (mostly) healthy food that is conveniently available as you walk around these beautiful cities. In the morning, small convenient shops will sell freshly squeezed orange juice for just over a dollar. The proprietor will measure out the juice as he squeezes it into a plastic cup. Then he will pour it into a plastic sandwich bag and stick a straw in it and you're good to go. Okay, you can't really set it down, but it is convenient and it cuts down on waste. In the morning you will also find street-side stands selling cups of an assortment of fresh fruit for about $1.50. You can have this fruit topped with condiments such as honey, granola, or whipped cream, or just eat it plain. Either way, it's a treat. In the afternoon, the fruit stands are replaced by stands selling *chicharrrones*, potato chips, and corn on the cob. Condiments for corn on the cob, or *elotes*, include margarine, chili powder, and mayonnaise. Expect a strange look if you ask for it plain.

You may consider eating at these street vendors to be a roll of the dice. However, that is basically true of anything you eat that you do not make yourself. The food here likely contains ingredients that your system is not used to. In terms of sanitation, any street vendor or restaurant that is busy should be okay. Like you, Mexicans have no desire to frequent an establishment if it is going to make them sick.

Vendors selling fresh fruit are a common sight in the morning.

GUANAJUATO

Mexican Food

EL ABUE RESTAURANTE

473-732-6242
Calle San José #14, Guanajuato, Gto. 36000
Open: Daily 12:30 PM –10:30 PM
Price: Moderate to Expensive
Cuisine: Mexican-Italian
Serving: L, D
Credit Cards: MC, V
Handicap Access: No
Located in an attractive house right off the beautiful Plaza Baratillo, this Mexican-Italian fusion restaurant offers one of the best dining experiences in Guanajuato. The owners have developed recipes from those of their grandparents who were from Italy and the Oaxacan region of Mexico. The mood is set with quiet music and good service. Dishes are made with quality ingredients and careful attention is paid to presentation here, creating a wonderful dining experience. The atmosphere is elegant but not stuffy. The margaritas are very good, as are the salads. There are continental favorites on the menu, such as filet mignon, as well as Italian and Mexican classics such as lasagna and *chiles en nogada.* Among the surprisingly delicious specialties you will find here are enchiladas *el abue,* dried fruit and meat rolled in tortillas and topped with a red Oaxacan mole sauce. The menu also includes several pasta selections, including fettuccine Poblano. The pastas and breads are made daily here. If you're not full, top your whole meal off with apple pie à la mode. Also, if you're looking for a bargain, come for the menu del día lunch during the week.

LA CABAÑA

473-732-7359
Ex-Hacienda de San Antonio #37, Guanajuato, Gto. 36000
Open: Daily 8:30 AM–11:30 PM

Vendors selling corn on the cob are a common sight in the evening.

Price: Moderate
Cuisine: Mexican
Serving: B, L, D
Credit Cards: MC, V
Handicap Access: Yes
Just east of the Ex-Hacienda San Gabriel de Barrera, you will find this Mexican restaurant, which offers a menu of traditional favorites and a relaxed atmosphere. This restaurant caters to families, and it has a small playground so that parents can eat while the kids play. It also offers event facilities with equipment such as audio/video systems and video screens. This restaurant is also equipped with satellite television and they show all the biggest sporting events, particularly soccer games. The décor is very colonial, with an open air dining area and cabaña-style chairs and tables.

EL CERRO DE LAS RANAS

473-732-5546
Juan Valle #7, Guanajuato, Gto. 36000
Open: Mon.–Sat. 9 AM–10 PM
Price: Inexpensive
Cuisine: Mexican
Serving: B, L, D
Credit Cards: None
Handicap Access: No
This small restaurant serves up all the traditional Mexican favorites, with plenty of chicken and beef dishes. If you want a quick, cheap meal, try the chicken *flautas*, which are fried rolled tacos made with flour tortillas. This restaurant also has a daily menu del día, which makes a great way to taste a variety of classic Mexican specialties at a small price. It also has a bar where you can get your favorite drinks as well.

Many stores sell fresh-squeezed orange juice in the morning.

EL CHAHISTLE

473-733-2535
Carretera Guanajuato Km. 7.8, Guanajuato, Gto. 36000
Open: Mon.–Sat. 8 AM–11 PM; Sun. 10 AM–7 PM
Price: Inexpensive to Moderate
Cuisine: Mexican
Serving: B, L, D
Credit Cards: MC, V
Handicap Access: Yes
This is a relaxed Mexican restaurant with a homey atmosphere. It is furnished with handmade wooden chairs and tables in a narrow dining room decorated with *artesenia*. They specialize in traditional Mexican dishes such as *pozole* and *milanesa*. Of course, you will also find enchiladas here, as well as a wide variety of tacos. They are also quite proud of their hamburger, though hamburgers in Mexico tend to be hit and miss, with the majority of them falling on the miss side. It's usually best to stick with Mexican food when eating at a Mexican restaurant, and for that, this restaurant is a good choice. For those traveling with children, this restaurant has a playground where the kids can play while parents enjoy the meal.

LA CLAVE AZUL RESTAURANTE

473-732-1561
Segunda de Cantaritos #31, Guanajuato, Gto. 36000
Open: Mon.–Thurs. 1:30 PM–10 PM; Fri.–Sat. 1:30 PM–12 PM
Price: Inexpensive
Cuisine: Mexican
Serving: L, D
Credit Cards: None
Handicap Access: No
This small and interesting restaurant is

Enchiladas *Mineras:* Specialty of Guanajuato

Mexico is known for its spicy culinary inventions. Mexicans love their spicy food and they seem to put chili on just about everything. They put chili on corn on the cob, fresh fruit, popcorn, and even in beer. However, while zesty flavors are a common ingredient in all Mexican food, culinary specialties are surprisingly varied by region. Along the coasts, food tends to be quite simple and incorporates a lot of seafood. There, simple seviche and fish tacos are perfect for a hot day at the beach. Inland, dishes revolve much more around beef, pork, and chicken and often have intricate sauces. What might surprise you about the food of Central Mexico is that many so-called Mexican dishes that you would probably find very familiar are almost unknown here. Both nachos and the deep-fried burritos known as chimichangas were developed in Texas. In fact, the burrito itself is not something you are likely to find very far south of the border. Generally speaking, tortillas are almost always made of corn and the flour tortillas you do find are of comparable size—nothing like the plate-size tortillas necessary to make burritos. Consequently, if you were to ask for a burrito, your server might find it strange that you're ordering a small donkey.

Many cities in Mexico have specific dishes associated with them. For example, the city of Puebla is famed for its chiles en nogada stuffed with pork. In Oaxaca, tamales are wrapped in banana leaves instead of corn husks. Guanajuato is known for a dish called enchiladas *mineras,* or "miner's enchiladas." This is a hearty dish that was likely a favorite among miners after a grueling day deep in the earth. It is comprised of cheese enchiladas in a red sauce piled high with grilled chicken, roasted carrots, and potatoes on a bed of shredded lettuce, and topped with crumbled *queso fresco* and Mexican sour cream. Needless to say, this dish looks like a complicated jumble of food. However, it's actually a wonderful blend of flavors that can really satisfy an appetite after a day of touring around. You will find this dish on the menu of just about every Mexican restaurant in town. Give it a try to experience Guanajuato's tastiest tradition.

Enchiladas mineras is the specialty dish of Guanajuato.

tucked into a narrow alley just off Plazuela San Fernando. The interior of the restaurant resembles an old colonial tavern with stucco walls, a rounded arch, and niches filled with modern art. Here and there are small, dark wooden tables and chairs creating an intimate atmosphere. There is a full bar here so you can get your favorite drink. However, there is no menu. Each day, the restaurant offers a different traditional Mexican dish for about $10. It's worth every *centavo*.

CONDE RUL

473-732-9725
Jardín del la Unión #6, Guanajuato, Gto. 36000
Open: Daily 8 AM–11 PM
Price: Moderate to Expensive
Cuisine: Mexican
Serving: B, L, D
Credit Cards: MC, V
Handicap Access: Yes
This restaurant is located right on the Jardín de la Unión at the Hotel Luna, making it an ideal place to meet up with friends. It offers both outdoor seating on the plaza as well as indoor seating in a comfortable dining room. The menu offers primarily Mexican dishes such as enchiladas and chicken mole. However, there are several international dishes on the menu as well, such as spaghetti and steaks. This restaurant also offers a good breakfast menu and the Jardín de la Unión is a lovely place to start your day.

LAS LEYENDAS

473-732-3146
Plazuela San Fernando #34, Guanajuato, Gto. 36000
Open: Daily 12:30 PM–10:30 PM
Price: Moderate to Expensive
Cuisine: Mexican
Serving: L, D
Credit Cards: MC, V
Handicap Access: Yes

This Mexican restaurant is located in the Plazuela San Fernando and offers open-air seating on the plaza as well as a small indoor dining area. The plaza seating is where it's at though, with a relaxed atmosphere and a chance to enjoy Guanajuato's beautiful weather. The menu is strictly Mexican with plenty of chicken and beef dishes as well as *antojitos*, or appetizers, such as *taquitos, sopes* (kind of a small, thick tostada), *quesadillas,* and *flautas.* However, perhaps the most popular dish here is the *arranchera mocajete.* This is a *mocajete* (pronounced mocha-HEH-tay, a stone grinding bowl) filled with chicken, chorizo, beans, and *arranchera* steak, and topped with thick slices of *queso fresco* (a soft white cheese) and a nopál. Delicious stuff.

LAS MERCEDES

473-733-9059
Calle de Arriba #6, Guanajuato, Gto. 36000
Open: Daily 8 AM–10 PM
Price: Expensive
Cuisine: Mexican
Serving: B, L, D
Credit Cards: MC, V
Handicap Access: No
This elegant Mexican restaurant is located in a house in the hills overlooking Guanajuato. The dining area is impeccably decorated and furnished in a colonial style that is both comfortable and sophisticated. The house is lit with small lamps and fixtures that hang from a wood-beamed ceiling. The walls are covered with paintings and *artesenia* knick-knacks. The dining experience is further complemented by the view, which overlooks the city. The menu is filled with traditional Mexican favorites such as chicken mole and enchiladas that are beautifully presented. Reservations are highly recommended.

LA PIRINOLA

473-733-9752
Avenida Juárez #25, Guanajuato, Gto. 36000

Open: Daily 8 AM–9 PM
Price: Inexpensive to Moderate
Cuisine: Mexican
Serving: B, L, D
Credit Cards: MC, V
Handicap Access: With difficulty
Just west of Plaza de la Paz on the right side of the street, you will find this small Mexican restaurant that happens to be a favorite among locals. Here, traditional Mexican favorites are served up with the relaxed and casual feel of an everyday taco shop. The breakfast also includes such standard dishes as *huevos a la Mexicana* and *huevos rancheros*. Lunch and dinner entrees such as chicken mole, steak a la *Tampiqueña*, and of course enchiladas *mineras* are all served in generous portions. They also offer a variety of wines, beers, and spirits to accompany your meal. This restaurant has a spin-off restaurant in the Plazuela San Fernando called Pirinola II, which also serves delicious traditional specialties. However, this restaurant has the benefit of being located in one of the best plazas in the city. At Pirinola II, you will also find a very good *menu del día*.

RESTAURANTE TERESITA

473-731-2183
Paseo de la Presa #76, Guanajuato, Gto. 36000
Open: Daily 8 AM–10 PM
Price: Expensive
Cuisine: Mexican
Serving: B, L, D
Credit Cards: AE, MC, V
Handicap Access: Yes
Located at the Villa Maria Cristina hotel, this fine dining restaurant combines sophistication with traditional Mexican cuisine. The gourmet menu changes daily and meals are attractively presented on white dishes. The dining area is a room set in off-white colors contrasted with dark-stained woods. High ceilings and an elegant fireplace combine to create an ambiance

reminiscent of aristocratic colonial times. There is also an intimate wood-paneled bar area offering fine wines, whiskeys, and tequilas. An interesting array of desserts as well as port wines and Sherries make the perfect way to round off your culinary experience.

TIC TIC

473-732-2320
Avenida Juárez #119, Guanajuato, Gto. 36000
Open: Daily 8 AM–11 PM
Price: Inexpensive to Moderate
Cuisine: Mexican
Serving: B, L, D
Credit Cards: MC, V
Handicap Access: Yes
This traditional Mexican restaurant is located on the west side of the historic district near the Hidalgo Market. It offers a relaxed family atmosphere and all of the traditional favorites. For breakfast, they offer a variety of dishes served up with a Mexican flair. For lunch or dinner, the chicken mole is wonderful, as are the enchiladas *mineras*. However, the specialty of the house is *pozole verde*, a hominy soup in a tomatillo broth with chunks of pork. Of course, there is an assortment of wines and Mexican beers to complement your meal as well.

TRUCO 7

473-732-8374
Calle del Truco #7, Guanajuato, Gto. 36000
Open: Daily 8:30 AM–11 PM
Price: Inexpensive to Moderate
Cuisine: Mexican
Serving: B, L, D
Credit Cards: MC, V
Handicap Access: With difficulty
This small but cozy restaurant has a rather bohemian atmosphere to it and seems to be popular with the university crowd. It occupies a building that was originally built for the extremely wealthy Valenciana silver

Bagel Cafetín is a popular place to have a coffee and log on to the Internet.   Mary Delgado

mining family. The dining area is small and a bit crowded, which seems appropriate since the walls are jam-packed with all kinds of rustic knickknacks and paintings by local artists. The menu offers up all of the traditional favorites. Try the tortilla soup, it is very good here. This restaurant also offers espresso drinks and delicious pastries such as the traditional Mexican dessert *pastel de tres leches,* a white cake that is saturated with sweet milk. If you've never tried it, this might be the place to do so.

Coffee Shops

BAGEL CAFETÍN

473-733-9733
Callejón de Potrero #2, Guanajuato, Gto. 36000
Open: Mon.–Sat. 9 AM–4 PM
Price: Inexpensive
Cuisine: Coffee shop
Serving: B, L
Credit Cards: MC, V
Handicap Access: No
Right up the street from the Museo Iconográfico del Quijote and the Templo de San Francisco, you will find this interesting little coffee shop. Decorated with modern art deco furniture, it looks more like a late night drinking lounge but it's actually a great place to stop and get a bagel sand-wich. They offer all your favorite espresso and coffee drinks, including frappucinos, as well as juices and Italian sodas. Because the Spanish school Escuela Mexicana is just up the street, you are bound to run into international language students here, mak-ing it a great place to meet people. This shop is also equipped with free wireless Internet access, so if you happen to have a laptop on you, this is an excellent place to come and catch up on your E-mail. Just ask at the cash register for the login code.

CAFÉ CONQUISTADOR

473-734-1358
Pocitos #35, Guanajuato, Gto. 36000
Open: Daily 9 AM–10 PM
Price: Inexpensive
Cuisine: Coffee shop
Serving: B, L, D
Credit Cards: MC, V
Handicap Access: Yes
If you're a coffee lover, you're likely to be drawn to this hole-in-the-wall restaurant by the aroma of fresh roasted coffee beans. Besides espresso drinks and café Americano (American-style coffee), this little café offers baguette sandwiches and pastries. You can also buy coffee by the kilo.

International

BOSSANOVA CREPERIA CAFÉ

473-733-1423
Plazuela San Fernando #46, Guanajuato, Gto. 36000
Open: Mon.–Sat. 10 AM–12 PM; Sun. 10 AM–8 PM
Price: Moderate
Cuisine: French
Serving: B, L, D
Credit Cards: MC, V
Handicap Access: Yes
If you happen to find yourself in Plazuela San Fernando in the morning with an hour to kill, point yourself in the direction of the tables with the distinctive yellow table-cloths, have a seat, and get ready to enjoy yourself. This rather relaxing open-air café is reminiscent of something you might expect to find in a square in Paris. Coincidentally, the specialty here is crepes. In fact, they serve 50 varieties of crepes here, as well as some pretty good espresso drinks. The fruit crepes are very good, but if you're looking for something really deca-dent, try the chocolate crepe. If that wasn't enough, this café does more than just crepes and coffee. The menu also includes salads and pastas as well as fine wines and a

Crepes are works of art at Bossanova.

selection of beers. There is also indoor seating available and, in fact, the dining room is attractive. However, this is perhaps the most relaxing plaza in Guanajuato, so you might as well enjoy it. All dishes are prepared with fresh ingredients, no cans.

EL CAFÉ GALERÍA
473-732-2566
Calle Sopeña #10, Guanajuato, Gto. 36000
Open: Daily 8:30 AM–11:30 PM
Price: Moderate
Cuisine: International
Serving: B, L, D
Credit Cards: MC, V
Handicap Access: Yes
This restaurant is located in a small cubby-hole of a space across the street from Teatro Juárez, but most of their business takes place at the outdoor tables set up just to the left of the theatre's steps. This area is a

popular place for foreigners to congregate and have a coffee or a drink. Tables can be hard to get here in the early evening. The menu includes several choices that are more common north of the border, such as hamburgers and French fries. However, there are also plenty of local choices such as enchiladas *mineras* and chicken mole. The food is good but the main attraction is the location, which has a lot of foot traffic and is right next to where street performers often set up to entertain crowds.

CAFÉ ATRIO
473-731-1213
Agora del Baratillo s/n Planta Baja, Guanajuato, Gto. 36000
Open: Daily 9 AM–11 PM
Price: Inexpensive
Cuisine: International
Serving: B, L, D

Credit Cards: MC, V
Handicap Access: No
This is a somewhat tough restaurant to pin down because it has such a varied menu. It's mainly a snack bar, though they offer several items that are not typical of such an establishment. It's an informal place with several lounge chairs, as well as several small tables. In the morning, it's a bit like a college cafeteria with bagels, coffee, and juices. For lunch, they offer pastas, salads, tacos, nachos, and even Buffalo wings. From Monday through Thursday, they offer complimentary coffee with the purchase of a slice of pie. Later in the evening, this restaurant transforms into a cocktail bar with jazz and lounge music.

LA CAPELLINA

473-732-7224
Sopeña #7, Guanajuato, Gto. 36000
Open: Daily 1:30 PM–12 AM
Price: Moderate
Cuisine: International
Serving: L, D
Credit Cards: MC, V
Handicap Access: Yes
If you begin to feel that all of the restaurants in Guanajuato have different versions of the same menu, you might want to look across the street from Teatro Juárez, where you will find this little gem of a restaurant. This building was built in 1673 and was used to melt gold and silver. Today, it is a simply decorated restaurant offering up an array of interesting dishes. Despite the fact that it is located in a 17th-century building, this restaurant is something fairly new to Guanajuato. The cuisine here offers a nice mix of Mexican, Italian, Moroccan, and even Thai influences. The menu includes soups, salads, pastas, seafood, meats, and vegetarian dishes. These items range from handmade pizza to salmon with *guajillo* chile to beef filet prepared in red wine. And speaking of wine, there is a nice wine list to complement your meal as well. Come here

on the weekends to enjoy bossanova and Cuban music as well as Latin jazz.

CHAO BELLA

473-732-6764
Positios #52, Guanajuato, Gto. 36000
Open: Tues.–Sat. 2 PM–10 PM; Sun. 2 PM–6 PM
Price: Moderate
Cuisine: Italian
Serving: L, D
Credit Cards: MC, V
Handicap Access: No
This beautifully decorated Italian restaurant is located in a house typical of Guanajuato's historic district. Therefore, dining areas are spread out among several small rooms with just a few tables in each, creating an intimate ambiance. The menu features many authentic Italian pasta dishes such as lasagna and fettuccini, as well as salads and pizzas. There is also a good selection of wines and other spirits to complement your meal.

FRASCATI

473-732-2158
Jardín de la Unión #1, Guanajuato, Gto. 36000
Open: Daily 1 PM–12 AM
Price: Expensive
Cuisine: Italian
Serving: L, D
Credit Cards: AE, V, MC
Handicap Access: Yes
This restaurant is conveniently located right on Jardín de la Unión on the second floor of the Hotel San Diego. It is accessible by the stairs in the front lobby or by the elevator at the back of the lobby. This restaurant has locations throughout Mexico and they serve mainly Italian dishes. The décor is modern with an upscale feel, though the 1980s rock ballads playing low over the sound system didn't add to this ambiance. If you can, get a window seat, which looks onto the main plaza. The open

air from these windows blows in a cool breeze as you look out over the plaza. The menu offers plenty of Italian favorites, such as lasagna, cannelloni, and shrimp linguini as well as hand-tossed pizzas. There is also complimentary fresh bread and a nice wine list to complement the meal. And if you're not full at the end of your meal, you might consider trying the giant ice cream brownie dessert, which is practically a meal in itself.

EL GALLO PITAGORICO

473-732-6758
Constancia 10-A, Guanajuato, Gto. 36000
Open: Tues.–Sun. 2 PM–11:30 PM
Price: Moderate to Expensive
Cuisine: Italian
Serving: L, D
Credit Cards: MC, V
Handicap Access: No
Behind the Templo de San Diego, if you follow the steep hill up to the right of Bar Ocho and, at the restaurant sign, follow an even steeper set of stairs, you will find an Italian restaurant hidden away up here that has an excellent view of the city, particularly at night. The problem with that is that you will have to walk these steps in the dark, so do be careful. The restaurant is decorated with plenty of Mexican handicrafts, but the menu offers a nice array of Italian specialties such as lasagna and penne *arrabiata*. There are also seafood and steak dishes as well as a large selection of wines and liquors. Getting here can be a chore, but the payoff is equally rewarding. Reservations are recommended.

IK-ETZNAB ALTA COCINA

473-102-5146
www.ik-etznab.com
Camino a Ojo de Agua, Guanajuato, Gto. 36000
Open: Tues., Wed., Sun. 1 PM–6 PM;
Thurs.–Sat. 1 PM–7 PM
Price: Expensive
Cuisine: International
Serving: L, D
Credit Cards: MC, V
Handicap Access: No
If you're tired of the same old traditional Mexican dishes that are served all over the place in Guanajuato, perhaps you may be in the mood for some elaborately prepared haute cuisine. If so, head over to this strangely named restaurant (whose name is a Mayan word meaning "mirror wind"). The dining room here is designed to offer a wonderful view of the Santa Rosa Mountains while you enjoy a unique dining experience full of texture, flavor, and creativity. This being haute cuisine, the dishes are small and rich. The menu varies by season as Chef Iván Monzón brings to bear his years of experience cooking in Spain, France, and around Mexico.

EL JARDÍN DE LOS MILAGROS

473-732-9366
www.eljardindelosmilagros.com.mx
Calle Alhóndiga #80, Guanajuato, Gto. 36000
Open: Tues.–Sun. 1 PM–10 PM
Price: Expensive
Cuisine: International
Serving: L, D
Credit Cards: MC, V
Handicap Access: Yes
Located in a 17th-century hacienda, this restaurant offers visitors an elegant dining experience in a truly colonial setting. Attractive dining areas are set among gardens with stone walls and white *zapote* trees as well as in a large dining room. The menu is an interesting mix of Spanish, Mexican, and Mediterranean flavors such as their chief dish, mahi mahi in cilantro sauce with apples and Spanish pistachios. Great attention is paid to the texture, taste, and presentation of the dishes here. They also offer a wide selection of wines to complement these meals. Reservations are highly recommended.

MARISCOS LA JAULA

473-734-0180
Bulevar Guanajuato #39, Guanajuato, Gto.
36000
Open: Mon.–Sun. 10 AM–8 PM
Price: Inexpensive to Moderate
Cuisine: Seafood
Serving: B, L, D
Credit Cards: None
Handicap Access: With difficulty
This restaurant may not look like much,
being located as it is in a tent. However,
when you look past the aluminum fencing
and the folding chairs, what you find is a
pretty good seafood restaurant in the heart
of Mexico. Despite the fact that there hasn't
been a lot invested in furnishings here, it is
clean and it has a laid-back atmosphere
that is conducive to having a good time, and
they offer free wireless Internet. There is
also plenty to choose from here for any
seafood lover, including seviche, shrimp
cocktails, and even paella. Come on Friday
afternoons for live music, as well.

EL MIDI

Plazuela San Fernando #22, Guanajuato,
Gto. 36000
Open: Mon.–Fri. 2 PM–6 PM
Price: Inexpensive
Cuisine: French
Serving: L, D
Credit Cards: No
Handicap Access: Yes
This restaurant is owned and run by a
woman named Veronique, who was born in
the south of France. She left there many
years ago, but she has brought the healthy
attitude of the Mediterranean to Central
Mexico. This is a buffet-style restaurant
that has a beautiful salad bar with fresh
vegetables and fresh bread. Most items
here are vegetarian but there are some
entrees for the meat eaters out there. In
addition to salads, they serve a variety of
pies, tarts, and other pastries. This restaurant is also well known for its *aguas frescas*,
which are slightly less sweet than what you
generally find hereabouts. Plus, Veronique
offers such wonderful combinations as
strawberry-guava and lime-cucumber.
There are tables on the plaza where you can
sit with a salad and enjoy the day.

PIZZA PIAZZA

473-731-1213
Plaza San Fernando, Guanajuato, Gto.
36000
Open: Daily 11 AM–10 PM
Price: Inexpensive
Cuisine: International
Serving: L, D
Credit Cards: None
Handicap Access: No
This being a college town, there are plenty
of pizza joints to be found in Guanajuato.
Now, there's New York pizza—thin and
crispy—and Chicago pizza—thick and
loaded—and then there's Mexican pizza.
This pizza tends to be thin and doughy with
not as much cheese as you are probably
used to. I suspect that most pizza connois-
seurs will find Mexican pizza disappoint-
ing, just as burger connoisseurs will find
Mexican burgers rather disgusting.
However, with that understood, the pizza at
Pizza Piazza is pretty good, particularly
when you consider the inexpensive price.
The restaurant is reminiscent of the pizza
parlors you might have eaten in as a
kid—kind of dark inside with faux wooden
booths and hanging Coke light fixtures.
There is no seating on the plaza, but at the
back of the restaurant a large wooden door
opens onto the plaza. There's also an old
jungle gym inside the restaurant that would
never meet American safety standards, but
the kids will have fun playing on it if you
keep an eye on them.

REFUGIO CASA COLORADA

473-734-1151
Cerro de San Miguel #13, Guanajuato, Gto.
36000

The Plaza de la Paz bustles with foot traffic.

Open: Mon.–Sat. 8 AM–11 PM; Sun.
6 AM–10 PM
Price: Expensive
Cuisine: International
Serving: B, L, D
Credit Cards: AE, MC, V
Handicap Access: Yes
Located at the Refugio Casa Colorada hotel behind the El Pípila statue, this gourmet restaurant specializes in haute cuisine and fine wines. The restaurant has a comfortable inside dining area but you might prefer sitting on the patio where the panoramic view of the city is a complement to any meal. This restaurant also has separate private rooms available for business meetings and special occasions that seat up to a hundred people.

EL RINCÓN DE LOS SABORES
473-118-6776
Alhóndiga #84, Guanajuato, Gto. 36000
Open: Mon.–Sat. 2 PM–11 PM; Sun. 10 AM–
6 PM

Price: Expensive
Cuisine: Seafood
Serving: L, D
Credit Cards: AE, MC, V
Handicap Access: Yes
This elegant restaurant uses seafood as a base to create a diverse menu of traditional Mexican dishes and international flavors. Here you will find seafood with pastas, fresh vegetables, and other fine ingredients that create a fusion of aromas and tastes. There are several dishes that feature meats and poultry, as well. Dining is surprisingly informal here, done in an open-air dining area with shade umbrellas and wrought iron chairs and tables, perfect for enjoying the wonderful weather of Guanajuato.

TASCA DE LA PAZ
473-734-2225
Plaza de la Paz #28, Guanajuato, Gto. 36000
Open: Daily 8 AM–12 PM
Price: Moderate
Cuisine: International

Food and Water

Getting used to the food in Mexico can sometimes take a period of adjustment, particularly if you are not used to the spices. A little common sense will go a long way toward making sure you don't get sick while you're enjoying yourself with sun and fun. Spend the first few days of your trip taking it easy. Many people go on vacation, suddenly find themselves free of the workaday hours and the social mores of home—and sometimes tend to cut loose and overdo it. Resist this urge—at least for a little bit. Give yourself time to adjust to jet lag, new cuisine, and the other strains traveling to a new place puts on your body.

Some hotels have purified water systems, and others generally offer complimentary bottled water. Try to carry bottled water wherever you go so that you have it on hand to keep yourself hydrated. Be sure to brush your teeth with bottled water if you're staying at a hotel without a purified system (if the hotel has one it will be advertised). Restaurants serve ice made of purified water, so it's fine to have ice in your Coke. You may see street vendors selling flavored *aguas frescas* (fresh waters) with flavors such as *sandía* (watermelon), *limón* (lemonade), *melón* (cantaloupe), and *fresa* (strawberry). These are delicious and can be quite refreshing—but there is no guarantee that they are made with purified water. It's a good idea to ask just to be sure, though the answer is likely to be yes either way. The bottom line is that by consuming these refreshments, you are taking a calculated risk, and you need to be aware of that.

In fact, any time you consume peeled, raw fruits and vegetables, or eat from a small "locals" restaurant or street vendor, you are taking a risk of getting sick. You can help to prepare your body for these risks by eating plenty of yogurt for several weeks prior to your trip. Scientific studies have shown that the live active cultures in yogurt have properties that protect the intestinal tract from gastrointestinal infection.

Street vendors offer good home-style food at a cheap price.

Serving: B, L, D
Credit Cards: MC, V
Handicap Access: Yes
This restaurant offers outdoor seating on the Plaza de la Paz, a perfect place for taking in the early morning sun on a springtime day, or enjoying an afternoon on this historic plaza. Because this is an open square surrounded by colonial buildings with plenty of foot traffic, this is a good place to people watch and get a feel for this beautiful town. The menu is a mix of Mexican and Spanish cuisine, including all the traditional favorites such as enchiladas *mineras,* steak *milanesa,* paella, and a variety of Spanish tapas. The menu also offers a good selection of wines and beers, making it a good choice to start off an evening, as well.

YAMUNA

473-732-1873
Calle del Sol #10, Guanajuato, Gto. 36000
Open: Mon.–Sat. 9 AM–8 PM
Price: Moderate
Cuisine: Vegetarian/Indian
Serving: B, L, D
Credit Cards: MC, V
Handicap Access: Yes
This vegetarian restaurant has a joyful atmosphere and serves a variety of dishes that are sort of an Indian-Mexican fusion of flavors. It is decorated with fine Indian linens as well as Indian art on the walls, quite a strange and wonderful find in the heart of Mexico. They serve breakfast beginning at 9 AM and serve a multiple-course lunch beginning at 1 PM. This meal comes with basmati rice and a salad and has different entrée options every day. Of course, you may also order any of these options à la carte. If you're a vegetarian, or you're just looking for a lighter meal that is something a little different, this restaurant is a great option.

Bakeries

ORRANTI LUIS

473-732-0114
Avenida Juárez #138, Guanajuato, Gto. 36000
Open: Mon.–Sat. 10 AM–8:30 PM; Sun. 11 AM–5 PM
This traditional Mexican bakery is a great place to stop for some snacks. Just grab one of the circular trays and a pair of tongs and have at it. The walls are lined with racks where you will find Mexican pastries of all sorts, from cookies to doughnuts, to *bolillo* bread used to make tortas.

PANADERIA Y PASTELERIA LA INFANCIA

473-732-6754
Cantarranas #60, Guanajuato, Gto. 36000
Open: Daily 8:30 AM–6 PM
This small bakery offers an array of Mexican pastries and they are located near several small plazas where you can sit and enjoy your choices. They also sell soft drinks and juices.

Ice Cream

BASTIEN CUE HUMBERTO

473-732-0116
Avenida Juárez #36, Guanajuato, Gto. 36000
Open: Daily 11 AM–9 PM
This ice cream shop offers a large assortment of ice cream, frozen yogurt, and popsicles. Afterward, the Plaza de San Francisco just up the street is a great place to go and enjoy your treat.

NEVERIA Y MESCELANEA SIGLO XXI

473-732-3895
Jardín de la Unión #13, Guanajuato, Gto. 36000
Open: Daily 11 AM–10 PM
This ice cream shop has the advantage of being located right on Jardín de la Unión.

Fresh-baked bolillo bread makes a great snack.

There may be no better way to spend an afternoon in Guanajuato than sitting on the benches in this plaza with an ice cream in your hand, watching all the people walk by.

SAN MIGUEL DE ALLENDE

Mexican Food

BUGAMBILIA
415-152-0127
Hidalgo #42, San Miguel de Allende, Gto. 37700
Cuisine: Mexican
Open: Daily 12 PM–11 PM
Price: Moderate to Expensive
Serving: L, D
Credit Cards: MC, V
Handicap Access: Yes
This is one of the more elegant Mexican restaurants in San Miguel. Unlike many restaurants in town, this one offers a spacious dining area as well as an attractive patio. It has a lively, boisterous ambiance that is perfect for a night out with friends. This restaurant offers a wide-ranging menu of traditional Mexican favorites. The *chiles en nogada* (stuffed poblano chile with walnut cream sauce) are a good bet, as is the chicken mole. And the *sopa azteca* (tortilla soup) may be the best in town. The margaritas tend to be made on the strong side, and you can finish your meal by trying the homemade ice cream brought in from Dolores Hidalgo. If you plan on eating here on the weekend, it's a good idea to make reservations in advance.

LA CAPILLA
415-152-0698
Cuna de Allende #10, San Miguel de Allende, Gto. 37700
Cuisine: Mexican Fusion
Open: Wed.–Mon. 1 PM–11 PM
Price: Expensive
Serving: L, D
Credit Cards: MC, V
Handicap Access: Yes
Nestled against La Parroquia in the heart of San Miguel, this elegant restaurant offers innovative cuisine in a comfortable atmosphere. With its unbeatable view of the cathedral and mountains beyond, the rooftop terrace offers a wonderful place to dine. From red snapper in mango sauce to Poblano chicken stuffed in goat cheese, most dishes are constructed around poultry and seafood and are presented in an elegant style. If you're just looking for somewhere to have a drink, there is also a piano bar here.

CASA DE SIERRA NEVADA EN EL PARQUE
415-152-7155
Santa Elena #2, San Miguel de Allende, Gto. 37700
Cuisine: Mexican
Open: Daily 7 AM–11 PM
Price: Moderate
Serving: B, L, D
Credit Cards: MC, V
Handicap Access: Yes
This fine dining restaurant is located beneath the columns of the Hotel Casa Sierra Nevada adjacent to Parque Benito Juárez. The menu features a variety of exotic

Mexican fusion specialties such as *mole de Marilú* and carpaccio of fresh salmon and sautéed shrimp, as well as traditional favorites such as *sopa azteca* (also known as tortilla soup) and *leche quemada a la naranja* (orange-flavored burnt milk fudge). This restaurant is refined and elegant while maintaining an informal atmosphere. The patio overlooking the garden is a particularly pleasant place to enjoy lunch. There is also a bar here that is open from 1 PM to 10:30 PM. On Thursdays, it features live music from 2 PM to 4 PM and again from 8 PM to 10 PM, with Thursday night two-for-one happy hour specials running from 6 PM to 8 PM.

EL CORREO
415-152-4951
Correo #23, San Miguel de Allende, Gto. 37700
Cuisine: Mexican
Open: Wed.–Mon. 8 AM–11 PM

Price: Inexpensive
Serving: B, L, D
Credit Cards: None
Handicap Access: Yes
This small restaurant specializes in a relatively small number of classic Mexican dishes. Don't expect any burritos, nachos, or chimichangas here, though. These dishes are purely old Mexico, such as *sopes* (kind of a thick tostada), moles, and enchiladas. Here, you will also find a homey ambiance. Located just a half block east of the Jardín, it is also convenient. Reservations are accepted but not necessary.

MAMA MIA
415-152-2063
Umarán #8, San Miguel de Allende, Gto. 37700
Cuisine: Mexican
Open: Daily 8 AM–2 AM

Mariachi music complements any Mexican meal.

Price: Inexpensive to Moderate
Serving: B, L, D
Credit Cards: MC, V
Handicap Access: Yes

A popular saying among the residents of San Miguel is that you don't know this city until you've been to Mama Mia. If you're looking for a place with great atmosphere, this is a good bet, offering a wide range of menu items. From 8 AM to 1 PM, there is an inexpensive Mexican buffet breakfast as well as a nice selection of á la carte options. In the evening, the restaurant has a much more Italian flavor, with delicious specialties such as vegetarian lasagna and a variety of pastas. The restaurant has several bars that feature a variety of live music—from jazz to flamenco—and tends to attract a young crowd. And located just a few steps from the Jardín, it has the benefit of being convenient as well.

PUEBLO VIEJO

415-152-4977
Umarán #6, San Miguel de Allende, Gto. 37700
Cuisine: Mexican
Open: Daily 8 AM—11 AM; 1 PM—3 AM
Price: Moderate
Serving: B, L, D
Credit Cards: MC, V
Handicap Access: Yes

This restaurant is designed to offer the experience of spending a day in a 19th-century Mexican village. It is perhaps the best place in town for breakfast, with such specialties as eggs Benedict and superb blueberry pancakes, as well as dishes with a more Mexican flavor, such as *huevos rancheros* and *huevos a la Mexicana*. Upstairs, you will find La Azotea terrace bar with wonderful views of the city.

OLÉ-OLÉ

415-152-0896
Loreto #66, San Miguel de Allende, Gto. 37700

Cuisine: Mexican
Open: Daily 1:30 PM—9 PM
Price: Inexpensive
Serving: L, D
Credit Cards: None
Handicap Access: Yes

This colorful restaurant is tucked away several blocks north of San Francisco Plaza along Juárez. Decorated with bullfighting memorabilia, including several mounted bull heads, you will not mistake this place for a swanky French restaurant. The cuisine is fajitas and that's about it. Chicken, beef, shrimp, and vegetables in large portions, with a friendly staff to make sure you have a good time. Top it off with a cold beer and you have yourself a Mexican meal you won't soon forget. If the lighting is too dim in the front dining room, venture to the back of the restaurant where large skylights give the feeling of sitting in a colonial courtyard. And remember to bring cash because credit cards aren't accepted here.

EL RINCONCITO

415-154-4809
Refugio #7, San Miguel de Allende, Gto. 37700
Cuisine: Mexican
Open: Mon., Wed.–Sat., 1 PM–9 PM; Sun. 1 PM–7 PM
Price: Inexpensive
Serving: L, D
Credit Cards: none
Handicap Access: Yes

Its name means "the little corner" and this small family-run restaurant presents an inviting atmosphere that will make you think of it as your neighborhood corner restaurant. The menu offers traditional Mexican options that are done well and satisfying. It is a bit off the beaten path but that works to its advantage since prices here are very reasonable, and it does not have the overbearing ambiance that is synonymous with tourist traps.

RINCÓN DE DON TOMÁS

415-152-3780
Portal de Guadalupe, San Miguel de
Allende, Gto. 37700
Cuisine: Mexican
Open Mon.-Sat. 8:30 AM–10 PM; Sun.
8:30 AM–9 PM
Price: Moderate to Expensive
Serving: B, L, D
Credit Cards: MC, V
Handicap Access: Yes
This busy restaurant is conveniently located
right on the Jardín. The entire plaza-facing
side of the restaurant is open, allowing for
prime people watching while you dine. The
extensive menu offers a wide range of
options, the majority of which are traditional Mexican specialties. The fajitas are
highly recommended. In case you're only
looking for a place to relax and watch the
activity of the Jardín, there is also a nice
dessert and coffee menu as well as a full
bar—be sure to try a fresh-squeezed margarita. The restaurant's biggest drawback,
however, is that it seems to be a popular
spot for smokers. Getting stuck downwind
of a group puffing away is enough to make
you wish you'd gone elsewhere. In any case,
the food is good, the atmosphere is pleasant, the service is friendly, and the location
justifies the prices, which are slightly
higher than smaller nearby restaurants.

TORTA MUNDO

Umarán #29, San Miguel de Allende, Gto.
37700
Cuisine: Mexican
Open: Mon.–Sat. 10:30 AM–6:30 PM
Price: Inexpensive
Serving: L
Credit Cards: None
Handicap Access: Yes
This hole-in-the-wall restaurant specializes in tortas, Mexican sandwiches made
with fluffy, fresh-baked bread. There are
no frills here, but the tortas are quick, delicious, and make a great lunch when you're
on the go. There are about a half dozen
plastic tables on the outdoor patio where
you can plan your next adventure.

Coffee Shops

EL BUEN CAFÉ

415-152-5807
Jesús #23, San Miguel de Allende, Gto.
37700
Open: Mon.–Sat. 8:30 AM–4:30 PM
Price: Moderate
Cuisine: Coffee Shop
Serving: B, L
Credit Cards: MC, V
Handicap Access: Yes
This is a wonderful little neighborhood
coffee shop conveniently located near the
center of town. It's mainly a breakfast
restaurant, but they also do lunch as well as
a variety of bakery goods. The restaurant
has seating for about 40 people.

CAFÉ DEL JARDÍN

415-152-5006
Portal de Allende #2, San Miguel de
Allende, Gto. 37700
Cuisine: Coffee Shop
Open: Daily 7 AM–12 AM
Price: Inexpensive
Serving: B, L, D
Credit Cards: None
Handicap Access: Yes
This small restaurant is located on the west
side of the Jardín Principal. This is a great
place to come and enjoy a *café con leche*.
There is seating on the patio where you can
sit back and plan the day's adventure. They
serve all kinds of coffee and espresso
drinks, along with desserts and a small
selection of foods such as sandwiches, sal-
ads, and pizza. Because of its great location,
it also tends to be crowded.

CAPPUCCINO'S

415-154-8000
San Francisco #1, San Miguel de Allende,

Gto. 37700
Cuisine: Coffee Shop
Open: Daily 9 AM–10 AM
Price: Inexpensive
Serving: B, L
Credit Cards: None
Handicap Access: With difficulty
This small coffee shop is located right off
the Jardín. It is located in a nook of a shop
with a few tables and a courtyard. Besides
fresh brewed coffee, they also sell whole
bean coffee and a wide variety of teas.

LA FINISTERRA CAFÉ

415-152-5784
Ancha de San Antonio #9, San Miguel de
Allende, Gto. 37700
Cuisine: Coffee Shop
Open: Wed.–Mon. 9 AM–6 PM
Price: Inexpensive to Moderate
Serving: B, L
Credit Cards: None
Handicap Access: No
This lovely shop is located at the back
through the foyer. It's a narrow almost hall-
way of a restaurant and you may have to do a
little navigating around diners to get to the
counter. The left wall is covered with works
by local artists, and the entire right wall is a
series of arched windows that look onto
gardens and let in plenty of natural light.
There is also patio seating. They have a
large breakfast menu as well as light lunch
items such as sandwiches and salads. They
also serve beer and wine.

LAS MUSAS CAFÉ

415-152-4946
Hernández Macías #75, San Miguel de
Allende, Gto. 37700
Cuisine: Coffee Shop
Open: Mon.–Sat. 9 AM–8 PM; Sun.
10 AM–2:30 PM
Price: Inexpensive
Serving: B, L
Credit Cards: None
Handicap Access: Yes

This restaurant is located near Bellas Artes
and has a nice garden patio that is great for
sipping coffee. They serve espresso drinks
and coffee as well as meals such as pasta
and tacos.

SAN AGUSTÍN CAFÉ

415-154-9102
San Francisco #21, San Miguel de Allende,
Gto. 37700
Cuisine: Coffee Shop
Open: Mon.–Fri. 8 AM–11 PM; Sat.–Sun.
9 AM–12 AM
Price: Inexpensive to Moderate
Serving: B, L, D
Credit Cards: None
Handicap Access: Yes
This restaurant across the street from the
Templo de San Francisco is a great place to
come anytime, particularly for dessert.
Here, you can indulge in the Mexican tradi-
tion of *churros y chocolate*, homemade
doughnuts and hot chocolate. They also
serve all kinds of coffee, as well as beer,
wine, and soft drinks. And, if you're in the
mood for a light meal, they also have a large
menu of *tapas*.

International

AZAFRÁN

415-152-7482
Hernández Macías #97, San Miguel de
Allende, Gto. 37700
Cuisine: International
Open: Thurs.–Tues. 11 AM–11 PM
Price: Expensive
Serving: L, D
Credit Cards: MC, V
Handicap Access: Yes
This highly modern restaurant and lounge
presents an atmosphere of contemporary
art and superb service. It was created by a
local designer and chef named Luis
Maubecín, who offers a gourmet meal for
the discriminating palate. The interna-
tional cuisine here has a Mediterranean

flair and tends to be a bit frilly. Enjoy drinks with a variety of atmospheres, such as a patio bar, lounge area, or in the garden.

CASA PAYO

415-152-7277
Zacateros #26, San Miguel de Allende, Gto. 37700
Cuisine: Argentinean
Open: Daily 12 PM—11 PM
Price: Moderate
Serving: L, D
Credit Cards: MC, V
Handicap Access: Yes
Casa Payo specializes in Argentine-style cuisine, and that means one thing: Meat. The charcoal grilled steaks are large and tasty and there are plenty of other choices for the devoted carnivore, such as barbecue ribs and chicken. The restaurant also offers a nice wine list of national and imported flavors. Live music each night adds to the relaxed atmosphere you will find here.

CHIMARRÃO

415-154-9091
Diez de Sollano #28, San Miguel de Allende, Gto. 37700
Cuisine: Brazilian
Open: Daily 12 PM—11 PM
Price: Moderate to Expensive
Serving: L, D
Credit Cards: MC, V
Handicap Access: Yes
This restaurant offers delicious Brazilian cuisine with an emphasis on fine meats of all sorts. You're sure to find the basics, such as beef, chicken, turkey, and pork. Additionally, you can come here to sample seasonal flavors that are not so everyday, such as lamb and rabbit. There is also a salad bar and a good wine list to complement any meal.

LA GROTTA

415-152-4119
Cuadrante #5, San Miguel de Allende, Gto. 37700
Cuisine: Pizza
Open: Daily 1 PM—11 PM
Price: Inexpensive
Serving: L, D
Credit Cards: None
Handicap Access: Yes
This popular pizza restaurant offers a couple of dining areas, including seating upstairs that has a great view of the street. That said, seating can be hard to get some nights, with the line stretching out onto the street.

HARRY'S NEW ORLEANS CAFÉ

415-152-2645
Hidalgo #12 (near the Jardín), San Miguel de Allende, Gto. 37700
Cuisine: Cajun Seafood
Open: Daily 12 PM—1 AM
Price: Moderate to Expensive
Serving: L, D
Credit Cards: MC, V
Handicap Access: Yes
This restaurant brings a taste of the Big Easy to old Mexico with traditional New Orleans dishes such as spicy Cajun jambalaya and seafood gumbo. The French influence doesn't stop there. There are many interesting choices here. The menu at Harry's is extensive, with everything from prime rib to Louisiana Rock Cornish game hen to duck. For dessert, be sure to try their chocolate truffle cake. Needless to say, you won't find many Mexican dishes, so this is not the place for local fare. Food is served both indoors and on the patio. There is a bar that is great for hanging out with friends. Happy hour is served Monday through Friday from 5 PM to 7 PM with two-for-one martini specials all day and night on Wednesdays. Live jazz is also featured Tuesday through Thursday nights, and on Sunday evenings as well.

L'INVITO

415-152-7333
Ancha de San Antonio #20, San Miguel de
Allende, Gto. 37700
Cuisine: Italian
Open: Daily 1 PM—11 PM
Price: Moderate
Serving: L, D
Credit Cards: MC, V
Handicap Access: Yes
This small Italian restaurant offers Italian
specialties that range from classic dishes,
such as spaghetti and meatballs, to more
interesting dishes such as chicken à la
Rossini with a creamy lemon sauce. The
owner and chef, Silvia Bernardini, prepares
her dishes with attention to detail to attain
subtle flavors, as opposed to relying on a
copious use of spices. The menu also
includes a variety of salads and desserts.

EL MARKET BISTRO

415-152-3229
Hernández Macías #95, San Miguel de
Allende, Gto. 37700
Cuisine: French
Open: Mon.—Fri. 1 PM—11 PM; Sat.—Sun.
1 PM—12 AM
Price: Moderate to Expensive
Serving: L, D
Credit Cards: MC, V
Handicap Access: Yes
This restaurant features an attractive courtyard as well as a small bar (or *Petit Bar*) with
a fireplace—a nice place to have a cup of
coffee during a chilly San Miguel evening.
There are two menus—full and light—which
offer a nice variety of options that focus on
traditional French cooking, including
dishes such as chateaubriand béarnaise,
tournedos montagnarde, braised sweet-
breads, and salmon à la Provençale. The
Petit Bar has a nice wine list and the courtyard offers meals with an upscale but informal feel. Live music is offered on the
weekends.

EL PEGASO RESTAURANT BAR

415-152-1351
Corregidora #6, San Miguel de Allende,
Gto. 37700
Cuisine: International
Open: Mon.—Sat. 8:30 AM—10 PM
Price: Inexpensive to Moderate
Serving: B, L, D
Credit Cards: MC, V
Handicap Access: Yes
This casual, inviting restaurant is a favorite
among the local expatriate crowd. It is
eclectically decorated with a fireplace and
walls covered with work from local artists.
In fact, you can buy any of it right off the
wall. Breakfast is a busy time at El Pegaso,
and there is good reason. They do it well,
with Mexican specialties as well as dishes
more standard north of the border, such as
eggs Benedict, oatmeal, and lox and bagels.
The lunch and dinner menu also features
Mexican dishes as well as international cuisine, with items from hamburgers to Asian
specials. They also have pastrami and
corned beef sandwiches as well as kung pao
chicken and beef Thai salad. In addition,
there is an extensive dessert menu. Drop by
if you're hankering for some cheesecake,
raspberry cream pie, or mile-high lemon
meringue pie.

ROMANO'S

415-152-7454
Hernández Macías #93, San Miguel de
Allende, Gto. 37700
Cuisine: Italian
Open: Tues.—Sat. 5 PM—11 PM
Price: Inexpensive to Moderate
Serving: D
Credit Cards: None
Handicap Access: Yes
Another popular place to eat, this restau-
rant offers pizzas and pastas in generous
portions with both indoor and outdoor din-
ing. Pastas are made on the premises and
most of the ingredients here are organic.
The pizzas and bread are baked in a wood

burning oven. Being the popular place that it is, it does tend to get busy so making reservations in advance is probably a good idea. Also, remember to bring your pesos because credit cards are not accepted here.

TÍO LUCAS

415-152-1996
Mesones #103, San Miguel de Allende, Gto. 37700
Cuisine: Steak
Open: Daily 12 PM–12 AM
Price: Moderate
Serving: L, D
Credit Cards: MC, V
Handicap Access: Yes
This restaurant is known for its live blues and jazz music that starts nightly at 9 PM. There is also live accordion music on Friday and Saturday from 3 PM to 5 PM. Though a fairly wide variety of items are on the menu, it is mainly known for its steaks, which are served in large portions. Another innovation is the house Caesar salads, which are prepared at your table in large

salad bowls. It's a fun touch at first but can take several minutes longer than the novelty lasts. This is a very good restaurant but certainly not a place to go if you are looking for an intimate evening out. The seating in the main dining room can get noisy and more than a bit cramped. Make sure you have reservations if you are planning to dine here on the weekend. The outdoor patio offers a nice alternative, with its open-air seating and overhanging tree covered in glowing red lamps. This is a nice place to have a margarita and enjoy the music. Be warned, however, the drinks here tend to be on the strong side.

Bakeries

ANTARES PASTELERÍA

415-154-8910
Ancha de San Antonio #4A, San Miguel de Allende, Gto. 37700
Open: Mon.–Sat. 10 AM–8:30 PM; Sun. 11 AM–5 PM
If you are looking for a cake or pastries for a

Mexican bakeries offer a variety of delicious baked goods.

special occasion, this is the place. They sell all types of beautifully presented fruit tarts, pastries, breakfast rolls, cheesecake, gelatin deserts, cookies, and I could go on. They make fine-looking wedding cakes, as well.

LA BUENA VIDA

415-152-2211
Alhóndiga #84, San Miguel de Allende, Gto. 37700
Open: Mon.–Sat. 8 AM–5 PM
If you enter the building across from Bellas Artes and look to the left, you'll find this charming little bakery that is great for breakfast or lunch. They sell many types of breads, rolls, cookies, and other sorts of pastries. There are also several tables on a shaded patio where you can sit and enjoy it all.

LA CASITA FELIZ

415-152-6555
Guadiana #15B, San Miguel de Allende, Gto. 37700
Open: Mon.–Sat. 10 AM–8 PM; Sun. 10 AM–6 PM
This bakery sells a large array of cookies, cakes, and pastries. It is located just down the street from the Insituto Allende, so this is an ideal place to come for snacks between classes.

LA COLMENA PANADERÍA

415-152-1422
Reloj #21, San Miguel de Allende, Gto. 37700
Open: Mon. 8:30 AM–2 PM and 5 PM–9 PM;

Tues.–Sat. 6 AM–2 PM and 5 PM–9 PM
This is what the Mexican bakery experience is all about. Just grab a tray and load it up with whatever you want. And since the Jardín Principal is just a half block away, it makes the perfect place to sit and enjoy your pastries.

Ice Cream

DOLCE CAPRICCIO

Correo #2, San Miguel de Allende, Gto. 37700
Open: Daily 8:30 AM–9 PM
This small Italian shop is located near the Jardín. Here you can get Italian ices, espresso drinks, and bakery treats.

DOLPHY

415-152-2744
Plaza Principal #24, San Miguel de Allende, Gto. 37700
Open: Daily 10 AM–10 PM
This ice cream shop is located on the north side of the Jardín. They sell ice cream, doughnuts, coffee, and other healthy favorites. It is a great place to come on a hot afternoon.

SANTA CLARA

415-152-5141
Ancha de San Antonio #1, San Miguel de Allende, Gto. 37700
Open: Daily 10 AM–9 PM
This ice cream and frozen yogurt shop also doubles as a small postal store, with a fax machine and E-mail service.

The ice cream vendors of Dolores Hidalgo sell many strange and wonderful flavors.

Ice Cream of Dolores Hidalgo

In the Plaza Principal in the town of Dolores Hidalgo, surrounded by the monuments to Mexico's independence, there is a monument of a different kind. Tucked away in the southwest corner of the plaza, there is a monument to the palate. Here, vendors loiter behind stands filled with some of the best homemade ice cream you will find anywhere. These ice cream stands have become a reason in and of themselves for visiting Dolores Hidalgo. The beautiful plaza is the perfect venue for kicking back and enjoying a large waffle cone of your favorite flavor. Or, better yet, why not take this opportunity to try flavors that you've never had—and likely won't have the chance to try anywhere else.

For just a little over a dollar, you can get a small cup of ice cream, or there are larger options available as well. There are, of course, plenty of the more traditional flavors. For the truly timid, there is vanilla, strawberry, or chocolate. There is also mango, pistachio, or caramel with pecans. These are all wonderful flavors and probably a good choice if you're going to have a large cone. However, while you're there you might think about asking for a sample of some of the more unusual flavors that are available. You'll be surprised to find that these strange flavors actually make for some truly interesting ice cream. For example, avocado ice cream is rich and creamy with just the subtle flavor of the green fruit. Corn has bits of corn throughout but it's not bad. Even *mole* flavored ice cream is worth a taste if you otherwise like this traditional dish. Other unusual flavors worth trying include beer and tequila. These two are actually not so much an ice cream but rather shaved ice flavored with these beverages. In any case, these flavors are subtle but present and the taste of alcohol is also present, particularly in the tequila-flavored dessert. Perhaps you don't want to wolf down a large container of this stuff, but it's good for a try. Flavors to stay away from would include pork rind, fish, and shrimp. The shrimp ice cream is particularly disagreeable, with chunks of shrimp throughout. Speaking as someone who loves shrimp, it is not a flavor or texture that lends itself to good ice cream. And when you stop to consider that there aren't any fresh shrimp anywhere near Dolores Hidalgo, you realize that for the good of your own well-being, this is a delicacy that is better left alone.

That said, if you find yourself in Dolores Hidalgo, take time to sample the local flavors. It's an experience that is unique as well as delicious.

A street vendor selling toys

7

Recreation

If you have gone to the trouble to visit San Miguel de Allende or Guanajuato, chances are you are not there looking for a Jet Ski or golf destination. Simply put, if that is what you're looking for, there are plenty of destinations in Mexico better suited to your expectations. However, this region of Central Mexico has plenty of natural resources that make it a great destination for those looking to dig a bit deeper for their satisfaction. The wide varieties of natural wonders are enough to blow the mind of just about any botanist or bird-watcher. The nature reserves located nearby are full of endangered plants, and the region is lucky enough to sit smack dab on the migratory path of a number of neotropical birds from farther north. Furthermore, the geologic activity underneath the ground of this region provides it with natural springs that are particularly suited for the health spas that have popped up. Rock climbing is quickly becoming a popular sport here, with so many sheer cliff faces nearby. In addition, the nature reserves have been developed to accommodate hikers, campers, and horseback riders, with facilities to suit all skill levels. And if relaxation and rejuvenation is the purpose of your visit, there are more than enough masseuses, yoga instructors, and personal growth coaches located here to meet your needs. If all else fails, sit under the shade of the nearest plaza with an ice cream cone and all will be good.

If you are attending a Spanish school or other affair put together by an organization, you will likely have your recreation taken care of in advance. Spanish schools, cooking schools, and the like have itineraries that are planned out from the moment you get up until late in the day. These groups not only tour the city's historical and cultural venues but quite often they also organize relief efforts to local indigenous villages and fill your day with so many activities that you will probably cherish any free time as an opportunity to relax.

Ecotourism

Even though the state of Guanajuato has always had a reputation as a place that is rich in natural beauty, this fact is easy to overlook since it is located in a country known for gorgeous beaches and jungle landscapes, which this landlocked state is decidedly short on. However, Guanajuato is blessed with a highly varied landscape, with forests and arid desert areas pocked with volcanic craters. Furthermore, this area lies on the migratory path of several species of neotropical birds from Canada, the United States, and as far away as Alaska. As these birds fly south for the winter, bird-watchers from just as far descend on Guanajuato hoping to catch a glance of a rare specimen. All of this makes San Miguel de Allende, Guanajuato, and Dolores Hidalgo, as well as their surrounding environs, wonderful cities from which to launch an expedition into the natural wonders of Central Mexico.

The reserves of this region offer plenty of opportunity for outdoor recreation.

CERRO DE LA BUFA

Off Carretera Panorámica (southeast of Guanajuato)
Open: Daily 24 hours
This is an impressive rock formation located on the outskirts of Guanajuato. Residents of the city consider this an enchanted place with many legends surrounding it. It is also a popular location for hiking. There are trails that will take you along old quarries that were used to build the city's oldest buildings. There are also a variety of climbing routes suitable for beginning and advanced climbers. Camping is also allowed here free of charge. However, keep in mind that this is a semidesert climate so the nights can get quite cold. To get to La Bufa, take the Carretera Panorámica toward the Hospital ISSSTE, southwest of Presa de la Olla. Turn east at the electrical substation and the site will be right in front of you. Be sure to bring plenty of water as well as light snacks.

EL CHARCO DEL INGENIO BOTANICAL GARDENS AND ECOLOGICAL RESERVE

415-154-4715
www.laneta.apc.org/charco
Jesus 32, San Miguel de Allende, Gto. 37700
Open: Daily from sunrise to sunset
This 250-acre ecological reserve is located just outside of San Miguel de Allende. Here you will find a wealth of impressive vistas as you explore its abundant plants and wildlife, as

well as aqueduct ruins that once served the city. Many of the plants you find here are endangered. There are also enormous cliffs that rise up from the foliage that make great places to enjoy these majestic landscapes; they look over San Miguel, the broad Rio Laja Valley, and the Sierra de Guanajuato in the distance. The reason for the abundance of wildlife here can be found in the canyons, where permanent spring waters give rise to a wide range of flora, from cactus to aquatic plants, as well as in the wetlands, where the Las Colonias Dam has created a permanent body of water in the heart of the botanical garden. Here, trees and shrubs grow along the water's edge and more than 20 species of migratory birds take shelter. Entrance to the park costs about a quarter and children under 10 get in free. A series of paths take visitors from the information center located at the entrance to points of interest throughout the reserve. These include the Plaza of the Four Winds, a community and ceremonial space with panoramic views; the impressive cliffs of the canyon; and the reservoir with its resident and migratory birds. These paths are patrolled by the reserve security staff and are ideal for walking, running, mountain biking, and to access rock climbing areas. Adjacent to the botanical gardens, there is a nature park that has a recreational area with vehicle access and facilities for camping, picnics, and horse-back riding. To get here from downtown San Miguel de Allende, go east on Salida a Querétaro and turn left at the traffic circle with the equestrian statue. Continue straight on the cobbled stone and dirt roads for about 500 yards, then follow the signs guiding you left to the park. The easiest way to get here using public transportation is to take a taxi.

LA GRUTA
Carretera a Dolores Hidalgo Km. 9.5, San Miguel de Allende, Gto. 37700
Open: Sunrise to midnight
La Gruta is located in a private park 15 minutes out of San Miguel de Allende. The taxi ride here will cost you about $14 round trip. This is a series of three caves with a series of pools that are fed by a thermal spring. These pools vary from lukewarm to steaming. The pools are the product of the volcanic activity that is happening under the ground around this region, and they get hotter the farther into the caves you go. Many also believe that these pools have rejuvenating effects on the body. The caves are well lit, and you can swim into them and pick the water temperature that you prefer. Admission is about $7. There are changing rooms here and you can also rent a locker, and you can eat at a small outdoor restaurant that sells typical Mexican food. You can rent this site between 6 PM and 12 AM for private parties of up to 10 people for around $190. Make reservations through Señora Flor de María Perez, at 415-185-2099.

SANTUARIO CAÑADA DE LA VIRGEN
415-154-8771
South of San Miguel de Allende
Open: Daily sunrise to sunset
Cañada de la Virgen is an archaeological and nature preserve that lies southwest of San Miguel de Allende. The archaeological site consists of five groups of pre-Hispanic monuments that were once the northern reaches of the Toltec empire. These monuments include pyramids as high as 60 feet, terraced basements, an ancient ball court, and an avenue that is the length of nearly 11 football fields. These sites have also yielded many smaller artifacts, such as pottery and metal tools, that have been a boon to archaeologists trying to piece together the ancient past of this region. However, 900 years of neglect have

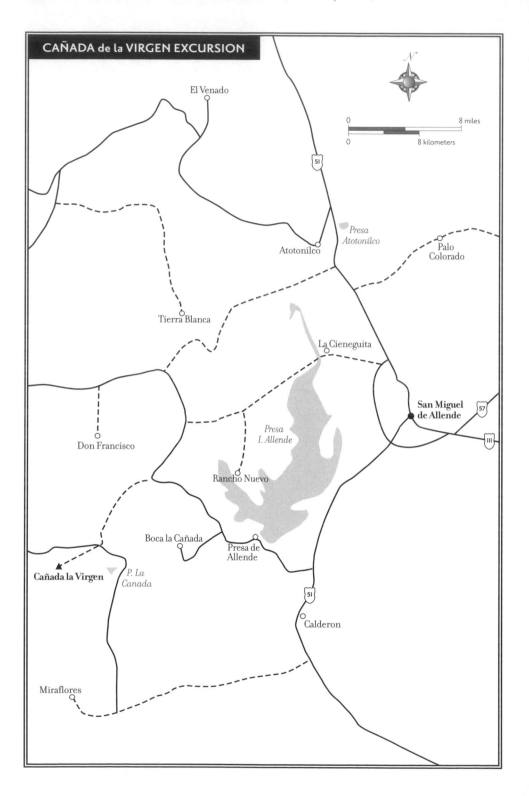

CAÑADA de la VIRGEN EXCURSION

El Venado

N

0   8 miles

0   8 kilometers

51

Presa Atotonilco

Palo Colorado

Atotonilco

Tierra Blanca

La Cieneguita

San Miguel de Allende

57

Don Francisco

Presa I. Allende

III

Rancho Nuevo

Boca la Cañada

Presa de Allende

Cañada la Virgen

P. La Canada

51

Calderon

Miraflores

taken their toll on these sites and therefore they are currently not open to the public, though the INAH (National Institute of History and Anthropology) has plans to do so in the near future. This area is also one of the largest ex-haciendas in the state of Guanajuato and is ideal for outdoor activities such as hiking, camping, and horseback riding. There is a group in San Miguel de Allende that specializes in ecotours and spiritual excursions to this location (415-154-8771). They offer a wide range of services and tours, though they require guests to sign a wilderness agreement to protect the natural habitat. To get here on your own, take the road to Celaya south out of San Miguel de Allende, past the Presa de Allende Reservoir. Then take the road to the right and continue for another 9.3 miles.

SIERRA DE LOBOS
477-774-2121
North of León
Open: Daily sunrise to sunset
Located about 34 miles northwest of Guanajuato and only 18 miles north of the city of León is the Sierra de Lobos Nature Reserve. This reserve is an area of more than 250,000 acres and has been important for the protection and preservation of the Mexican wolf, which is also how this area got its name. Other animals that call this reserve home include pumas, white-tailed deer, flying squirrels, and a wide variety of birds. Numerous trails in the park will lead you along sheer cliffs and dams located within the park. If you are interested in an extended stay, there are also hotels located within the reserve. The grounds of this nature reserve are scarred by crags, ponds, and mountain streams, making it ideal for a wide range of outdoor activities, including rock climbing, fishing, hiking, and camping. However, keep in mind that it rains here quite regularly during the summer and gets quite cold during the winter. To get here, take León 37-S north toward Ocampo and look for the signs. You can get here by public transport by going to the central bus station in León and taking the bus to Ocampo. Tell the bus driver you want to get off at Vergel de la Sierra. Here you will find a hotel and visitor's center that offers guided tours for a nominal fee. Or, if you prefer, hike the trails independently.

VALLE DE SANTIAGO
South of Guanajuato
Open: Daily 24 hours
You will find the protected ecological zone of Valle de Santiago 54 miles south of Guanajuato, off Highway 110 and Highway 45. There is a village here called Camébaro, which was settled in 1607. Later in the 17th century, the Hospital de Tarascos was established here to care for the indigenous people who had fallen victim to a devastating epidemic of disease. The region is blessed with various microclimates, which have given rise to a wide array of wildlife, and it is pocked with volcanic craters. In fact, it is sometimes referred to as the *Siete Luminares*, or the Seven Lights, because of the seven volcanic craters in the area. These include La Alberca, which is famous for its sulfur waters; La Hoya de Cintura, filled with thermal springs; and La Hoya de las Flores, where you will find vestiges of a pre-Hispanic ceremonial town as well as several springs. And then there is a crater named Parangueo el Viejo, which has a tunnel nearly 1000 feet long that leads to a salt lake in the interior. The terrain here is mountainous with volcanic rock formations ranging from 6 feet to 66 feet, making it ideal for hiking, rappelling, mountain biking, and other outdoor activities.

Bullfighting

Because of the long Spanish occupation of Mexico, the culture here is deeply influenced by the culture of Spain. Consequently, bullfighting has been one of the most popular pastimes in the country for the last 400 years. Bullfighting in Mexico is very similar to Spanish-style bullfighting. The event begins with the *picadors* circling the bull on horseback, jabbing its shoulder muscles with lances. Next, running fighters called *banderilleros* enter the ring, thrusting barbed darts called *banderillas* into the bull's neck and shoulder region. Finally, the matador enters the ring. Matadors perform precise moves to impress the crowd and attract the bull in a manner that is considered graceful. The event ends with the matador killing the bull with a sword. These events also include other events such as rodeos, pig chases, and dances. However, these events have also become a source of controversy in recent years. Animal rights groups have railed against the sport, arguing that it is dangerous for the matador, the horses these picadors ride, and of course, is inhumane toward the bulls. These groups have had their influence and, in fact, for a time it was illegal for anyone under the age of 18 to attend a bullfight. However, that law has since been rescinded. In any case, bullfighting remains a prominent sport in Mexico from November to March.

PLAZA DE TOROS ORIENTE

Recreo #52, San Miguel de Allende, Gto. 37700

This plaza is located in a residential area and seats approximately 3,500 people. There are different prices for sitting in the *sombra* (shade) or the *sol* (sun). The *sombra* is more expensive. The seats are made of concrete but you can rent a cushion or bring one of your own. Most fights are scheduled during the winter season and during various festivals throughout the year. There will be posters advertising the fights posted around town. These posters will indicate whether the bullfights will feature *corridas de toros* with full matadors, or *novilleros*, which are aspiring matadors fighting bulls younger than four years old. There are usually four to six bullfights in a day's program.

ZONA RECREATIVA DE LAS PALOMAS

473-732-0294

Just north of Guanajuato

Open: Daily sunrise to sunset

Drive 15 minutes north of Guanajuato, off Highway 110, and you will come upon the nature reserve of Las Palomas, in La Cuenca de la Esperanza. This is a vast wildlife preserve and recreational zone popular with nature enthusiasts. It lies on the migratory path of several species of neotropical birds from Canada, the United States, and Alaska. There are said to be 172 different species of birds in this preserve, almost half of which are migratory. There are also other interesting animal species, such as white-tailed deer and lynxes. This reserve is crisscrossed by a series of rugged trails that are ideal for bird-watchers and naturalists, as well. These trails will also lead you to some of Guanajuato's most famous mines, such as the La Valencia, the Mina de Guadalupe, and the Real de Santa Ana. The preserve has trained guides that can provide you with in-depth information about the birds as well as the rest of the flora and fauna of the Guanajuato Sierras, for a nominal fee. In recent years, this area has seen development to accommodate increasing interest. There are now facilities here where you can rent bicycles, binoculars, camping gear, and even cottages. There are also sanitary facilities, food vendors, and marked camping areas.

Local plazas can be great places for kids to cut loose.   Mary Delgado

FAMILY FUN

Outside of the day camp listed below, there is very little here geared specifically toward kids. This is not to say these towns are not kid friendly. In fact, just the opposite is true. The large plazas are ideal places to set your kids free and let them run around. And you will never have to look far to find a street vendor selling balloons, plastic airplanes, and other toys to keep your kids occupied. Talk about family fun, this is a great way to spend a lazy afternoon relaxing in the warm Mexican weather. Throw in the museums and the myriad small shops, bakeries, and ice cream stores that line the street and your kids will never be wanting for something to do.

Spanish Summer Day Camp for Children

CENTRO BILINGUE DE SAN MIGUEL

415-152-5400
Correo #46, San Miguel de Allende, Gto. 37700
This program is designed to introduce children to Spanish in a fun, safe, and educational environment. Here, kids learn the language immersed in a cultural setting, dancing, cooking, doing arts and crafts, as well as other activities. Class sizes are limited to 10 students. This program costs $200 per week or $700 for four consecutive weeks.

FITNESS FACILITIES

AXIS GYM

415-154-5874
San Francisco #40, San Miguel de Allende, Gto. 37700
Open: Mon.–Fri. 7 AM–9 PM; Sat. 8 AM–2 PM
This is rather a small gym with weights and stationary bikes.

LYDIA WONG

415-152-5558
www.sanmiguelyoga.com
Mesones #101, San Miguel de Allende, Gto. 37700
Open: Times vary
Lydia Wong offers you the chance to rejuvenate yourself while on vacation. She offers holistic body work that can improve your state of mind, body, and spirit. She has many years of experience teaching these techniques and has worked with such celebrities as Jack Nicholson and Anjelica Houston. She offers classes in Feng Shui, Yoga, and Tai Chi.

MALANQUÍN COUNTRY CLUB

415-152-0516
Ancha de San Antonio
Open: Tues.–Sun. 8 AM–6 PM
This country club is located about 2 miles south of town on the road to Celaya. It has four clay tennis courts, a swimming pool, and a driving range. It also has a 9-hole golf course. Greens fees for nonmembers are around $40. Nonmembers can only tee off after 1 PM on the weekends. A caddie is about $7 plus tip and an electric cart is about $15. This club also offers a day camp for kids.

RAMIRO'S CLUB

415-152-2707
Potrero #8, San Miguel de Allende, Gto. 37700
Open: Mon.–Fri. 6:30 AM–10 PM; Sat. 6:30 AM–2 PM
This is a relatively large gym with a racquetball court and a personal trainer available for a nominal fee.

SAN MIGUEL HEALTH AND FITNESS CENTER

415-153-8395
Stirling Dickinson #27, San Miguel de Allende, Gto. 37700
Open: Mon.–Fri. 6:30 AM–10 PM; Sat. 8 AM–3 PM; Sun. 9 AM–1 PM
This is a large gym with modern equipment including weights, treadmills, and stationary bikes.

YOGA CON ANABEL

415-152-8129
Salida a Celaya, San Miguel de Allende, Gto. 37700
Open: Mon.–Thurs. 9:15 AM–10:30 AM; Sat. 9: 30 AM–11 AM

This experienced yoga instructor offers classes at a convenient central location. Bilingual classes are available and all levels are welcome.

SPAS

Artists and cultural tourists have long flocked to San Miguel de Allende and Guanajuato to enjoy their cultural treasures and creative atmosphere. For centuries, Mexicans have been aware of the restorative effects of the mineral-rich waters, volcanic mud, and native herbs in the area around San Miguel de Allende. The presence of these components has been attracting healers and herbalists to the area for decades. Today, these cities are quickly becoming a destination for spa vacationers seeking a reprieve from their frantic daily life. The spa industry here incorporates these elements into their treatments and therapies to enhance the spa experience. These treatments are designed to help you achieve both physical and inner harmony, release toxins, subdue stress and anxiety, as well as allay the disorders associated with the hectic modern lifestyle. This results in an experience that soothes your mind, pampers your body, and lifts your spirit. It can also be a key ingredient in making the perfect romantic getaway by creating the perfect setting for lovers to reconnect. Whether you aim to achieve a healthier lifestyle, experience a new culture, relieve stress, or simply pamper yourself, you will find what you are looking for in the spas throughout the region.

Guanajuato

AZUL SPA

473-733-3449
Carretera a Juventino Km. 5, Guanajuato, Gto. 36000
Open: Tues.–Sat. 10 AM–6:30 PM; Sun. 10 AM–2 PM
Offers: Aromatherapy, body treatments such as mud wraps, facials, and massages

HACIENDA DE CABOS

473-732-0350
Calle Padre Hidalgo #3, Guanajuato, Gto. 36000
Open: Mon.–Sat. 10:30 AM–2 PM and 4:30 PM–8 PM
Offers: A variety of unique services including microexfoliation, metabolic stimulation, and cellulite reduction

MAO-RÁN SPA & HOLISTIC HEALTH

473-102-3000
Carretera Panorámica Carrizo San Javier, Guanajuato, Gto. 36000
Open: Mon.–Sat. 10 AM–7 PM
Offers: A variety of massages, including Swedish, shiatsu, and hot stone massages. Other treatments include body detoxification and antiaging treatments

QUINTA LAS ALONDRAS SPA

473-733-3030
www.quiintalasalondras.com.mx

Autopista Guanajuato Silao Kilometer 1, Guanajuato, Gto. 36000
Open: Mon.–Sat. 10 AM–7 PM
Offers: A wide range of treatments including facials, body treatments, and massages

VILLA MARÍA CRISTINA

473-731-2183
Paseo de la Presa #76, Guanajuato, Gto. 36000
Open: Mon.–Sat. 10 AM–6 PM
Offers: A variety of services including facial moisturizer, oxygenating facial, and body massages

San Miguel de Allende

BAMBU DAY SPA

415-103-0240
Ancha de San Antonio #15, San Miguel de Allende, Gto. 37700
Open: Mon.–Fri. 9 AM–3 PM; Sat. 10 AM–2 PM
Offers: Massages and body treatments as well as facials, manicures, and pedicures

CLINICA IZCUINAPAN PET CARE & SPA

415-120-0043
Calle Relampoga #22, San Miguel de Allende, Gto. 37700
Open: Mon.–Fri. 9 AM–7 PM; Sat. 9 AM–2 PM
Offers: This is a combination veterinary center, dog groomer, and canine spa

JASMINE DAY SPA

415-154-4578
Jesús #25-A, San Miguel de Allende, Gto. 3770
Open: Mon.–Sat. 10 AM–6 PM
Offers: Body treatments, massages, manicures, pedicures, and facials

HACIENDA EL SANTUARIO SPA

415-185-2036
www.haciendaelsantuario.com
Carretera a Dolores Hidalgo Km. 13, San Miguel de Allende, Gto. 3770
Open: Mon.–Sat. 10 AM–7 PM
Offers: A variety of facials and massages

EL QUINTO SOL DÍA SPA

415-152-1608
Calle Farolito #10, San Miguel de Allende, Gto. 37700
Open: Mon.–Sat. 10 AM–7 PM
Offers: Facials and massages, Jacuzzi and sauna

THE SPA HEALTH AND BEAUTY CENTER

415-152-3427
www.smaspa.com
Hospicio #46, San Miguel de Allende, Gto. 3770

Open: Mon.–Sat. 9:30 AM–7 PM; Sun. 10 AM–4 PM
Offers: A variety of treatments including body wraps of algae and rose petal extracts, exfoliation, massages, and aromatherapy

TOURS

Guanajuato and San Miguel de Allende are so stunning that you might be apt to take a seat in one of their many plazas and just take in what's around you. Certainly, this is a great way to appreciate these beautiful colonial towns. However, the region is so packed with points of interest that you really should make the effort to experience as much as you can. Tours can be an efficient way to see these sites that you would otherwise have missed. San Miguel is blessed with several formal tour companies (listed below) that employ bilingual tour guides that are wonderful at explaining the region's history and culture. Guanajuato is not so lucky. There are almost no formal, independent tour companies here, though you are likely to be approached by enterprising individuals as you stroll the plazas

Guanajuato

GUANAJUATO OFFICE OF TOURISM

473-732-1574
www.guanajuato-travel.com
Plaza de la Paz #4, Guanajuato, Gto. 36000
The main tourist information office in Guanajuato is located at the south end of Plaza de la Paz next to the Basilica. This office is open daily from 8 AM to 8 PM; it offers information in English about a variety of inexpensive tours around Guanajuato, as well as to the statue of Cristo Rey and other nearby points of interest.

If you plan to take no other tour, you should really set a day aside for a tour of the Paseo de la Independéncia. It costs about $20 for an 8-hour tour that takes you first on a tour of Dolores Hidalgo, makes a brief stop at the sanctuary of Atotonilco, and then on to San

The altar of the Atotonilco sanctuary

Miguel de Allende, where you are set loose for about an hour. The tour does make brief stops at artesenía shops and selected ice cream vendors in Dolores (and one gets the sense that the guides get kickbacks for this), but you are not required to purchase anything. The tour's biggest drawback is that the guide picks the place to eat in San Miguel, and it is not always the best restaurant around. In cases such as this, it's best to just wait it out and find a restaurant to your liking once you are set free on the streets of San Miguel.

Keep in mind that while the tourist office in Guanajuato is staffed by people who speak English, most of the tour guides generally do not conduct tours in English. Not to worry. The tours are still well worth the cost in money and time. If you need translation, there is usually at least one fellow sightseer along for the ride who is bilingual. Or, better yet, use this trusty guide to get yourself informed on what's what.

MELLADO HORSEBACK RIDING
473-105-0417
Subida San José #16, Guanajuato, Gto. 36000
This small tour company offers horseback excursions in the hills surrounding Guanajuato. They will guide you along back trails to spots with breathtaking panoramic views of the city and the surrounding environs. The staff is fully bilingual and packages start at around $20. Group rates are also available.

San Miguel de Allende Tourism Companies

COYOTE CANYON ADVENTURES
415-154-4193
www.coyotecanyonadventures.com
This adventure tour group is located on a ranch about 10 miles outside of San Miguel de Allende. They offer several kinds of tours and excursions, including horseback riding, hiking, mountain biking, ATV adventures, and even hot air balloon rides. Prices vary depending on the excursion and duration, which can last from a half day to a full week of overnight camping.

GONZALEZ TOURS AND TRANSPORTATION
415-152-5552
http://transportesgonzalez.tripod.com
Tesoro #89, San Miguel de Allende, Gto. 37700
This company offers private transportation to the León airport for up to eight people for between $70 and $100, depending on the number of people in your group. Transport to the Mexico City airport runs between $200 and $250, again depending on the number of people in your group. You can also arrange for transport to and from locations such as Querétaro and Guadalajara through this company, or even chauffeur service to the United States. They also offer a variety of historic tours in San Miguel and the surrounding cities.

LIFEPATH SPA RETREATS
415-154-8465
www.lifepathretreats.com
Recreo #11, San Miguel de Allende, Gto 87700
LifePath is a center for personal growth and healing located in San Miguel de Allende. This

organization offers lectures, classes, workshops, and retreats devoted to the wellness of the body, mind, and spirit. They offer a quiet atmosphere of deep reflection where professionals provide psychological and spiritual guidance. It is staffed with trained individuals with years of experience specializing in psychology, Oriental medicine, counseling, and massage therapy. They also feature visiting practitioners and personal growth special events.

POLANCO TOURS
415-152-4193
www.internetsanmiguel.com/polanco/polanco.htm
Cri Cri #25, San Miguel de Allende, Gto. 37700
This company offers transportation to and from the León airport for $72 for up to two people, with a cost of $10 for each additional person. They also offer art tours by appointment for $20 per hour, covering scenic and historic sights in San Miguel, Atotonílco, Dolores Hidalgo, the ghost mining town of Pozos, and Guanajuato. You can also schedule cooking classes with this company to learn about the fine art of authentic Mexican cooking.

SANTUARIO CAÑADA DE LA VIRGEN
415-154-8771
www.canadadelavirgen.com
Orizaba #2, San Miguel de Allende, Gto. 37700
This group specializes in tours of the Santuario Cañada de la Virgen. They offer several different horseback riding excursions in the subtropical microclimate of the canyons and meandering Virgen River. At certain times of the year, they also offer a ride to the hacienda ruins. Children must be at least 10 years old for these trips. For those interested in astronomy, they offer guided stargazing tours conducted by a knowledgeable astronomer complete with a telescope and star chart. These tours vary according to the season, weather, and known astronomical events. They also offer guided hiking and camping tours to remote camp locations. All guests are required to sign a wilderness agreement to protect the natural habitat of this preserve.

SOL Y LUNA
415-154-8599
www.solylunatours.com
Hospicio #10, San Miguel de Allende, Gto. 37700
This company offers airport shuttle service to Mexico City and León. They also offer a variety of unique tours such as kayaking in the nearby botanical gardens, horseback riding in and around the city, bullfights, hot springs, and several other options. They rent out everything from cars to cell phones to bicycles to camping equipment. Contact them for rates and details.

VIAJES SAN MIGUEL
415-152-2537
www.viajessanmiguel.com
Ollano #4, San Miguel de Allende, Gto. 37700
This company offers a shuttle to the León airport starting at $26. Private door-to-door service to any of the surrounding airports, including Mexico City, is also available. They also offer a variety of cultural, historical, and ecological tours.

All manner of goods are sold at Mercado Hidalgo.

8

Shopping

If you're looking for shopping, San Miguel de Allende is the right place to be. There you will find hundreds of small shops radiating out from the Jardín Principal. This town is particularly known for metalwork, such as wrought iron, bronze, and brass. Downtown you will find many shops with handicrafts, where you can buy silver and gold jewelry as well as fine *talavera* pottery. The pottery is mainly composed of urns, plates, washbasins, tile, and bowls—a perfect addition to your home's décor. San Miguel has the unique distinction of being an isolated colonial Mexican city with a large population of well-to-do foreigners and a steady stream of foreign tourists, so you can find all kinds of interesting shops here, catering to a wide range of tastes and sophistication. Keep in mind that many shopkeepers abide by the Mexican siesta, a practice that is completely foreign to anyone coming from north of the border. This means that they will close down the shop in the early afternoon, usually around 2 or 3 PM, and reopen a few hours later, staying open until the early evening. If you see a shop is closed in the early afternoon, don't assume that the shopkeeper has taken the day off. Chances are good that you can return in a couple of hours and be able to look around. Also keep in mind that Americans have an $800 duty-free allowance when reentering the United States, and Canadians have a C$500 allowance once they have been out of the country for a week.

If you are in the market for Mexican ceramics, Dolores Hidalgo is one of Mexico's main centers for the production of talavera. The town has several workshops where you can go to watch the process of making the Mexican earthenware, and buy it right from the factory. The town also has several producers of Mexican furniture, many of which take custom orders and will ship their wares to you wherever you happen to live. Guanajuato is home to two of the most respected talavera artisans in Mexico; they also have workshops for you to visit and shop. The town has many fine shops of different varieties, though nowhere near the volume or variety that you will find in San Miguel de Allende. Still, there is good shopping to be had in Guanajuato. What follows is a small selection of the kind of specialty shops you will find.

Talavera is an important element in Mexican decoration.

BOOKS

San Miguel de Allende

EL COLIBRÍ

415-152-0751
Sollano #30, San Miguel de Allende, Gto. 37700
Open: Mon.–Sat. 10 AM–2 PM and 4 PM–7 PM
This store has a selection of English language paperbacks and magazines.

LAGUNDI

415-152-7395
Umarán #17, San Miguel de Allende, Gto. 37700
Open: Mon.–Sat. 10 AM–2 PM and 4 PM–8 PM; Sun. 11 AM–3 PM
This shop has a selection of art books and English-language magazines.

LIBROS EL TECOLOTE

415-152-7395
Jesús #11, San Miguel de Allende, Gto. 37700
Open: Tues.– Sat. 10 AM–6 PM; Sun. 9 AM–4 PM
This small boutique bookstore has a nice selection of English language books, including guidebooks, books on the arts and architecture, and children's books.

CERAMICS AND FOLK ART

Dolores Hidalgo

ARTESANIAS GAMEZ

418-182-3752
Avenida José Alfredo Jíminez #15, Dolores Hidalgo, Gto. 37800
Open: Mon.–Fri. 9 AM–5:30 PM
This workshop produces many interesting pieces, from animal figures to adorn your walls to large, multicolored planters. They also produce many unique vases and talavera pots.

ARTESANÍAS LICEAGUI

418-182-1700
Avenida Norte #5-C, Dolores Hidalgo, Gto. 37800
Open: Mon.–Fri. 9 AM–5:30 PM
This talavera shop offers a large selection of traditional Mexican ceramic ware. Most of the collection here has a white base color with a lot of blue trim, with intricate but modest flower work. They offer anything from teacups to 3-foot vases and multilayered fountains.

ARTESANÍAS VÁZQUEZ

418-182-0305
Puebla #58, Dolores Hidalgo, Gto. 37800

Dolores Hidalgo is famous for its ceramic work.

Open: Mon.–Sat. 8 AM–8 PM; Sun. 10 AM–3 PM
This ceramic workshop has a large selection of traditional Mexican talavera in several showrooms. The owner speaks English. You can also find work from this shop at their store in Guanajuato.

AZULEJOS TALAVERA CORTÉS
418-182-0900
Calle Distro Federal #8, Dolores Hidalgo, Gto. 37800
Open: Mon.–Fri. 8 AM–4:30 PM; Sat. 8 AM–2 PM
This is the largest talavera operation in Dolores Hidalgo. You can also enter the actual work area where the artists are making their ceramic wares and see the process as it happens.

CARRILLO VERTIX HERMANOS
418-182-0122
Puebla #54, Dolores Hidalgo, Gto. 37800
Open: Mon.–Sat. 8 AM–8 PM; Sun. 10 AM–3 PM
This shop has a large showroom of mostly handmade Mexican tiles and talavera sinks.

CERAMICA DAEL

418-182-9887
Nicolas Bravo #15, Dolores Hidalgo, Gto. 37800
Open: Mon.–Sat. 10 AM–8 PM
This ceramic shop specializes in ceramic figurines of cherubs. These cherubs range from small statuettes to candleholders to fountains.

CERAMICOS GUANAJUATO

418-182-5143
www.ceramicosguanajuato.com
Avenida Sur #20, Dolores Hidalgo, Gto. 37800
Open: Mon.–Sat. 10 AM–8 PM
This talavera shop sells a wide range of Mexican ceramic tiles, from solid colors to intricate, multicolored pieces. They also sell talavera pots, vases, and flatware in a wide range of styles, from the traditional blue and white to pieces adorned with sunflowers or fruit.

D' TALAVERA

418-182-0749
Puebla #62, Dolores Hidalgo, Gto. 37800
Open: Mon.–Sat. 9 AM–7 PM
This shop specializes in highly traditional talavera with intricate designs and bright natural colors. They have decorative plates and large urns, as well as a large selection of other objects.

JUAN F. GUERRERO VAJILLAS

418-182-0305
Calzada de los Héroes, Dolores Hidalgo, Gto. 37800
Open: Daily 9 AM–7 PM
If you come to Dolores Hidalgo shopping for talavera, make sure you stop in here. They produce high quality ceramic ware at reasonable prices.

MERCADO DE ARTESANIAS 15 DE SEPTIEMBRE

418-182-1194
San Luis Potosí #3-B, Dolores Hidalgo, Gto. 37800
Open: Daily 9 AM–6 PM
This store sells a wide range of Mexican artesenia, including lamps, ceramic urns, ironwork, silverwork, and talavera.

TALAVERA CASTILLO

418-182-2698
www.talaveracastillo.com
Calzada de los Héroes #124, Dolores Hidalgo, Gto. 37800
Open: Daily 9 AM–6 PM
This shop produces an extremely varied array of high-quality ceramic work, including pieces that are appropriate for cooking and eating off, many decorative vases and accessories, planters, and a selection of tiles.

TALAVERA CORTÉS

418-182-0900
www.talaveracortes.com.mx
Distrito Federal #8, Dolores Hidalgo, Gto. 37800
Open: Daily 9 AM–6 PM
This is a Mexican ceramic tile workshop that produces high-quality tiles right on the premises. There is a wide range of styles, some of which join together to form pictures such as flower pots or Diego Rivera reproductions. Some styles are colorful, some are quite understated.

Guanajuato

ARTESANÍAS VÁZQUEZ

473-732-5231
Cantarranas #8, Guanajuato, Gto. 36000
Open: Mon.–Sat. 8 AM–8 PM
This shop offers a nice selection of pieces made in their workshop in Dolores Hidalgo.

CASA DE CAPELO

473-732-0612
Carretera a Dolores Hidalgo Km. 5, Guanajuato, Gto. 36000
Open: Daily 10 AM–6 PM
This is the workshop of the famous Guanajuato ceramist Javier de Jesús Hernández, known simply as Capelo. He is also a painter and a University professor, and he has worked out of this workshop for more than 30 years. Here you will find a small showroom of museum quality talavera. These pieces are made according to Spanish colonial majolica designs guaranteed to beat U.S. standards for lead content.

GORKY GONZÁLEZ QUIÑONES

473-731-0462
www.gorkypottery.com
Pastita Ex-Huerta de Montenegro s/n, Guanajuato, Gto. 36000
Open: Mon.–Fri. 10 AM–2 PM and 4 PM–6 PM; Sat. 10 AM–12 PM
This is the workshop of the world-renowned ceramist known simply as Gorky. This workshop is located in the Pastita area east of the city center. They have a large showroom with all manner of ceramic artwork. If you make an appointment, you can also tour the workshop during the week to see the pieces being made. Like Capelo, the pieces here are produced according to the majolica design standards of the Spanish colonial period. These two artists are the only ceramists in Mexico still working by these techniques. Also, the talavera here meets U.S. standards for lead content.

MAYÓLICA SANTA ROSA

Carretera a Dolores Hidalgo Km. 13, Guanajuato, Gto. 36000
Open: Mon.–Fri. 10 AM–2 PM and 4 PM–6 PM; Sat. 10 AM–12 PM
This workshop has a showroom that covers two floors displaying talavera at reasonable prices.

The showroom of Gorky González Quiñones

Talavera Pottery

The colorful Mexican earthenware that you see in gift shops and art stores is called talavera. This form of handicraft was brought to Mexico by Spanish guild artisans during the 16th century. These Spanish artisans worked with Mexico's indigenous populations, who already had long traditions of firing earthenware of their own that went all the way back to the Olmecs, widely considered the mother of Mesoamerican civilizations. The Spanish version of ceramic ware is called majolica. These techniques originated with the Moors, who conquered Spain in the 8th century, but they were refined with knowledge gained from such diverse places as Italy and China. Mexican ceramic ware draws its name from the 16th-century pottery center, Talavera de la Reina. This was a small Spanish town where innovative techniques were developed over time that led to big strides in the art of fine ceramics. Ceramics covered with intricate blue and white designs are emblematic of the older Spanish tradition. Mexican indigenous artisans later added multicolored floral, celestial, and other motifs to their talavera. Since the colonial period, these age-old techniques have been passed down from generation to generation by master craftsmen. The city of Guanajuato is home to the only two talavera artisans in Mexico that still craft their work to majolica forms and standards, Gorky González Quiñones and Capelo. These artisans fire their products at extremely high temperatures to produce very durable products.

This ceramic work comes in many forms, including sinks, planters, jars, platters, pitchers, and vases. Additionally, these artisans make all types of indoor and outdoor tile. These items are hand painted in a wide range of styles and sizes and can make a wonderful addition to the décor of your home. The city of Dolores Hidalgo is renowned throughout Mexico as a special place to shop for talavera, rivaled only by the city of Puebla, south of Mexico City. Dolores Hidalgo has many workshops where you can go and see the process of manufacturing these ceramics, as well as haggle with sellers to get a deal. However, talavera is notorious for being made with glazes with high lead content. Therefore, if you plan to use your talavera for anything besides decorative purposes, you should buy it from the more reputable artisans who guarantee that their work meets U.S. standards. The

San Miguel de Allende

CASA DE LAS ARTESANÍAS DE MICHOACÁN

415-155-9211
Calzada de la Aurora #23, San Miguel de Allende, Gto. 37700
Open: Mon.–Sat. 10 AM–7 PM
This store is run by a nonprofit organization associated with the Mexican state of Michoacán. They specialize in selling folk art from that state, including ceramics, wood carvings, copper goods, and furniture.

HACIENDA STYLE

415-154-7962
Zacateros #83-A, San Miguel de Allende, Gto. 37700
Open: Daily 10 AM–8 PM
This is a manufacturer and wholesaler of original handmade majolica ceramics. Their designs range from old-world Mexican to more modern designs that look more Midwest American than anything else. This is the only factory outlet for ceramics in San Miguel.

peace of mind is worth the extra money. Furthermore, you should treat talavera as you would fine china. Place it in the dishwasher with care, making sure that it won't rattle around. Also, it is microwave safe but it will absorb plenty of heat, so use oven mittens when taking it out.

Talavera pottery comes in a wide variety of forms.

EXIM

415-154-5282
Hidalgo #6-A, San Miguel de Allende, Gto. 37700
Open: Mon.–Sat. 10 AM–8 PM; Sun. 10 AM–7 PM
This shop offers a large selection of Mexican handicrafts, including candleholders, wall decorations, and furniture. The entire inventory here is handmade of ceramic, glass, and other materials.

GALERÍA MARIPOSA

415-152-4488
Recreo #36, San Miguel de Allende, Gto. 37700
Open: Mon.–Sat. 10 AM–7 PM
This shop sells traditional Mexican folk art from around the country. Among the items you will find here are Oaxacan *alebrijes*, carved animal figurines that are sometimes monstrous and always intricately painted with minute dot patterns. This shop also has a small number of works by local painters.

SURFACES

415-152-2068

www.ceramicaantique.com

Calzada de la Aurora, San Miguel de Allende, Gto. 37700

Open: Mon.–Sat. 10 AM–5 PM

This tile shop manufactures and sells a wide variety of high-quality handcrafted Mexican tiles. They have styles that include Mexican, Moroccan, and Italian and have an interactive design display as well as a large tile gallery. They do custom orders and have a knowledgeable staff on hand for consultations.

TALAVERA LA HIDALGUENSE

415-152-3546

Calle Antonio Plaza #21-A, San Miguel de Allende, Gto. 37700

Open: Mon.–Sat. 10 AM–7 PM; Sun. 10 AM–5 PM

This shop sells a good selection of talavera made in Dolores Hidalgo, at reasonable prices.

ZÓCALO MEXICAN FOLK ART

415-152-0663

www.zocalotx.com

Hernández Macías #110, San Miguel de Allende, Gto. 37700

Open: Mon.–Sat. 10 AM–7 PM; Sun. 10 AM–3 PM

This store sells a wide variety of Mexican folk art from around the country. This includes highly traditional items such as talavera (decorative ceramic plates), clay *katrina* (female skeleton) Day of the Dead figurines, and Oaxacan alebríjes (intricately painted wooden animal figurines). You will also find more hard-to-find items here as well, such as carved masks and engraved glassware.

CLOTHING AND ACCESSORIES

San Miguel de Allende

ARTESANÍAS BÚFALO

415-152-1052

Zacateros #23-B, San Miguel de Allende, Gto. 37700

Open: Mon.–Sat. 10 AM–2 PM and 4 PM–8 PM; Sun. 10 AM–2 PM

This shop sells leather goods, mostly belts, but they also have wallets, vests, and purses.

BACARA

415-152-0062

Hidalgo #9, San Miguel de Allende, Gto. 37700

Open: Wed.–Sat. 10 AM–3 PM and 5 PM–8 PM

This store sells high-quality leather goods, including bags, boots, belts, and jackets. Most of their stock comes from the nearby city of León. They also have a selection of watches.

León: Shoe Capital of Mexico

The nearby city of León is the largest and most important industrial center in the state of Guanajuato. Due to its central location in the country, the number of industries located here has been expanding rapidly in recent decades. The city is widely known as the shoemaking and leather tanning capital of the country, because this industry has been prominent here since colonial times and it was the second most important economic activity here in the 18th century, behind agriculture. In 1888 a flood hit the city, causing many of the shoemakers to move their operations to cities such as Puebla and Monterrey. However, more than three hundred shoe manufacturers stayed put and eventually thrived. This industry went on to have more historic importance than simply to the development of León. For example, during World War II, several of the city's shoe factories dedicated their efforts to making footwear for the U.S. military. In fact, the shoe industry is so prominent here that there is a shopping mall dedicated solely to selling shoes.

BARBARITA BOUTIQUE

415-152-7463
Zacateros #47, San Miguel de Allende, Gto. 37700
Open: Mon.–Fri. 10 AM–6 PM; Sat. 10 AM–3 PM
This interesting boutique offers custom designed clothing and accessories, including clothing for plus-size women. They also carry a selection of skin care products.

GIRASOL CLOTHING BOUTIQUE

415-152-2734
San Francisco #11, San Miguel de Allende, Gto. 37700
Open: Daily 10 AM–6 PM
This boutique offers a collection of costume jewelry and brightly colored Mexican casual wear. Located only a half block off the Jardín Principal.

THE LEATHER SHOP

415-152-8679
www.mahabags.com
Umerán #1, San Miguel de Allende, Gto. 37700
Open: Daily 10 AM–8 PM
This shop sells high-quality leather goods. Much of what they offer is imported. They also sell indigenous hand-loomed textiles.

SAN MIGUEL DESIGNS

415-150-0058
www.sanmigueldesigns.com
Ignacio Cruces #4, San Miguel de Allende, Gto. 37700
Open: Daily 9 AM–12 PM or by appointment
This store sells clothing with prints that are steeped in Mexican culture. This includes items such as kimonos and shower curtains adorned with the image of the Virgin of Guadalupe, shirts and aprons peppered with Day of the Dead skeletons, and other such items.

Shoe Size Conversions

Men's Shoes

MEX	4.5	5	5.5	6	6.5	7	7.5	8	8.5	9	9.5
US	6	6½	7	7½	8	8½	9	9½	10	10½	11

Women's Shoes

MEX	2	2.5	3	3.5	4	4.5	5	5.5	6	6.5	7
US	5	5½	6	6½	7	7½	8	8½	9	9½	10

VILAR FOOTWEAR

415-152-2658
Recreo #5, San Miguel de Allende, Gto. 37700
Open: Mon.–Fri. 10 AM–2 PM; Sat. 10 AM–8 PM; Sun. 10:30 AM–2:30 PM
This shop offers shoes and boots in styles that vary from comfortable to daring, as well as jackets, handbags, and a range of other fashion accessories.

PLAZA DEL ZAPATO (SHOE MALL)

www.plazadelzapato.com.mx
Adolfo Lopez Matéos #1601, León, Gto. 37000
Open: Mon.–Sat. 10 AM–8:30 PM; Sun. 10 AM–6 PM
This mall has been exclusively devoted to selling shoes for more than 20 years; it has shoes for the whole family. There are more than 60 shoe stores (and a restaurant) offering footwear of all types from work boots to women's pumps. And while there are upwards of 20 stores solely devoted to women's shoes, there are many that sell men's shoes and a few that sell only children's shoes.

SAPICA SHOE FAIR

477-152-9000
www.sapica.com
Adolfo López Matéos #3401, León, Gto. 37000
This international shoe fair is held twice a year to celebrate and exhibit seasonal shoe lines. Several dozen exhibitors and companies from Europe and the United States participate in the event.

FURNITURE AND HOME DESIGNS

Dolores Hidalgo

BAZAR EL PORTÓN

418-182-2229
Calzada de los Héroes Km. 3.5, Dolores Hidalgo, Gto. 37800
Open: Mon.–Sat. 8 AM–6 PM; Sun. 10 AM–4 PM

This is a large store with a nice selection of thick wood furniture. There are pieces here made of cedar, pine, and mahogany. They take custom orders and ship their pieces, as well.

MUEBLES Y DECORACIONES
418-182-2195
Calzada de los Héroes Km. 3.5, Dolores Hidalgo, Gto. 37800
Open: Mon.–Sat. 8 AM–7 PM; Sun. 10 AM–5 PM
This furniture workshop specializes in cedar and pine furniture made right on the premises. This furniture is the thick, darkly stained Mexican style. Some of it is intricately carved. This shop has some silverwork and handicrafts, as well.

San Miguel de Allende

ARTE EN COBRE
Zacateros #55, San Miguel de Allende, Gto. 37700
Open: Mon.–Sat. 10 AM–2 PM and 4:30 PM–7:30 PM
This shop specializes in selling copper items from Michoacán. They offer copper plates, trays, bowls, and other items.

BUENAS NOCHES
415-154-9624
Calzada de la Aurora, San Miguel de Allende, Gto. 37700
Open: Tues.–Sat. 11 AM–5 PM
This interesting bath shop is owned and run by a couple of American expatriates. It stocks a range of imported and Mexican bath and bedroom furnishings, including Egyptian bed sheets and comforters, as well as large, soft bath towels, and scented soaps and candles.

CAMILA
415-152-2697
Sollano #30, San Miguel de Allende, Gto. 37700
Open: Mon., Tues., Thurs.–Sat. 10 AM–3 PM and 4 PM–7 PM; Sun. 10 AM–3 PM
This small shop specializes in etched glass flatware as well as tablecloths, linens, and an assortment of other decorative household accessories.

CARACOL COLLECTION
415-152-1617
Cuadrante #30, San Miguel de Allende, Gto. 37700
Open: Wed.–Mon. 12 PM–6 PM
This shop features a collection of fine and applied arts by Mexican artists and artisans from around the country and includes clothing and furniture. The collection exhibits many different traditions with pieces made of materials such as paper, silver, wood, and clay.

COBÁ
415-154-7516
Juárez #7, San Miguel de Allende, Gto. 37700
Open: Mon.–Sat. 10 AM–6 PM

This centrally located furniture store offers a large selection of antiques and imported furniture as well as a variety of art, ceramics, and other home décor items.

DE WA

415-152-5481
www.cdewayneyouts.com
Calzada de la Aurora, San Miguel de Allende, Gto. 37700
Open: Mon.–Fri. 10 AM–6 PM; Sat. 10 AM–4 PM
This furniture shop manufactures a line of fine wood, wrought iron, and upholstered furniture. This includes tables, cabinets, and chairs that are reproductions, as well as custom furniture. They also make accessories such as gorgeously beveled wood-framed mirrors and large metal urn lamps.

FINCA HOME

415-154-8323
www.fincahome.com
Calzada de la Aurora, San Miguel de Allende, Gto. 37700
Open: Mon.–Fri. 11 AM–6 PM; Sat. 11 AM–4 PM
This shop stocks hand-finished wrought iron and wood furniture such as armoires, chests, and end tables. They also offer imported leather furniture, and a selection of wrought iron and copper light fixtures and lighting accessories, as well as imported fabrics.

FUN ART

415-152-5770
Zacateros #26, San Miguel de Allende, Gto. 37700
Open: Mon.–Wed. and Fri., Sat. 10 AM–2 PM and 4 PM–8 PM; Sun. and Thurs. 10 AM–2 PM
This store sells a large selection of Mexican pewter ware. This is a shiny metal alloy made of tin and copper. Here you can buy pewter bowls, trays, candlesticks, vases, and other items.

GABY

415-152-2797
Zacateros #33, San Miguel de Allende, Gto. 37700
Open: Mon.–Sat. 11 AM–3 PM and 5 PM–8:30 PM; Sun. 11 AM–3:30 PM
This store sells a variety of home fixtures, including lighting fixtures, mirrors, and picture frames, made of brass and other metals. All items are produced in San Miguel de Allende. They also accept custom orders.

ICPALLI

415-152-1236
Correo #43, San Miguel de Allende, Gto. 37700
Open: Mon.–Fri. 10 AM–6 PM; Sat. 10 AM–2 PM
This store has a selection of high-quality furniture and home furnishings. This includes leather furniture, window treatments, lamps, shades, and rugs. They also stock pottery by Gorky González from Guanajuato.

ORIGEN

415-154-8387
Zacateros #12, San Miguel de Allende, Gto. 37700
Open: Wed.–Mon. 10 AM–8 PM
This shop has several showrooms of thick Mexican furniture as well as a large selection of decorative crafts, including wooden figurines, candleholders, and woven artistic hangings.

PRODUCTOS HERCO

415-152-1434
Reloj #12, San Miguel de Allende, Gto. 37700
Open: Mon.–Sat. 9 AM–2 PM and 4 PM–7 PM
Located a block off the Jardín in a building adorned with sculpted gargoyles, this store has a range of items to help you redecorate and remodel your bathroom and kitchen. This includes iron door knockers, pewter bowls, cast brass washbasins, and plenty of talavera trays and plates. They also have a selection of wood and wrought iron furniture.

SOLLANO 16

415-154-8872
www.sollano16.com
Sollano #16, San Miguel de Allende, Gto. 37700
Open: Mon.–Fri. 10 AM–2 PM and 4 PM–6 PM; Sat. 10 AM–2 PM
This shop is located in a beautiful colonial building with a large courtyard. They sell a variety of luxury goods including textiles, furniture, jewelry, and other accessories. They have a variety of antiques as well. Much of their inventory is imported from Europe, South America, and other exotic locations.

GIFT SHOPS

Guanajuato

EL VIEJO ZAGUÁN

473-732-3971
www.viejozaguan.com
Positos #64, Guanajuato, Gto. 36000
Open: Tues.–Sat. 10:30 AM–3 PM and 5 PM–8 PM; Sun. 11 AM–3 PM
Located in an historic house, with soft music playing in the background, this handsome little store has a selection of books, music, Mexican art, and coffee. Enjoy an espresso drink while you peruse their carved Oaxacan alebrijes and paintings by local artists, as well as reproductions.

LA RANA

473-732-2990
Positos #7, Guanajuato, Gto. 36000
Open: Mon.–Sat. 10 AM–7 PM; Sun. 10 AM–3 PM
Located in downtown Guanajuato, this store offers a variety of Mexican handicrafts

You will find many shops with interesting gift ideas.

including colorful woven baskets, blown glass vases, carved Oaxacan alebrijes, and a selection of talavera.

LOS MILAGROS BAZAR

473-734-1637
www.eljardindelosmilagros.com.mx

Calle Alhóndiga #80, Guanajuato, Gto. 36000
Open: Daily 12 PM–8 PM
Located inside El Jardín de los Milagros restaurant, this store has a variety of Mexican handicrafts and items dealing with folklore. They have finely woven scarves, alebrijes, and papercrafts, as well as other items.

San Miguel de Allende

ARTESA
415-154-4838
Canal #32, San Miguel de Allende, Gto. 37700
Open: Mon.–Sat. 10 AM–2:30 PM and 4:30 PM–8 PM; Sun. 10 AM–3 PM
This shop offers a variety of gift items such as colorful mirrors and picture frames, as well as decorative boxes made of brass and glass.

CASA DE PAPEL
415-154-5187
Mesones #57, San Miguel de Allende, Gto. 37700
Open: Mon.–Sat. 10 AM–8 PM; Sun. 10 AM–5 PM
This small gift shop sells quality cards and books in both English and Spanish. Here you will also find other gift shop essentials, such as posters, candles, wrapping paper, and other items.

CASA KATALINA GIFTS
415-150-0061
Jesús #26, San Miguel de Allende, Gto. 37700
Open: Tues.–Sat. 11 AM–6 PM
This gift shop located near the Jardín Principal offers a variety of jewelry, furnishings, and home decorating items.

LA CUBA VIEJA
415-152-2125
Hidalgo #4, San Miguel de Allende, Gto. 37700
Open: Daily 12 PM–8 PM
Located just a half block from the Jardín Principal, this shop offers fine Cuban cigars and gourmet coffee, combined with Mexican handicrafts and a gallery of oil paintings.

ESPIRAL
415-120-0871
Hernández Macías #56-A, San Miguel de Allende, Gto. 37700
Open: Mon.–Sat. 10 AM–2 PM and 4 PM–7 PM; Sun. 11 AM–3 PM
This downtown gift shop offers a variety of gift ideas that are made throughout Mexico. They offer many things to spruce up your kitchen and bathroom as well.

LA VICTORIANA
415-152-6903
Hernández Macías #72, San Miguel de Allende, Gto. 37700

Mercado Hidalgo

Along Avenida Juárez across the street from the Church of Belén, you will find Mercado Hidalgo, the city's primary market. This market was built at the beginning of the 20th century on the site of an old bullfighting ring and was inaugurated in 1910 by President Porfirio Diaz. It has a pink cantera stone neoclassical façade, though from the inside it looks more like a converted aircraft hangar. The building is about 75 yards long and has three entrances.

It is said that this building was originally meant to be a train station. However, when it was finished the main marketplace formerly located at Plaza de la Reforma was moved here. The ground floor of the market is filled largely with vendors selling produce, meats, and candies. There are also food stalls located here. Around the upper periphery and scattered throughout the ground floor are merchants selling clothing, crafts, and souvenirs. However, don't expect a shopping mall when you come here. This is a chaotic and cramped place where you can find cheap toys and gifts, and where you may see vendors selling odd items such as knockoff DVDs and dog-eared pornographic magazines. It's certainly not the most pleasant place in Guanajuato, but it is interesting. If you do find something you like, don't be afraid to barter for it.

The Mercado Hidalgo is the city's primary market.

Open: Mon.–Sat. 9 AM–8 PM; Sun. 11 AM–3 PM

This store sells a wide variety of items including bath and body products, cards, handmade jewelry, and children's clothing. They also offer botanical and homeopathic medicines that are made right on the premises.

JEWELRY

Guanajuato

ANGELUS PLATA

473-732-2960

Pasaje Barón Von Humboldt, Guanajuato, Gto. 36000

Open: Mon.–Sat. 11 AM–2 PM and 5 PM–8 PM

You will find this jewelry store just west of the Jardín de la Unión. They specialize in unique silverwork and many of their pieces incorporate polished wood as well as semi-precious stones, such as amber and jade. They have many necklaces, bracelets, and rings, as well as other items such as key rings and letter openers.

CASA DEL SOL

473-732-0115

Obregón, Guanajuato, Gto. 36000

Open: Wed.–Mon. 10 AM–8 PM

This shop sells reproductions of antique jewelry, mostly in silver. Among their items, they offer *pajaritos,* or bird-shaped jewelry, and baroque silverwork.

San Miguel de Allende

AZUL Y PLATA JEWELRY DESIGNS

415-154-8192

Cuna de Allende #15, San Miguel de Allende, Gto. 37700

Open: Wed.–Mon. 10 AM–8 PM

This shop offers an array of tasteful fine jewelry designs.

CANDELA

415-154-5701

Cuna del Allende #3, San Miguel de Allende, Gto. 37700

Open: Sun.–Thurs. 10:30 AM–8 PM; Fri.–Sat. 10:30 AM–11 PM

This shop offers silver jewelry produced in Mexico City. New designs arrive regularly.

CERROBLANCO

415-154-4888

Canal #21, San Miguel de Allende, Gto. 37700

Open: Mon.–Sat. 11 AM–2 PM and 5 PM–8 PM

This shop offers an array of fine silver and gold jewelry. Many pieces are embossed with precious and semiprecious stones. It is run by third-generation jewelry designers who design all of their own pieces. Their work has been sold at Nordstom and Saks Fifth Avenue stores.

DARLA

415-154-5550
Recreo s/n, San Miguel de Allende, Gto. 37700
Open: Daily 10 AM–3 PM and 4 PM–7 PM
This is a little shop but it offers some of the most distinctive pieces you will find in San Miguel de Allende. The owner is originally from Boston and is a designer who creates one-of-a-kind pieces, mostly of sterling silver. Here you will also find unique handbags and accessories. Prices are fair and discounts are sometimes offered.

JOYERÍA DAVID

415-152-0056
Zacateros #53, San Miguel de Allende, Gto. 37700
Open: Mon.–Sat. 9 AM–7 PM
This shop offers an array of silver and gold jewelry. Prices here are based on the prevailing international silver market.

JOYERÍA PARÍS

415-152-2637
Umerán #8, San Miguel de Allende, Gto. 37700
Open: Mon.–Sat. 10 AM–2 PM and 4 PM–8 PM; Sun. 10 AM–2 PM
This shop has a unique selection of fine jewelry of silver and gold and other materials, with cut precious and natural stones at fair prices.

KELLI BROWN JEWELRY

415-154-7069
www.kellibrownjewelry.com
Hacienda Calderon, San Miguel de Allende, Gto. 37700
Open: By appointment
Raised in Austin, Texas, the daughter of a noted architectural designer and an art dealer, Kelli Brown grew up with a passion for design and beauty. Today, she creates bold jewelry in gold and silver with precious and semiprecious stones. The result is an old-world feel of booty from a pirate's chest. The shop is located in a hacienda that is more than 300 years old. Call for an appointment and Kelli will even arrange for you to be picked up from your hotel.

PIEDRAS

415-154-9193
www.piedrassanmiguel.com
Tanque #14, San Miguel de Allende, Gto. 37700
Open: Varies
This jewelry store is run by an American expatriate and a San Miguel native. It features jewelry made of beautiful semiprecious stones such as freshwater pearls, Mexican fire opal, and jade, as well as less traditional materials, such as petrified wood. They use these materials to make earrings, bracelets, and thick, draping necklaces with a distinctive Mexican feel. Hours of operation vary.

9

INFORMATION

U.S. EMBASSY
(01-55) 5080-2000
Reforma #305, Mexico City D.F. 06500
Open: Mon.–Fri. 9 AM–2 PM and 3 PM–5 PM

CANADIAN EMBASSY
(01-55) 5724-7900 or 800-706-2900
Schiller #529, Mexico City D.F. 11560
Open: Mon.–Fri. 9 AM–1 PM and 2 PM–5 PM

EMERGENCY SERVICES

Guanajuato

EMERGENCY
Dial 068

POLICE DEPARTMENT
473-732-0292
Alhóndiga #10, Guanajuato, Gto. 36000

FIRE DEPARTMENT
473-732-3357
Pozuelos s/n, Guanajuato, Gto. 36000

ÁNGELES VERDES (AMBULANCE)
473-732-0119
Casa Martha s/n, Guanajuato, Gto. 36000

STATE OFFICE OF TOURISM
473-732-1574
Plaza de la Paz #14, Guanajuato, Gto. 36000

Mexican money is colorful.

San Miguel de Allende

U.S. CONSULATE

415-152-2357
Hernández Macías #72, San Miguel de Allende, Gto. 37700
Open: Mon.–Fri. 9 AM–1 PM; closed Mexican and American holidays

EMERGENCY HOTLINE IN ENGLISH

415-152-2890
Available: Mon.–Fri. 8 AM–4 PM

POLICE DEPARTMENT

415-152-022
Salida a Querétaro, San Miguel de Allende, Gto. 37700

FIRE DEPARTMENT

415-152-3238
Salida a Querétaro, San Miguel de Allende, Gto. 37700

RED CROSS (AMBULANCE)
415-152-1616
Libaramiento Zavala Zavala s/n, San Miguel de Allende, Gto. 37700

BANKS

Guanajuato

BANAMEX
473-732-1707
Calle los Ángeles #21, Guanajuato, Gto. 36000
Open: Mon.–Fri. 9 AM–4 PM; Sat. 10 AM–2 PM
Features two 24-hour ATMs.

BANORTE
473-732-9222
Calle Alhóndiga #10, Guanajuato, Gto. 36000
Open: Mon.–Fri. 9 AM–4 PM; Sat. 10 AM–2 PM
Money exchange hours are Monday through Friday 9 AM to 1:30 PM. Features one 24-hour ATM.

HBC
473-732-0187
Plaza de la Paz #59, Guanajuato, Gto. 36000
Open: Mon.–Sat. 8 AM–7 PM
Features two 24-hour ATMs.

SERFIN-SANTANDER
473-732-7385
Avenida Juárez #13, Guanajuato, Gto. 36000
Open: Mon.–Fri. 9 AM–3 PM
Features one 24-hour ATM.

San Miguel de Allende

BANAMEX
415-152-1040
Canal #4, San Miguel de Allende, Gto. 37700
Open: Mon.–Fri. 9 AM–4 PM; Sat. 10 AM–2 PM
Features three 24-hour ATMs.

BANORTE
415-152-0019
San Francisco #17, San Miguel de Allende, Gto. 37700
Open: Mon.–Fri. AM–4 PM; Sat. 9:30 AM–2:30 PM
Money exchange hours are Monday through Friday 9 AM to 1:30 PM. Features one 24-hour ATM.

Street vendors add to the life of the city.

BANCOMER

415-152-0847
Juárez #11, San Miguel de Allende, Gto. 37700
Open: Mon.–Fri. 8:30 AM–4 PM
Features two 24-hour ATMs. A photocopy machine is also available during bank hours.

HBC

415-152-0847
San Francisco #31, San Miguel de Allende, Gto. 37700
Open: Mon.–Sat. 8 AM–7 PM
Features one 24-hour ATM.

SERFIN-SANTANDER

415-152-1161
San Francisco #32, San Miguel de Allende, Gto. 37700
Open: Mon.–Fri. 9 AM–3 PM
Features one 24-hour ATM.

BUS TERMINALS

Guanajuato

CENTRAL DE AUTOBUSES

473-733-1329
Carretera a Silao #8, Guanajuato, Gto. 36000

San Miguel de Allende

CENTRAL DE AUTOBUSES

415-152-2206
Calzada de la Estación #90, San Miguel de Allende, Gto. 37700

CALLING HOME AND MEXICO

To call directly to the United States from Mexico, dial 001 then the area code and phone number. Conversely, to call Mexico from the United States, dial 011-52 then the area code and phone number.

It isn't a good idea to dial direct long distance or international calls from your hotel room in Mexico. Hotels often add their own surcharges, even to local calls. This also applies to bringing and using your cell phones while in Mexico. It may seem extremely convenient to pull your phone out of your pocket and dial away, but you will likely wish you hadn't at the end of the month when you get a phone bill packed with hefty international roaming charges. Even receiving calls on your cell can result in excessive charges. Public phones in the larger towns are provided by a company called Ladatel; it offers long-distance calls with a *tarjeta de teléfono* (phone card) issued through TelMex, the national phone company of Mexico. You can buy prepaid Ladatel phone cards in pharmacies, convenience stores, and supermarkets. Another option is to obtain a calling card through your own phone company before leaving on your trip.

ELECTRICITY

Mexico's electrical system is the same as in the United States and Canada: 110 volts AC. The outlets are compatible with any electrical appliance, recharger, or extension cords you may bring. However, the outlets in older or smaller hotels may not have outlets suitable for polarized plugs (in which one prong is slightly larger than the other). Pick up an adapter at any hardware or discount store before your trip.

GETTING MARRIED IN MEXICO

As "destination weddings" have become more of a popular practice in the United States, San Miguel de Allende has become an increasingly popular destination to hold such an event. Not only is the city the perfect setting for a storybook wedding, but other Mexican hotspots are nearby, making for a great honeymoon. And if you're going to ask your guests to do some traveling anyway, why not bring them to a place as interesting and wonderful as San Miguel de Allende?

As with any wedding (outside of Las Vegas), getting married in Mexico requires planning, coordination, and the completion of documents. One solution to make the process easier is to complete the legal paperwork in the United States and simply perform the ceremony in Mexico. However, if you want your ceremony to be more than symbolic, there are several requirements that you need to fulfill at the location in Mexico where you will be married.

Keep in mind that religious weddings are not officially recognized in Mexico and thus do not change your legal marriage status. Therefore, to have your wedding legally recognized in Mexico and back home, you'll need a civil ceremony performed by a Spanish-speaking judge who resides in the city where you are getting married. You can also arrange to have this ceremony performed at an outside site for an additional fee.

In addition to the judge, you'll need at least two witnesses who are 18 or older, plus fulfill several other legal requirements that you'll have to get out of the way for your marriage to be legally binding. To complete these requirements, it is necessary to arrive in Mexico several days before the ceremony. You'll need certified copies of your birth certificates as well as passports and copies of your tourist cards. If you have been married previously, you'll need papers indicating that you have been legally divorced for at least a year. There is also medical lab work that needs to be performed in Mexico.

With all of these ancillary details, it's probably a really good idea to hire a wedding coordinator to help you out, especially if you don't speak Spanish. Several wedding planners work out of San Miguel de Allende, and many of the hotels in the city offer their own wedding planners. Check the hotel Web sites for more details.

The following are some wedding planners that you might want to check out:

CELEBRATIONS SAN MIGUEL
415-154-8367
(U.S.) 512-351-4537
www.celebrationssanmiguel.com
Centro, San Miguel de Allende, Gto. 37700
This company is owned and run by an experienced wedding planner from Austin, Texas. They offer complete wedding planning services and several wedding packages. They will also work with you to scout out the best location in San Miguel to meet your needs.

SAN MIGUEL WEDDINGS
415-154-8121
www.sanmiguelweddings.com
Coda #5-A, San Miguel de Allende, Gto. 37700
This company offers a bilingual staff as well as creative catering and equipment rental. They will help you with your itinerary, set appointments, and plan the ceremony and reception.

LOS SECRETOS
415-152-0823
(U.S.) 706-659-2054
www.smasecretos.com

Centro, San Miguel de Allende, Gto. 37700
This business offers a full host of wedding planning services, including photography, music, and hotel reservations.

WEDDINGS SAN MIGUEL

415-152-5807
www.weddingssanmiguel.com
Jesús #23, San Miguel de Allende, Gto. 37700
This business is owned and run by Kris Rudolph, the owner of the Buen Café. She has been catering weddings in San Miguel de Allende for more than 10 years. She offers a full range of wedding planning services. Her knowledge of local venues, regulations, and traditions are invaluable for making your wedding go off without a hitch.

INTERNET ACCESS

If you plan on bringing a laptop computer, many hotels offer wireless Internet access as part of their amenities. However, there is always an added risk when traveling with a laptop. For an alternate option, several cyber cafes in both San Miguel de Allende and Guanajuato offer Internet access for a nominal fee. In Guanajuato, these tend to be concentrated near the university, along Calle Pocitos, and near the Plaza de San Roque. If you do use these machines, it's always a good idea to click on "Internet Options" and clear the cache before logging off. You don't want any of your personal information sitting on the computer after you have left. However, your best bet is to log into personal accounts sparingly on public computers, since unscrupulous hackers have been known to bug computers in cyber cafes and even hotels with software designed to gain access to personal information—especially banking and e-trade accounts. Here are some cyber cafes where you can get on the Internet.

Guanajuato

GRUMARA

473-732-0607
Jardín Reforma 12, Guanajuato, Gto. 36000
Open: Mon.–Sat. 10 AM–10 PM
This Internet shop has about a half dozen computer stations and a printer available.

INTERNET STATION Y2K

473-732-1478
Juan Valle #4, Guanajuato, Gto. 36000
Open: Mon.–Sat. 9 AM–11:30 PM
This public Internet shop is often filled with college kids but if you can get to a station, they do have high-speed Internet connections here.

JUAN ARTURO REYES POSADA

473-733-9588
Calle 28 de Septiembre s/n, Guanajuato, Gto. 36000

Open: Mon.–Sat. 9 AM–11:30 PM
This is kind of a hole in the wall but they have several computer stations equipped with high-speed Internet access as well as a printer.

San Miguel de Allende

CAFÉ ETC.

415-154-8636
Reloj #37, San Miguel de Allende, Gto. 37700
Open: Mon.–Sat. 9 AM–7 PM
This café has about a half dozen computers with DSL connections. A scanner and printer are also available. They sell sandwiches and espresso drinks, as well. There is also a bilingual staff here to assist you.

ESTACIÓN INTERNET

415-152-7312
www.estacioninternet.com
Correo #12-A, San Miguel de Allende, Gto. 37700
Open: Daily 9 AM–9 PM
This computer center has several computers available for rental at an hourly rate. There is also a printer and scanner available.

INTERNET SAN MIGUEL

415-100-3077
Mesones #57, San Miguel de Allende, Gto. 37700
Open: Mon.–Sat. 9 AM–9 PM; Sun. 10 AM–6 PM
This cyber café located in the city's historic center has eight PCs with high-speed Internet connection, as well as a public Ethernet port for customers with laptops. You can also stop in here to get espresso drinks, as well as desserts, fresh juices, and even beer and wine. The staff is bilingual, so that's also a plus.

PUNTO G

415-152-4493
Hidalgo #23, San Miguel de Allende, Gto. 37700
Open: Daily 9 AM–12 AM
This computer center features 14 computer stations with high-speed Internet hookup. They have inexpensive international phone service as well. There is a bilingual staff here to assist you.

LANGUAGE

It goes without saying that Spanish is the primary language spoken in this region of Mexico (though you do find indigenous people who primarily speak native languages). You will likely find that English is only spoken by the better educated upper class, those who have spent time working in the United States, and those locals who deal with tourists on a daily basis. All in all, this is probably less than 10 percent of the urban population, even in San

Miguel de Allende. This doesn't mean that they won't try to communicate with you in English. The ability to speak English is a valued skill in Mexico and people want to practice it every chance they get. But you will often find that they run through the English phrases they know pretty quickly. Your waiter will understand the names of the items you order off the menu, but he probably won't be able to describe them to you or tell you exactly how they are prepared. This doesn't mean that you won't be able to get along here without knowing any Spanish. In fact, there are many expatriates who live in San Miguel de Allende full time who don't speak Spanish. However, knowing some Spanish will likely enrich your experience and can really come in handy if you find yourself in a pinch. It is worth your while to make an attempt to learn at least the most basic Spanish phrases. Not only will this help you communicate better, it will also go a long way toward ingratiating you with your Mexican hosts. And that's never a bad thing.

Helpful Phrases

When it comes to conversation, Mexicans tend to appreciate formalities more than their neighbors to the north. When approaching someone for information, don't forget to greet them with the time-appropriate salutation (*buenos días, buenas tardes, buenas noches*), even if it's the only Spanish you can think of at the moment. Try not to say simply *"Hola,"* which comes across as abrupt. Also, contrary to what you were taught in high school Spanish, if you want to know how much something costs, try not to say *"¿Cuanto cuesta?"* This is a dead giveaway that you're a gringo, meaning that you've probably just added a few pesos to the price of the item. Instead say, *"¿A cuanto?"* This phrase just might pass you off as a *chilango* (Mexico City resident), making the vendor think that you are wise to inflated prices.

Good morning. – *Buenos días.*
Good afternoon. – *Buenas tardes.*
Good evening. (After 8 PM) – *Buenas noches.*
Good-bye. – *Adios.*
Please. – *Por favor.*
Thank you very much. – *Muchas gracias.*
You're welcome. – *De nada.*
Do you speak English? – *¿Habla usted ingles?*
I don't understand. – *No entiendo.*
How do you say . . . in Spanish? – *¿Como se llama . . . en español?*
My name is. . . . – *Me llamo. . . .*
Where is . . . ? – *¿Dónde está . . . ?*
To the right. – *A la derecha.*
To the left. – *A la izquierda.*
Straight ahead. – *Derecho.*
What is the rate? – *¿A cuanto es?*
Shower – *Ducha*
Towels – *Toallas*
Soap – *Jabón*
Toilet paper – *Papel higiénico*
Key – *Llave*
Order – *Orden*
Fork – *Tenedor*

Spoon – *Cuchara*
Knife – *Cuchillo*
Napkin – *Servilleta*
Food - *Comida*
Coffee – *Café*
Tea – *Té*
Beer – *Cerveza*
Wine – *Vino*
Milk – *Leche*
Juice – *Jugo*
Money – *Dinero*
Expensive – *Caro*
Cheap - *Barato*
Post office – *Correo*
Driver's licence – *Licencia de manejar*
Gas station – *Gasolinera*
Border – *Frontera*
Passport - *Pasaporte*

LAUNDRY SERVICE

Guanajuato

LAVANDERIA ALFA
473-733-0766
Amezquita #8, Guanajuato, Gto. 36000
Open: Mon.–Fri. 9 AM–7 PM
Offers dry cleaning, ironing, and regular washing service.

LAVANDERIA AUTOMATICA INTERNACIONAL
473-732-6718
Manuel Doblado #28, Guanajuato, Gto. 36000
Open: Mon.–Fri. 8 AM–8 PM
Offers same day service.

San Miguel de Allende

EXPRESS LAUNDRY
415-152-7086
Canal #127, San Miguel de Allende, Gto. 37700
Open: Mon.–Fri. 8 AM–8 PM; Sat. 9 AM–2 PM
Offers same day service with free pickup and delivery.

LA PILA
415-152-5810
Jesús #25, San Miguel de Allende, Gto. 37700
Open: Mon.– Fri. 9 AM–7 PM; Sat. 9 AM–2 PM
Offers dry cleaning service as well as regular laundry service. They will pick up and deliver.

LAVANDERÍA EL RELOJ
415-152-3843
Reloj #34-A, San Miguel de Allende, Gto. 37700
Open: Mon. Fri. 8 AM–8 PM; Sat. 9 AM–2 PM
Reasonable prices and friendly service.

LAVANDERÍA FRANCO
415-154-4495
Zacateros #54-B, San Miguel de Allende, Gto. 37700
Open: Mon.–Fri. 9 AM–7 PM; Sat. 9 AM–5 PM
Offers same day service with free pickup and delivery.

MAIL

Guanajuato

POST OFFICE
473-732-7394
Calle Ayuntamiento #25, Guanajuato, Gto. 36000
Open: Mon.– Fri. 8 AM–6 PM; Sat. 8 AM–1 PM

COPIA TODO
473-732-2356
Avenida Juárez #8, Guanajuato, Gto. 36000
Open: Mon.–Fri. 9 AM–6:30 PM; Sat. 10 AM–3 PM
This shop offers a full range of copy and fax services.

San Miguel de Allende

POST OFFICE
415-152-0089
Calle Correo #16 (one block east of Jardín), San Miguel de Allende, Gto. 37700
Open: Mon.–Fri. 8 AM–4 PM; Sat. 8 AM–12 PM

BORDER CROSSINGS
415-152-2497
www.bordercrossingsma.com
Mesones #57, San Miguel de Allende, Gto. 37700
Open: Mon.–Fri. 9 AM–6:30 PM; Sat. 10 AM–3 PM

This mailing store is located one block off the Jardìn Principal. It offers packing and UPS shipping service and has a copy machine, wireless Internet access, and offers mailboxes for rental.

SOLUTIONS

415-152-6152
Recreo #11, San Miguel de Allende, Gto. 37700
Open: Mon.–Fri. 9 AM–6 PM; Sat. 9 AM–2 PM
This store offers shipping services including DHL, FedEx, and UPS. They also offer packing and storage services.

MEDICAL SERVICES

Guanajuato

CENTRO MEDICO LA PRESA

473-731-1135
Paseo de la Presa #85, Guanajuato, Gto. 36000
This private medical center offers a full range of healthcare services.

HOSPITAL GENERAL DE GUANAJUATO

473-733-1573
Carretera de Cuota Guanajuato-Silao Km. 6.5, Guanajuato, Gto. 36000
This is the public hospital of Guanajuato.

MEDICA INTEGRAL GUANAJUATENSE

473-732-2305
Plaza de la Paz #20, Guanajuato, Gto. 36000
This centrally located medical clinic has specialists in the fields of internal medicine and plastic surgery.

San Miguel de Allende

HOSPITAL CIVIL

415-152-0045
Reloj #56, San Miguel de Allende, Gto. 37700
This is the public hospital in San Miguel.

HOSPITAL DE LA FÉ

415-152-2329
Libramiento a Dolores Hidalgo #43, San Miguel de Allende, Gto. 37700
This is a private medical center serving the San Miguel area.

HOMEOPATHIC PHARMACY
415-152-0230
Mesones #67, San Miguel de Allende, Gto. 37700
Open daily 24 hours.

MONEY AND MONEY EXCHANGE

American dollars are accepted in some places in Guanajuato and San Miguel de Allende. However, your money will go further if you use pesos. For both convenience and the fact that you don't have much choice, prices are usually rounded off to equal 10 pesos to the dollar. This means that since the official exchange rate is currently fluctuating at more than 10.9 pesos for every dollar, you will generally be overpaying about 9 cents for every dollar you spend.

Mexican currency notes come in denominations of 20, 50, 100, 200, 500, and 1000. Breaking larger bills is a persistent problem in Mexico, particularly at smaller independent establishments. I once had to wait a half hour after finishing a meal while the restaurant owner ran around to nearby businesses trying to make change for a 500 peso note. The best strategy to avoid such a situation is to pay with larger bills when spending money at larger businesses and save your smaller bills and *monedas* (coins) for small establishments and street vendors.

The quickest and easiest way to get Mexican currency is simply to go to a Mexican ATM and withdraw pesos. Like many banks north of the border, ATMs are located in an entrance area between the outer and inner doors to the bank. After normal business hours—as is the case in the United States—insert your card into the slot next to the outer door, and you will be buzzed inside to do your withdrawal. Once you withdraw currency in Mexican denominations, your bank will convert it back to the dollar amount and charge you that way. These machines generally offer cash at the wholesale bank rate instead of the less-favorable tourist rate that you get when you trade cash or traveler's checks, making ATMs both convenient and, on the surface, financially favorable. However, keep in mind when you use your debit card, your bank may charge you a foreign transaction fee of up to 3 percent of the transaction. On top of that, the owner of the ATM will likely charge you a fee of up to 3 percent as well.

Before your trip, it's a good idea to shop around for a credit card that imposes a small foreign transaction fee or none at all. Foreign transaction fees are disclosed in the terms and conditions. In any case, it's probably not such a good idea to rely solely on ATMs as your source for money. You should always have a little extra cash on you in case of an emergency. Banks or *casas de cambio* (exchange houses) offer respectable exchange rates. Hotels offer the worst exchange rates. It's always a good idea to exchange at least $50 or $75 into pesos before leaving the United States so that you'll arrive in Mexico with pesos for your cab ride or a meal. Credit cards are widely accepted in San Miguel de Allende and Guanajuto. However, in smaller towns an acceptance of credit cards is less common. The benefit of using a credit card is that you will receive the more favorable wholesale rate. The drawback is that if you're spending money in a place that accepts credit cards, chances are that it's an establishment that is geared toward serving tourists—and thus you get less bang for your buck than at places that cater to locals.

Casas de Cambio (Money Changers)

DIVISAS DIMAS

473-732-1058
Avenida Juárez #33-A, Guanajuato, Gto. 36000
Open: Mon.– Fri. 9 AM–6 PM; Sat. 9 AM–2 PM

SERVICIOS POPULARES DE IRAPUAT

473-732-6137
Madero #6, Guanajuato, Gto. 36000
Open: Mon.– Fri. 9 AM–4 PM; Sat., Sun. 10 AM–2 PM

DICAMBIOS FOREIGN CURRENCY EXCHANGE

415-152-3657
Correo #13, San Miguel de Allende, Gto. 37700
Open: Mon.– Fri. 9 AM–4 PM; Sat., Sun. 10 AM–2 PM

INTERCAM CASA DE CAMBIO

415-154-6676
San Francisco #4, San Miguel de Allende, Gto. 37700
Open: Mon.–Fri. 9 AM–6 PM; Sat. 9 AM–2 PM

MONEX

415-154-9996
www.monex.com.mx
Mesones #80, San Miguel de Allende, Gto. 37700
Open: Mon.–Fri. 9 AM–3 PM

Tipping

Being a former waiter, I am all too familiar with the frustration of foreign tourists skipping out without tipping just because they aren't familiar with the local customs. That's just a bad excuse to be cheap. Furthermore, Mexico does not have the same labor laws that you find in the United States and there may be times when your waiter is earning tips and tips alone. Be polite, and plan on tipping service personnel the customary amount.

Bellboys should be tipped based on the pieces of luggage they carry to your room. Restaurant servers are customarily tipped around 15 percent of the total bill; however, if you're dining with a large group, a service charge may be automatically added to the bill. The tipping of chambermaids is optional though highly appreciated. You should tip the gas station attendant about $0.50 USD and/or let them keep the change when it equals less than a peso. If you take a tour, it's standard to tip the guide about 10 percent of the cost of the trip. This is particularly important if you have a guide who goes out of his way to make sure that you are well informed and have a good time. Taxi drivers are generally not tipped in Mexico, except if they give special service or provide you with good advice. Even then, it

Be sure to tip your waiters and tour guides.

is at your discretion, since many taxi drivers will bend over backward to give you advice even if you're not looking for it.

NEWSPAPERS

ATENCIÓN SAN MIGUEL
www.atencionsanmiguel.org
Insurgentes #25, San Miguel de Allende, Gto. 37700
This bilingual newspaper comes out every Friday. It is published by the American staff at the Biblioteca Publica. It costs about $0.75.

Poverty in Guanajuato

You will read over and over again throughout this book that the cities of Dolores Hidalgo, Guanajuato, and San Miguel de Allende are beautiful. This is without a doubt true. However, it is important to remember that these are not prefabricated amusement parks. They are real cities with

Poverty is a fact of life for many in Mexico.

PHARMACIES

Guanajuato

FARMACIA ISSEG

473-732-8248
Avenida Juárez #129-A, Guanajuato, Gto. 36000
Open: Daily 24 hours

FARMACIA REGINA

473-732-1001
Plaza de la Paz #38, Guanajuato, Gto. 36000
Open: Daily 9 AM–2:30 PM and 4 PM–8:30 PM

FARMACIA SAN FRANCISCO

473-732-3915
Alhóndiga #10, Guanajuato, Gto. 36000
Open: Daily 10:30 AM–11 PM

real histories and real people living in them with real problems. And one aspect of those histories and the current living conditions is that Guanajuato is one of the poorest states in Mexico, a country where nearly half the population lives on less than $1,800 a year. This is an important reason why so many Americans can claim an ancestral heritage here. Guanajuato has contributed more than its share of people to the vegetable fields and restaurant kitchens of the United States.

When visiting, you will see beggars on the sidewalks, including very old women in indigenous dress, women with several children, blind men, men in wheelchairs, women missing limbs, and children selling chewing gum. There is always the possibility that you will be approached for money. Of course, how you handle this situation is completely up to you. However, it may be a good idea to consider this before the situation arises. Certainly, this problem is not nearly as bad as it was just 10 or 15 years ago. In the mid-1990s, Mexico's economy was in an unusually poor state and destitute indigenous people came to the cities to panhandle and sell trinkets and gum to tourists. One day, I sat in a café in the Jardín de la Unión talking with some Americans that I had just met. Every now and then children would approach us asking for change, and one member of the group would tell these kids quite forcefully in English to get lost. While no one would have faulted him for saying no, it was clear that people around us found his behavior to be quite offensive, and I'm sure that it reflected poorly on everyone sitting at the table. Several days later I was in Dolores Hidalgo with a tour group. There was also a couple from Texas along, whose families had come from the area many years before and had done quite well in the United States. When they were approached by a girl asking for money, the woman proudly took her wallet out of her purse and handed the girl a 10 dollar bill. This was shortly followed by the approach of a young boy, to whom she quickly gave a dollar. Within minutes, the woman was being hounded by women and children asking for money.

These are situations that you will almost certainly not encounter today. While there are a few panhandlers in the cities, it is nowhere near the level of a decade ago. However, they are there. And if you are approached, however you decide to deal with them, it's probably best to do it discreetly.

San Miguel de Allende

BOTICA AGUNDIS
415-152-1198
Canal #26, San Miguel de Allende, Gto. 37700
Open: Daily 10:30 AM–11 PM

BOTICA DE SANTA TERESITA
415-152-0147
Reloj #28, San Miguel de Allende, Gto. 37700
Open: Daily 9 AM–2:30 PM and 4 PM–8:30 PM

FARMACIA GUADALAJARA
415-154-9047
Ancha de San Antonio #13, San Miguel de Allende, Gto. 37700
Open: Daily 24 hours

FARMACIA GUANAJUATO
415-154-6090
Insurgentes #74, San Miguel de Allende, Gto. 37700
Open: Daily 24 hours

SUPERMARKETS

Guanajuato

COMERCIAL MEXICANA
473-732-9628
Avenida Juárez #131, Guanajuato, Gto. 36000
Open: Daily 8 AM—10 PM

San Miguel de Allende

MEGA COMERCIAL MEXICANA
415-120-9047
Salida a Celaya and Libramiento Zavala Zavala, San Miguel de Allende, Gto. 37700
Open: Daily 8 AM—10 PM

SUPER GIGANTE
415-120-9047
Libramiento Zavala Zavala and Carretera a Querétaro, San Miguel de Allende, Gto. 37700
Open: Daily 8 AM—10 PM

WEATHER

If you're looking for a place with a temperate climate that you can always count on, you've come to the right place. This region is famous for its nice weather, typical of mountainous Central Mexico. Normally from April through June temperatures peak out in the mid-80s during the daytime, though daytime temperatures have been known to creep up into the high 90s in May and June. The dry mountain air makes this tolerable, and cool mountain breezes make the evenings wonderful during this time, when temperatures typically remain up into the high 50s. The evenings can get quite chilling from November through February. San Miguel de Allende is at 6,400 feet and Guanajuato is almost at 6,600 feet, and temperatures fall down into the mid-40s at night, even freezing overnight during the peak winter weeks. However, things tend to warm up quite quickly when the sun comes up, with daytime temperatures typically rising into the low to mid-70s. If you are coming from Canada or the Midwest United States, these temperatures will likely prompt you into shorts and a T-shirt, while you will see locals walking about bundled in sweaters and jackets. Just remember that the temperature drops when the sun goes down, so dress in layers.

The rainy season lasts from June to September and usually comes in the form of late afternoon and evening showers. If you're out and about at this time, bring an umbrella and be prepared to duck into a coffee shop to wait out the shower. Rainfall typically averages

Jacaranda trees add color in the springtime.

around 4 to 5 inches a month during this period. In fact, these quick showers can flood the streets, making you realize exactly why the sidewalks are abnormally high. For the most part, however, the weather is perfect for sightseeing, kicking back by the pool, or taking a long afternoon nap.

The high season for tourists lasts from December 15 to April 1, when days are sunny and clear and nights are crisp and cool. The low season lasts during the hotter days of April through August. However, the city gets particularly crowded during Holy Week before Easter, or *Semana Santa*. This is when visitors from all over Mexico go on vacation to traditional places like San Miguel de Allende, where the festivities and processions are among the best in all of Latin America.

WHAT TO BRING

Obviously, if you are traveling to Guanajuato, San Miguel de Allende, or Dolores Hidalgo, you are going to want to bring a camera and a comfortable pair of shoes. If you are going to visit during Christmas or soon thereafter, a jacket will certainly be a must. These towns are located at a high altitude and they tend to get cold at night. Two other items that you'll need if you plan on touring around are sunscreen and a roll of toilet paper. The sunscreen is obvious. The high altitude and the dry, sunny air can combine to wreak havoc on your skin. As far as the toilet paper goes, some off-the-beaten-path restrooms will charge you a few pesos and give you a couple of squares, but in some places there just *isn't* any. Better to come prepared than find yourself in a situation where you have to improvise. Additionally, you'll want to have a tube or bottle of disinfectant hand lotion or disinfectant wipes to freshen up with. This comes in handy in a variety of situations.

One saying seems to have gotten truer in recent years: There are two types of luggage: carry-on luggage and lost luggage. We all know people who have taken trips and ended up spending days waiting for their luggage to arrive at their destination. It's best to pack light and carry all of your belongings aboard with you as you make your way south. But this is not always a possibility. A good trick is to make arrangements with your hotel and ship your belongings ahead. This costs extra, of course, but the peace of mind that it buys is really priceless.

General Index

Lodging by Price

Dining by Price

GUANAJUATO

Inexpensive
Bagel Cafetín, 180
Café Atrio, 181–182
Café Conquistador, 180
Cerro de las Ranas, El, 174
Clave Azul Restaurante, La, 175–177
Midi, El, 184
Pizza Piazza, 184

Inexpensive—Moderate
Chahistle, El, 175
Mariscos La Jaula, 184
Pirinola, La, 177–178
Tic Tic, 178
Truco 7, 178–180

Moderate
Bossanova Crepería Café, 180–181
Cabaña, La, 173–174
Café Galería, El, 181
Capellina, La, 182
Chao Bella, 182
Tasca de la Paz, 185–187
Yamuna, 187

Moderate—Expensive
Abue Restaurante, El, 173
Conde Rul, 177
Gallo Pitagorico, El, 183
Leyendas, Las, 177

Expensive
Frascati, 182–183
Ik-Etznab Alta Cocina, 183
Jardín de los Milagros, El, 183
Mercedes, Las, 177
Refugio Casa Colorada, 184–185
Restaurante Teresita, 178
Rincón de los Sabores, El, 185

SAN MIGUEL DE ALLENDE

Inexpensive
Café del Jardín, 191
Cappucino's, 191–192
Correo, El, 189
Grotto, La, 193
Musas Café, Las, 192
Olé-Olé, 190
Rinconcito, El, 190
Torta Mundo, 191

Inexpensive—Moderate
Finistera Café, La, 192
Mama Mia, 189–190
Pegaso Restaurant Bar, El, 194
Romano's, 194–195
San Agustín Café, 192

Moderate
Buen Café, El, 191
Casa de Sierra Nevada en el Parque, 188–189
Casa Payo, 193
L'Invito, 194
Pueblo Viejo, 190
Tío Lucas, 195

Moderate—Expensive
Bugambila, 188
Chimarrão, 193
Harry's New Orleans Café, 193
Market Bistro, El, 194
Rincón de Don Tomás, 191

Expensive
Azafrán, 192–193
Capilla, La, 188

Dining by Cuisine